AI for Healthcare with Keras and Tensorflow 2.0

Design, Develop, and Deploy Machine Learning Models Using Healthcare Data

Anshik

Apress®

AI for Healthcare with Keras and Tensorflow 2.0: Design, Develop, and Deploy Machine Learning Models Using Healthcare Data

Anshik
New Delhi, India

ISBN-13 (pbk): 978-1-4842-7085-1
https://doi.org/10.1007/978-1-4842-7086-8

ISBN-13 (electronic): 978-1-4842-7086-8

Managing Director, Apress Media LLC: Welmoed Spahr
Acquisitions Editor: Celestin Suresh John
Development Editor: Laura Berendson
Coordinating Editor: Divya Modi

Cover designed by eStudioCalamar

Cover image designed by Pixabay

Distributed to the book trade worldwide by Springer Science+Business Media New York, 1 New York Plaza, Suite 4600, New York, NY 10004-1562, USA. Phone 1-800-SPRINGER, fax (201) 348-4505, e-mail orders-ny@ springer-sbm.com, or visit www.springeronline.com. Apress Media, LLC is a California LLC and the sole member (owner) is Springer Science + Business Media Finance Inc (SSBM Finance Inc). SSBM Finance Inc is a **Delaware** corporation.

For information on translations, please e-mail booktranslations@springernature.com; for reprint, paperback, or audio rights, please e-mail bookpermissions@springernature.com.

Apress titles may be purchased in bulk for academic, corporate, or promotional use. eBook versions and licenses are also available for most titles. For more information, reference our Print and eBook Bulk Sales web page at www.apress.com/bulk-sales.

Any source code or other supplementary material referenced by the author in this book is available to readers on GitHub via the book's product page, located at www.apress.com/978-1-4842-7085-1. For more detailed information, please visit www.apress.com/source-code.

Printed on acid-free paper

This book is dedicated to my beloved parents,

Smt. Meenakshi Bansal

and

Sh. Jitender Kumar

About the Author

Anshik has a deep passion for building and shipping data science solutions that create great business value. He is currently working as a senior data scientist at ZS Associates and is a key member on the team developing core unstructured data science capabilities and products. He has worked across industries such as pharma, finance, and retail, with a focus on advanced analytics. Besides his day-to-day activities, which involve researching and developing AI solutions for client impact, he works with startups as a data science strategy consultant. Anshik holds a bachelor's degree from Birla Institute of Technology and Science, Pilani. He is a regular speaker at AI and machine learning conferences. He enjoys trekking and cycling.

About the Technical Reviewers

Dev Bharti is a seasoned, hands-on technical leader with close to 20 years of experience in delivering data, insights, and AI solutions for consumer products and goods, healthcare, manufacturing, pharmaceutical, and retail industries. He leads enterprises from conception to delivery through data governance, data science, and AI-based initiatives. His broad skills allow him to build, mentor, and lead multi-disciplinary teams comprising scientists, engineers, partners, product managers, and subject domain experts. He is currently pursuing his PhD from Oxford Brookes University on Federated Learning (AI).

Himanshu is currently an AI tech lead at Legato Healthcare (an Anthem Incorporation Company). He has over 7 years of experience and has an MBA in Marketing and Analytics. He is the co-founder of Infinite Epochs Research Lab and the author of four books in the machine learning domain. Himanshu is also a corporate trainer and guest faculty at institutes like Edureka, Imarticus, NMIMS, and IMT.

Ashish Soni is an experienced AIML consultant and solutions architect. He has worked and solved business problems related to computer vision, natural language processing, machine learning, artificial intelligence, data science, statistical analysis, data mining, and cloud computing. Ashish holds a B. Tech. degree in Chemical Engineering from Indian Institute of Technology, Bombay, India; a master's degree in Economics; and a post graduate diploma in Applied Statistics. He has worked across different industry areas such as finance, healthcare, education, sports, human resources, retail, and logistics automation. He currently works with a technology services company based out of Bangalore. He maintains a blog (Phinolytics.com) that focuses on data science and artificial intelligence applications in the field of finance.

Mitahee Divesh Kumar is currently working as an associate NLP engineer at Legato Health Technologies (an Anthem Company). He has over 3 years of experience in the field of data science and machine learning in the domain of natural language processing and computer vision. He is currently solving health care-related problems using AI.

Introduction

Like most readers of this book, your knowledge of healthcare is probably limited to your doctor visits and then reluctantly eating that bitter/sour medicine prescribed to you. But beyond that experience is a vast machinery of different stakeholders that have made it possible for us to receive the basic need of humankind: healthcare. If you want to understand how the healthcare system works and see how to apply AI to some of the most pressing problems in this space, read along.

Through this book, I will share my knowledge of the healthcare space gained from working with leaders from the top pharma companies in the world. I'll explain how they are using AI to automate, reorganize, and restructure different processes.

This book is a practitioner's book. You will explore seven case studies covering multiple problems that often occur in healthcare analytics. I start by introducing you to the healthcare ecosystem so that the basic fundamentals are in place and then I offer a fun exercise of identifying what's hot in the industry right now using company descriptions.

You'll then move on to the problems often faced when working with EHR data (MIMIC-III). You'll use a multi-task setup to account for a heterogeneous patient population on downstream tasks like readmission prediction. Next, you will be introduced to the ICD code system, which is used for patient healthcare reimbursement, and you'll leverage the mighty transformer models to identify them.

Chapter 5 discusses the Graph Convolutional Network and how you can leverage its structure learning capability to read food receipts submitted by sales reps of a pharma company.

Chapter 6 and 7 cover more nuanced aspects such as the availability of training data and privacy preservation. You will be introduced to semi-supervised learning using Snorkel and TensorFlow's Federated API in detail.

Chapter 8 is all about medical images and how to get the best of them using AI. You will learn about different image formats like DICOM and NIFTI, image modalities (X-Ray, CT, MRI, etc.) and different shapes (2-D, 3-D, and 4-D). You will solve two cases, image classification and segmentation using 2-D and 3-D images.

The last case study deals with how you can make your text alive by building a search engine on Covid research reports. You start by learning about different QnA systems and then you dive deeper by creating a closed-domain QnA system. You will learn about query paraphrasing, semantic retrieval, and reranking to fetch the right document on which you use a pretrained QnA model on SQUAD dataset.

Finally, you will deploy your model. In the last chapter, you will learn how web apps came into existence and how cloud technology is taking over. Docker-based app deployment using Flask is discussed.

—Curiosity fuels the world

Anshik

CHAPTER 1

Healthcare Market: A Primer

This chapter presents an overview of the healthcare system with special focus on the US health market. Healthcare systems are organized to meet the care and health needs of people. The systems include several stakeholders that come together to provide efficient care for people.

By the end of this chapter, you will understand how a healthcare environment functions and what role each group plays. You will also be aware of regulatory laws on data protection, which will help you make better decisions as a developer on what kind of data can be used. Lastly, you will understand the industry landscape. We will also discuss how AI is changing the healthcare system around us and for the good.

Different Stakeholders of the Healthcare Marketplace

As shown in Figure 1-1, there are different groups involved in bringing together a comprehensive medical system for consumers.

© Anshik 2021
Anshik, *AI for Healthcare with Keras and Tensorflow 2.0*, https://doi.org/10.1007/978-1-4842-7086-8_1

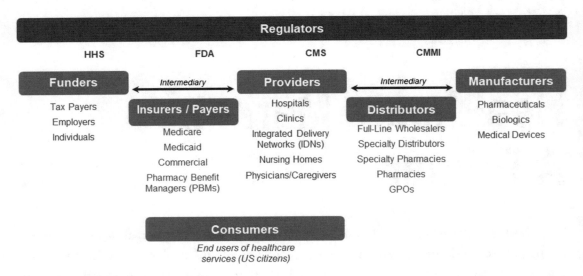

Figure 1-1. *Healthcare supply chain*

Let's dive deeper into the main actors of the healthcare delivery pipeline.

Regulators

All groups/actors are subject to regulation from various government and non-governmental agencies. Primarily, US healthcare is regulated by a variety of divisions and agencies that fall under the Department of Health and Human Services (HHS). The federal or central government manages various programs, research, direction, funding, and so on through HHS. This department in turn works with state and local governments along with private players to ensure that a constant balance is maintained between quality, access, and costs of healthcare.

The overall goal of HHS is guided by four key ideas, focusing on

- The patient as the consumer

- Providers as accountable entities

- Establishing payment for outcomes

- Prevention

The next few sections cover the three main functionaries of HHS.

Food and Drug Administration (FDA)

The primary role of the FDA is to ensure safety and approval of drugs, biological products, and medical devices. It is also tasked with making sure that food being served to US citizens is safe, pure, and wholesome.

The FDA also plays a role in advancing the public health through innovations that make medical products more effective, safer, and more affordable and by helping the public get better access to information needed to improve their health.

Center for Medicare and Medicaid Services (CMS)

The CMS manages federal and state payment programs, namely Medicare and Medicaid, respectively. It also helps to administer the Children's Health Insurance Program (CHIP) and it protects the transfer of sensitive patient health information without patient's consent or knowledge.

Center for Medicare and Medicaid Innovation (CMMI)

The innovation center allows the Medicare and Medicaid programs to test models that improve care, lower costs, and better align payment systems to support patient-centered practices. The innovation broadly centers around keeping patients healthy at home and for providers/physicians to keep patients healthy by providing higher value.

Payers

A *payer* or *payor* is an umbrella term used for organizations or state agencies that are responsible for making payments for any delivered healthcare service. They aim to control healthcare costs by maximizing the quality in patients' healthcare outcome.

The three main functions of payers are keeping patients healthy, managing costs of direct care, and maximizing outcomes. These functions are detailed in Figure 1-2.

- Preventative Health
- Predictive Medicine
- Tech-Enabled Health Education and Wellness (e.g. wearables)

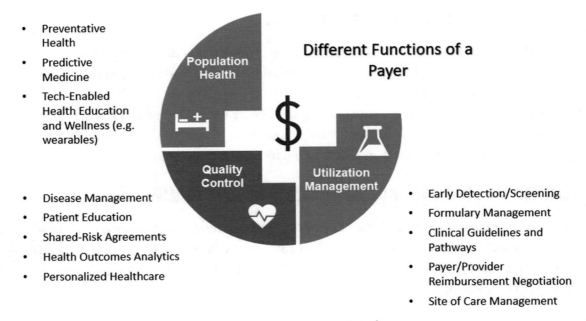

- Disease Management
- Patient Education
- Shared-Risk Agreements
- Health Outcomes Analytics
- Personalized Healthcare

- Early Detection/Screening
- Formulary Management
- Clinical Guidelines and Pathways
- Payer/Provider Reimbursement Negotiation
- Site of Care Management

Figure 1-2. *Different functions of a payer*

In 2018, more than two-thirds of national health expenditure was made by private insurance (which includes contributions from funders such as US households, private business, and government on the federal, state, and local levels), Medicare, and Medicaid programs.

In many markets, healthcare is a state issue, and in more developed markets, it is driven by public and private partnerships. The US spends roughly 8.5 % of its GDP on health out of public funds, which is comparable to spending by other countries. However, private spending is almost four times higher in terms of percentage of GDP than its counterpart in other countries.

Figure 1-3 shows the healthcare spend by different payers, with a major chunk dominated by private payers followed by government programs like Medicare and Medicaid.

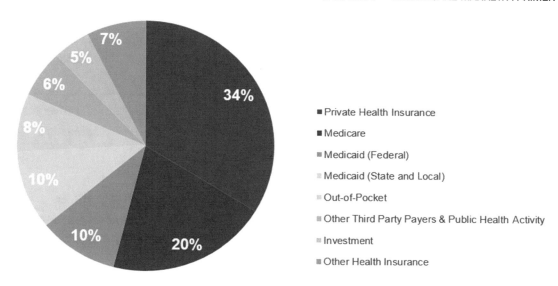

Figure 1-3. *2018 US healthcare spending distribution by payer*

As shown in Figure 1-3, since the majority spend of healthcare comes from insurance, it's good to have a look at the insurance options available for patients, which can vary depending upon age, income, and employment status.

Table 1-1 provides a complete overview of different insurance programs and costs. We are going to use claims data in our first case study, which is maintained by collaboration with payers, so you should have knowledge about different payer programs.

Table 1-1. *Insurance Options for Individuals, A Brief Comparison*

Type of Insurance	Insurance Name	Description	Eligibility	Costs
Government	Medicare	Federally funded health program covering adults with disabilities and those over age 65	Adults over age 65	Medicare Part A is free; low premiums for other parts

(continued)

5

Table 1-1. (*continued*)

Type of Insurance	Insurance Name	Description	Eligibility	Costs
Government	Medicaid	A joint health program run by states and the federal government that covers low-income individuals	Low-income adults and children	No or very low premiums
Private	Various private insurers	Insurance you buy on an exchange or directly from a health insurance company (UHG, Aetna, Kaiser, Anthem, etc.)	All U.S. citizens except Medicare and Medicaid recipients	Higher premiums overall
Private	Employer-sponsored	Insurance you buy through an employer	Anyone working for an employer that offers health insurance, and usually their dependents	Premiums are often subsidized by the employer
Others	Tricare	Provided to military service members and their families, operated by the U.S. Department of Defense	Defense personnel and family members; active or retired	Varies with ranks
Others	Veteran Affairs	Provided to veterans and some retired military service members, operated by Veterans Affairs	Active military, naval, or air service personnel who didn't receive a dishonorable discharge	Full for people with serious disabilities

Providers

Providers are individuals or organizations that provide healthcare services to patients. There are four prominent categories of providers in the healthcare market:

- Integrated delivery networks (IDNs): Hospital systems

- Integrated payer-provider networks (IPPNs): Physicians, nurses, and other caregivers

- Clinically integrated networks (CINs): Clinics, nursing homes

- Accountable care organizations (ACOs): Alternate sites like multi-specialty group practices like Mayo Clinic, Cleveland Clinic, etc.

These groups are not mutually exclusive; they might integrate at different levels to have more control over costs and quality of care. Examples include the Hospital Corporation of America, Dignity Health, etc. Table 1-2 lists the different types of providers.

Table 1-2. *Descriptions of Different Types of Providers*

Type of Provider	Description
IDNs	A network of hospitals and other provider facilities that work together to offer patient services across the continuum of care. These different facilities are owned by the parent company.
IPPNs	A network of hospitals, provider facilities, and a self-administered insurance plan that collects insurance premiums, provides medical services, and reimburses these procedures for some or all of the network's patients.
CIN	A network of loosely affiliated provider facilities (with different owners) collaborating within the same community to achieve the triple aim of healthcare. CINs are allowed to collectively contract with payers despite not being owned by the same parent company.
ACO	A network of hospitals, doctors, and other healthcare providers that contract with a payer (commercial or government). It coordinates care for a specific population of patients.

Regulation of Healthcare Information

Healthcare information within the US has received federal protection. This means federal agencies like the Department of Health and Human Services and the Federal Trade Commission looks after the generation, collection, and distribution of data (see `https://sitn.hms.harvard.edu/flash/2019/health-data-privacy/` for a history of US health data protection laws by Jordan Harroda and Dan Utter, titled *Health Data Privacy: Updating HIPAA to match today's technology challenges,* May 15, 2019, figure 1).

Key major events:

- Defining protected health information (PHI): In 2003, the HIPPA Privacy Rule defined what health information should be protected. This included payments, medical history, and payer information.

- Maintaining electronic health records: The Health Information Technology for Economic and Clinical Health Act (HITECH) introduced and incentivized health care records in electronic formats in 2009. Incentivization was managed through Medicare and Medicaid programs. Secondly, any security breach to EHRs came under the Breach Notification Rule if the breach affected more than 500 people.

- Final Omnibus Rule: Introduced in 2013, this rule gives more power to patients in a sense that those who pay for their healthcare on their own can have information private from the health plan so that no bias or differential treatment is practiced based on past medical history. It also empowers patients more as preauthorization is required from an individual before use. Also, a patient can ask for an electronic copy of their medical record (even if it is across different healthcare systems).

As technology is becoming more advanced, so are the ways to breach one's privacy. Moreover, we can federally control the use of healthcare data that are collected by organizations falling under government compliance laws but recent trends of being "always social" has led various people to be open about various aspects of their medical health, like reporting adverse events of drugs on Twitter. Digital devices and the burgeoning IoT ecosystem are beginning to generate a lot of data outside the clinical system, and this is currently not regulated under government laws.

This leads one to think that we need stricter laws, like GDPR, currently in the EU region, which protects "personal data" including all kinds of physical, physiological, genetic, mental, commercial, cultural, or social identity data, to become universal.

AI Applications in Healthcare

If I were to define why we are trying to solve problems in healthcare using AI, I would do that using just nine words:

- To reduce **costs**

- To improve **outcomes**

- To better **quality**

To act upon any of the above levers, AI will do screening, diagnosis, outcome/prognosis and response to treatment. Let me explain these terms briefly.

Screening

Screening is the identification of a disease before it starts showing any signs or symptoms. Early detection of diseases, especially chronic diseases, can lead to better outcomes at a much reduced cost.

This means an ideal screening should be done **in time** so that the outcome can be changed, with a highly **precise** model/process that is **cost-effective**.

Diagnosis

Diagnosis is a procedure through which a disease is found in a patient. It helps us reach the part of the body that is highly affected due the disease and hence it's quite an important step and one in which AI is frequently used.

Prognosis

Prognosis is another term to measure outcome of a treatment offered to the patient suffering from a disease. It can be measured by various metrics, like in how many days is the patient readmitted to the hospital or the chances of survival of the patient.

Response to Treatment

Different patients respond differently to treatments and hence based on a person's genetic makeup we are trying to develop more responsive treatment. This is also known as personalized medicine. A typical genetic data processing can take a large amount of time due to huge data and lack of algorithms to prune irrelevant information for analysis, but with advancements in data storage and processing technologies as well as innovative ML algorithms, personalize medicine is not a far-reaching aim anymore.

What Is the Industry Landscape?

As AI and tech advance, so do the methods to advance healthcare. Many companies use various technologies to solve multiple healthcare issues like health insurance coverage, managing care processes, accessibility, and so on.

I could share with you a list of top companies and what they are doing currently, but instead I will share with you a very effective yet simple way of looking at emerging trends in any industry.

We will use Crunchbase's dataset. Crunchbase is a platform for finding business information about private and public companies. Crunchbase information includes investments and funding information, founding members and individuals in leadership positions, mergers and acquisitions, news, and industry trends.

Crunchbase offers different versions of its Data API. Its Enterprise and Applications API is priced while free access is provided to limited data on its website through the Open Data Map. We will be using data from Open Data Map to get started.

You could look at information like funding, leadership, etc. But to understand the industry landscape, we are going to use company's short description.

Let's get started.

1) First, register with the Crunchbase Data API at this link and click the Get Started button: `https://about.crunchbase.com/crunchbase-basic-access/`

2) Fill the form, which looks something like Figure 1-4.

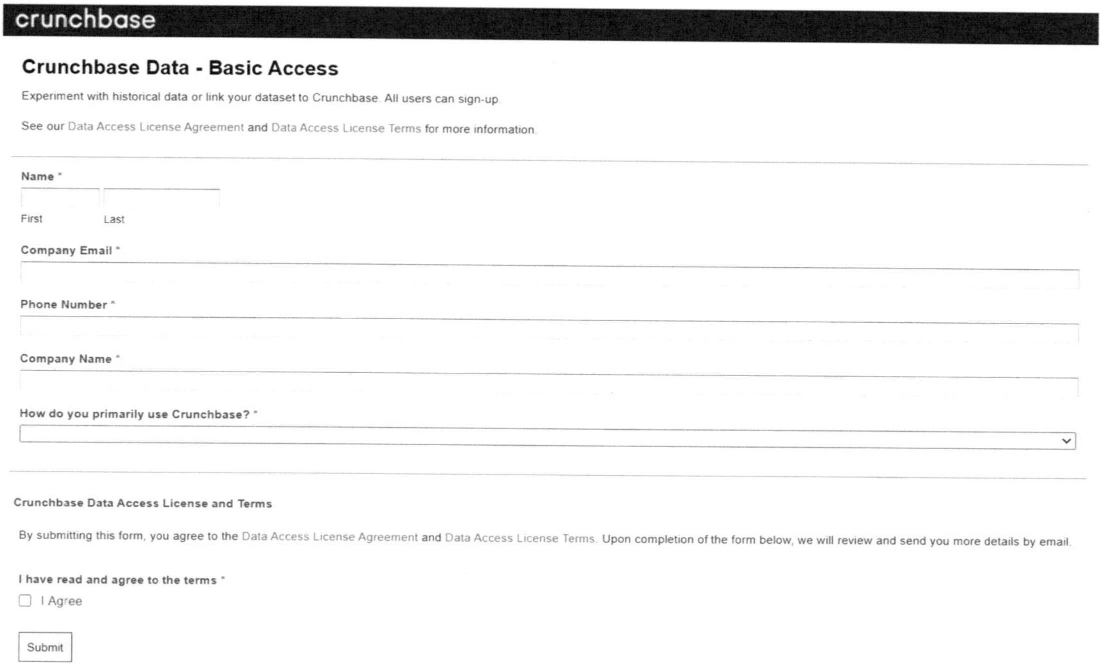
crunchbase

Crunchbase Data - Basic Access

Experiment with historical data or link your dataset to Crunchbase. All users can sign-up.

See our Data Access License Agreement and Data Access License Terms for more information.

Name *

First Last

Company Email *

Phone Number *

Company Name *

How do you primarily use Crunchbase? *

Crunchbase Data Access License and Terms

By submitting this form, you agree to the Data Access License Agreement and Data Access License Terms. Upon completion of the form below, we will review and send you more details by email.

I have read and agree to the terms *

I Agree

Submit

Figure 1-4. *Crunchbase basic data access form*

3) After the due diligence at Crunchbase's end, you will receive an email at your registered email address. This will be your user key.

```
# Loading required libraries
from urllib import parse
import requests
import pandas as pd
import numpy as np
import re

def create_urlquery_from_args(args):
    url_query = ""
    for k,v in args.items():
        # quote_plus helps us handle special characters like ~_. and spaces
        url_query += '&' + parse.quote_plus(k) + '=' + parse.quote_plus(v)
    return url_query
```

```
# Setup the basic url for rest api query
API_BASE_URL = 'https://api.crunchbase.com/'
API_VERSION = '3.1' # soon to be updated to v4
API_URL = API_BASE_URL + 'v' + API_VERSION + '/odm-organizations'
API_KEY = "xxxxxxxxx" #<--- Enter the user key you received from crunchbase
```

In order to know more about the endpoints available for the Odm API, please visit https://data.crunchbase.com/v3.1/reference#odm-organizations.

This can help you generate sample queries and show you the expected outcome:

```
# We are interested in getting organization name and their descriptions
query = 'healthcare' # this will search for keyword 'healthcare' in
organization name, it's aliases and short text
param_dict = {"query":query,"organization_types":"company","user_key":API_KEY}
rest_api_url = API_URL + '?' + create_urlquery_from_args(param_dict)

# Making Get Request
headers = {
    'accept': 'application/json',
    'content-type': 'application/json',
  }
resp = requests.get(rest_api_url, headers = headers)

# Checking api call status and seeing few values of the data
if resp.status_code != 200:
    raise ApiError('GET /tasks/ {}'.format(resp.status_code))

# Parsing JSON data
company_data = resp.json()

for items in company_data['data']["items"][:10]:
    print('{} ---> {}'.format(items['properties']['name'],
    items['properties']['short_description']))

# Let us create a dataframe from analysis
data = pd.DataFrame([[items['properties']['name'], items['properties']
['short_description']] for items in company_data['data']["items"]],
columns = ["name","short_description"])
```

Note there is paging information provided in the paging property of data, hence you can request again to get results of the next page. See Figure 1-5.

```
▼ {
  ▼ "metadata" : {
      "version" : 31
      "www_path_prefix" :
      "https://www.crunchbase.com"
      "api_path_prefix" :
      "https://api.crunchbase.com"
      "image_path_prefix" :
      "http://public.crunchbase.com/t_api_images/"
    }
  ▼ "data" : {
    ▼ "paging" : {
        "total_items" : 2034
        "number_of_pages" : 21
        "current_page" : 1
        "sort_order" : "custom"
        "items_per_page" : 100
        "next_page_url" :
        "https://api.crunchbase.com/v3.1/organizati
        ons?page=2&sort_order=custom&items_per_page
        =100&query=healthcare&organization_types=co
        mpany"
        "prev_page_url" : NULL
        "key_set_url" : NULL
        "collection_url" :
        "https://api.crunchbase.com/v3.1/organizati
        ons"
        "updated_since" : NULL
      }
    ▶ "items" : [...]
    }
}
```

Figure 1-5. *Paging property from Crunchbase API's JSON output*

So now you have the data necessary to draw preliminary insights from it. Let's get coding!

```python
# plotly library
import chart_studio.plotly as py
from plotly.offline import init_notebook_mode, iplot
init_notebook_mode(connected=True)
import plotly.graph_objs as go

# word cloud library
from wordcloud import WordCloud

# matplotlib library
import matplotlib.pyplot as plt

#stopwords
from nltk.corpus import stopwords

# Let us remove some frequent words from this domain
common_words = "|".join(["healthcare","medical","service","health","care","AI",
"data","solution","software","platform","provide","company","technology"])

data["short_description"] = data["short_description"].apply(lambda x:
re.sub(common_words,"",x.lower()))
data["short_description"] = data["short_description"].apply(lambda x: " "
.join([word for word in x.split() if word not in stopwords.words("english")]))

plt.subplots(figsize = (8,8))

wordcloud = WordCloud (
                    background_color = 'white',
                    width = 512,
                    height = 512,
                        ).generate(' '.join(data["short_description"]))
plt.imshow(wordcloud) # image show
plt.axis('off') # to off the axis of x and y
plt.savefig('word_cloud_trend.png')
plt.show()
```

Figure 1-6. *Word cloud from the short descriptions of the targeted companies*

You can see in Figure 1-6 that the solutions are targeting patients and hospitals and are mostly focused on accessibility and tackling chronic disease.

You can build upon this by seeing another version of the word cloud, this time weighted by the importance of a word, which in turn is decided by how frequently it occurs. If a word occurs very often in a document and also across the document, it is not as important as a word occurring sparsely across documents. This score is also called a words tf-idf score.

```
from sklearn.feature_extraction.text import TfidfVectorizer
vectorizer = TfidfVectorizer()
tf_idf_fit = vectorizer.fit_transform(data["short_description"])
```

```
weights = np.asarray(tf_idf_fit.mean(axis=0)).ravel().tolist()
words = vectorizer.get_feature_names()
weight_list = {x:y for x,y in zip(words, weights)}

wordcloud.generate_from_frequencies(weight_list)
plt.imshow(wordcloud) # image show
plt.axis('off') # to off the axis of x and y
plt.savefig('word_cloud_trend.png')
plt.show()
```

Figure 1-7 tells the same story. You can also find some mention of clinical data and medical devices as well as company names.

Figure 1-7. *Wordcloud weighted by a word's TF-IDF score*

You can definitely extend the analysis and play around with the data, but the idea was to share with you a method to look at the ever-expanding industry landscape from a lazy lens.

Conclusion

You have come a long way. I hope you are now curious about AI and also about healthcare. Healthcare, like any other system, has its own imperfections and gaps. In the next seven case studies, you are going to fill in those gaps. But before that, you will learn how to set up your systems and fetch the data necessary for the case studies. You will also get acquainted with the latest and greatest in TensorFlow 2.0 very briefly.

CHAPTER 2

Introduction and Setup

In Chapter 1, I covered the basics of the healthcare market, primarily that of the US. This introduction is simple enough that you can understand the healthcare system even in your own country; I say so as many countries with an underdeveloped system are taking inspiration from the US so their structure and order will likely remain fundamentally the same but with some indigenous flavor to the particular ecosystem.

Now let's shift gears to explore the behemoth of a library called TensorFlow and what is special about its new edition. The idea is not to cover each topic in length but to just pique your interest enough so you start exploring the ones you are interested in. You will also learn how to set up your systems and some best practices you can apply while you are learning.

Introduction to TensorFlow 2

TensorFlow started as an open source deep learning library from Google and has evolved into an ecosystem that contains four major components:

- TensorFlow Core
- TensorFlow JS
- TensorFlow Lite
- TensorFlow Extended

It was first made available under the Apache 2.0 License in November of 2015 and has since grown rapidly. It now consists of tools, libraries, and resources for the research community (and now even enterprises) looking to build ML- and DL-powered applications.

© Anshik 2021
Anshik, *AI for Healthcare with Keras and Tensorflow 2.0*, https://doi.org/10.1007/978-1-4842-7086-8_2

TensorFlow Core

TensorFlow Core is the core open source library to help you develop and train ML/DL models. TensorFlow 2 focuses on simplicity and ease of use, with updates like eager execution, intuitive higher-level APIs, and flexible model building on any platform.

There are multiple extensions and libraries to TensorFlow Core that help in building advanced models or methods using TensorFlow, such as

1) **TensorBoard**

   a) Track and visualize metrics such as accuracy and loss

   b) View changes in weights and biases over time

   c) Display data

   Official Documentation: www.TensorFlow.org/tensorboard/get_started

2) **TensorFlow Federated:** It is a framework that allows you to build DL/ML apps on decentralized data. This book offers a whole chapter on this where you will deep dive into this library.

   Official Documentation: www.TensorFlow.org/federated/get_started

3) **Neural Structured Learning:** It leverages the structure of a signal. In other words, it tries to leverage patterns or similarities between input data to train ML models. As a result, during training both labeled and unlabeled data is used.

   Official Documentation: www.TensorFlow.org/neural_structured_learning/framework

4) **Serving Models:** It is a system designed for production environments. Here *serving* means deployment, so it is a quick and dirty way to deploy your ML models for the world to see. It can be integrated with TensorFlow models and other third-party models and data. Have you ever thought about dockerizing your

ML model and are a little confused as to how to do it? The code snippet below (taken from official documentation) shows how easy it is to dockerize your app.

Official Documentation: www.TensorFlow.org/tfx

```
# Download the TensorFlow Serving Docker image and repo
docker pull TensorFlow/serving

git clone https://github.com/TensorFlow/serving
# Location of demo models
    TESTDATA="$(pwd)/serving/TensorFlow_serving/servables/TensorFlow/
    testdata"

# Start TensorFlow Serving container and open the REST API port
    docker run -t --rm -p 8501:8501 \
        -v "$TESTDATA/saved_model_half_plus_two_cpu:/models/half_plus_two" \
    -e MODEL_NAME=half_plus_two \
    TensorFlow/serving &

# Query the model using the predict API
    curl -d '{"instances": [1.0, 2.0, 5.0]}' \
        -X POST http://localhost:8501/v1/models/half_plus_two:predict

# Returns => { "predictions": [2.5, 3.0, 4.5] }
```

TensorFlow JS

TensorFlow JS enables ML models to run in the browser without any hassle of installing libraries/extensions/packages. Just open a webpage and your program is ready to run.

TensorFlow.js supports WebGL, which can speed up your code behind the scenes when a GPU is available.

You can connect or embed external hardware into your main device like a webcam (visual input) for laptops/computers or sensor input like a gyroscope or accelerometer for mobile devices. Isn't that amazing?

Figure 2-1 shows the different layers that make up TensorFlow JS.

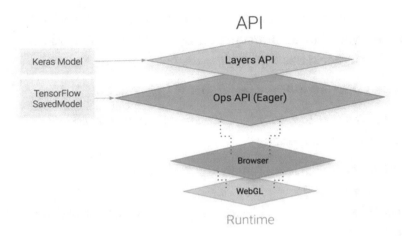

Figure 2-1. *TensorFlow JS*

TensorFlow Lite

TensorFlow Lite is a framework for on-device inference. TensorFlow Lite works with a huge range of devices, from tiny microcontrollers to powerful mobile phones. It enables on-device machine learning inference with low latency and a small binary size.

TensorFlow Lite consists of two main components:

- **TensorFlow Lite interpreter**
- **TensorFlow Lite converter**

TensorFlow Extended

TensorFlow Extended (TFX) helps you build a complete end-to-end machine learning pipeline via multiple independent and scalable components. These components are

- TensorFlow Data Validation
- TensorFlow Transform
- TensorFlow Model Analysis
- TensorFlow Serving
- ML Metadata

In Figure 2-2 you can see how many components from a typical machine learning pipeline are covered by TensorFlow Extended.

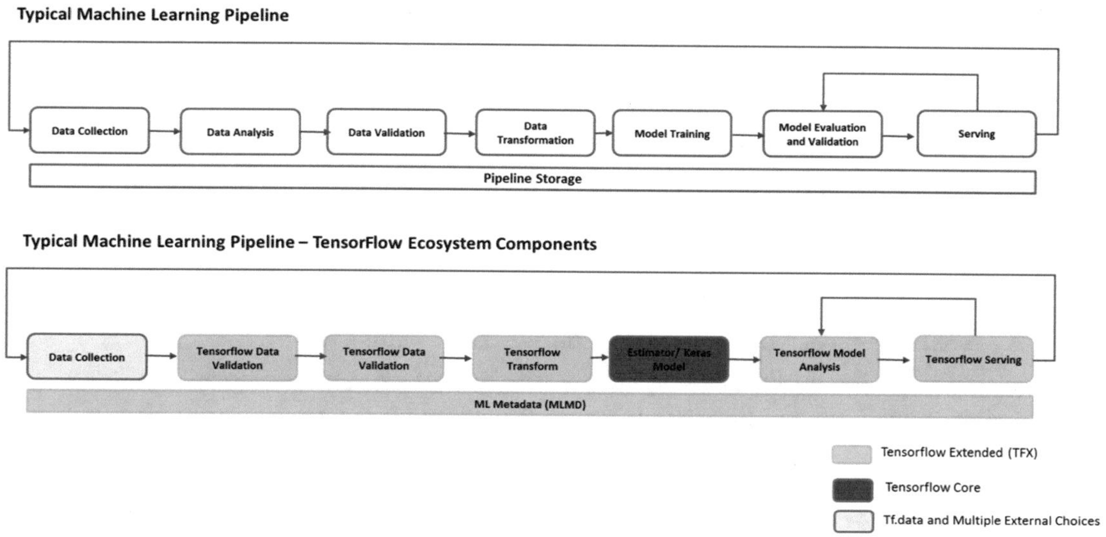

Typical Machine Learning Pipeline

Typical Machine Learning Pipeline – TensorFlow Ecosystem Components

Figure 2-2. Components of TensorFlow Extended

A very good overview of TensorFlow Extended can be found on YouTube by searching for "TensorFlow Extended An End to End Machine Learning Platform for TensorFlow."

TensorFlow 1.x vs 2.x

Well, first things first: If you are someone who has never worked with TensorFlow 1, the good news is you won't be confused by TensorFlow 2 code. But if you are someone like me who has used TensorFlow 1.x, then this section will help you understand the differences better.

If I had to summarize the difference in one line, I would say that TF 2.x offers higher-level APIs that abstract more lower-level details such as creating and manipulating computational graphs, tensor operations, etc. Let's build upon this.

What Is TF 1.x?

Let's start with how a typical workflow in TF 1.x is defined. In TF 1.x, we first need to build a blueprint of the neural network by building something called a computational graph. To build a computational graph, we **define** all the constants, variables, and operations that we need to perform.

After creating the computational graph, we execute the graph using a session object in which tensors and operations are **evaluated.** *Evaluation* in simple terms here means actual calculations of gradients and updates to parameters.

TensorFlow at a fundamental level allows you to play around with tensors. A tensor is basically an n-dimensional array. All types of data (that is, scalar, vectors, and matrices) are special types of tensors, which are

1. **Constants**: Constants are tensors whose values don't change.

2. **Variables**: Variable tensors can update their values within a session. Examples are weights and the bias of a neural network. Variables need to be explicitly initialized before use.

3. **Placeholders**: Placeholders are normally used to feed new training examples while training a neural network. We assign values to a placeholder while running the graph in a session. They don't to be initialized like variables.

Using these different tensors we define any NN or computational flow using TF 1.x. Here's an example showing TF 1.x code defining how a linear output from a hidden layer is created before it passes through the activation function:

```
import TensorFlow.compat.v1 as tf
tf.disable_v2_behavior()

    in_a = tf.placeholder(dtype=tf.float32, shape=(4))

    def nn_tfv1(x):
        with tf.variable_scope("matmul"):
            W = tf.get_variable("W", initializer=tf.ones(shape=(4,4)))
            b = tf.get_variable("b", initializer=tf.zeros(shape=(4)))
        return x * W + b

out_a = nn_tfv1(in_a)

with tf.Session() as sess:
    sess.run(tf.global_variables_initializer())

    hidden_output = sess.run([out_a],
        feed_dict={in_a: [1, 0, 1, 0]})
```

A couple of things to note:

1) A placeholder with a **particular** data type and of a **definite** shape is declared.

2) TensorFlow uses **scopes** to allow variable sharing. There are broadly two types of scopes: name or variable scopes. `tf.variable_scope()` adds a prefix to the names of all variables, operations, and constants. On the other hand, `tf.name_scope()` ignores variables created with `tf.get_variable()` because it assumes that you know which is the variable and in what scope you want to use them. Hence using a matmul scope we define W and b variables, since these are defined for matmul operation.

3) `global_variables_initializer()` allows variables to initialize, hold, and update values throughout the session.

4) We evaluate using the `run` **method** defined in the `Session` class as `run (fetches, feed_dict=None, options=None, run_metadata)`

5) If fetches is a list, `run` returns a list object. If it is a single tensor, then it returns a Python data type.

Also, `feed_dict` is used to pass in input data using the `tf` placeholder.

I think this provides a very high level but necessary overview of basics in TF 1.x. Now let's see how TF 2.x changed all of this.

Embracing TF 2.x

Let's discuss some key aspects that make TF2.x developer friendly.

Eager Execution

TensorFlow 2.x natively supports "eager execution." There is no longer the need to first statically define a computational graph and then execute it, which inhibits immediate error logging, faster debugging, and native Python control.

```
import TensorFlow as tf
    a = tf.constant([[1,0], [0,1]], dtype = float)
print(a)
```

```
tf.Tensor(
    [[1. 0.]
     [0. 1.]], shape=(2, 2), dtype=float32)
```

AutoGraph

AutoGraph takes eager-style Python code and automatically converts it to graph-generating code.

To use Python code, we need to add a decorator @tf.function. This converts that code to an equivalent static graph. @tf.function marks the code for just-in-time compilation (JIT), which enables compilation of a Python function to a TensorFlow function and hence overall with simple Pythonic logic we get the same optimization as that of a TF lower-level API.

For comparison, look at the following code:

```
def huber_loss(a):
  if tf.abs(a) <= delta:
        loss = a * a / 2
  else:
        loss = delta * (tf.abs(a) - delta / 2)
  return loss
```

Using decorator on the above function basically converts it to something like

```
def tf__huber_loss(a):
    with tf.name_scope('huber_loss'):

        def if_true():
          with tf.name_scope('if_true'):
            loss = a * a / 2
        return loss,

        def if_false():
          with tf.name_scope('if_false'):
            loss = delta * (tf.abs(a) - delta / 2)
        return loss,
    loss = ag__.utils.run_cond(tf.less_equal(tf.abs(a), delta), if_true,
        if_false)
    return loss
```

TensorFlow Datasets

TensorFlow datasets provide an easy way to deal with heterogeneous data such as columnar, text, image, etc. along with making it possible to handle large amounts and varieties of data and perform complex transformations.

Creation: Create data

- `from_tensor_slices()`: Individual (or multiple) NumPy (or tensors) and supports batches

- `from_tensors()`: Similar to above but doesn't support batches

- `from_generator()`: Takes input from a `generator_function`

Transformation: Transform data

- `batch()`: Divides the data into a sequence of predefined sizes

- `repeat()`: Duplicates the data

- `shuffle()`: Randomly shuffle the data

- `map()`: Applies a function to all the elements of the data

- `filter()`: Filters the data using a function/expression

Optimizations:

GPUs and TPUs radically cut back the time needed to execute one training step. Achieving peak performance needs an efficient input pipeline that delivers information for the ensuing step before the current step has finished. The tf.data API helps us achieve that. There's more information at `www.TensorFlow.org/guide/data_performance`. You are going to effectively leverage tf.data at various places in different case studies, so be watchful.

tf.keras

tf.keras offers a higher API level, with three different programming models: Sequential API, Functional API, and Model Subclassing.

- Sequential API: Sequential groups a linear stack of layers into a `tf.keras.Model`. Each layer is callable (with a tensor in input), and each layer returns a tensor as an output.

```
tf.keras.Sequential(
    layers=None, name=None
)
```

Arguments

`layers`	Optional list of layers to add to the model
`name`	Optional name for the model

- Functional API: Allows multiple inputs and outputs and building non-linear topology of neural networks such as one with residual networks.

```
tf.keras.Model(
    *args, **kwargs
)
```

Arguments

`inputs`	The input(s) of the model: a `keras.Input` object or list of `keras.Input` objects
`outputs`	The output(s) of the model
`name`	String, the name of the model

- Model Subclassing: It allows you to define your own custom layer. In order to create a custom layer, you must subclass `tf.keras.layers.Layer` and also implement the following functions:

  - `__init__`: Optionally used to define all the sublayers to be used by this layer. It takes all hyperparameters as arguments.

  - `build`: Used to create the weights of the layer. You can add weights with `add_weight()`.

  - `call`: Used to define the forward pass and computes the output of the layer after activation of linear input of weights and bias

> **Note**   Use `tf.Keras` instead of `Keras` for better integration with other TensorFlow APIs such as eager execution and `tf.data`, etc.

Estimators

The Estimators API was added to TensorFlow in Release 1.1 and provides a high-level abstraction over lower-level TensorFlow core operations. It works with an Estimator instance, which is TensorFlow's high-level representation of a complete model. See Figure 2-3.

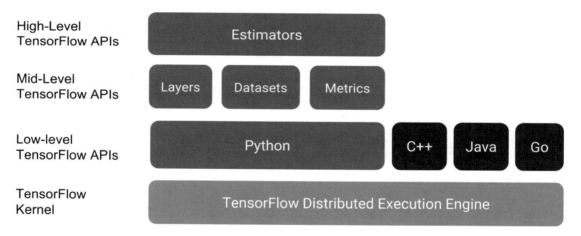

Figure 2-3. *TF Stack*

Keras is similar to the Estimators API in that it abstracts deep learning model components such as layers, activation functions, and optimizers to make it easier for developers. See Figure 2-4.

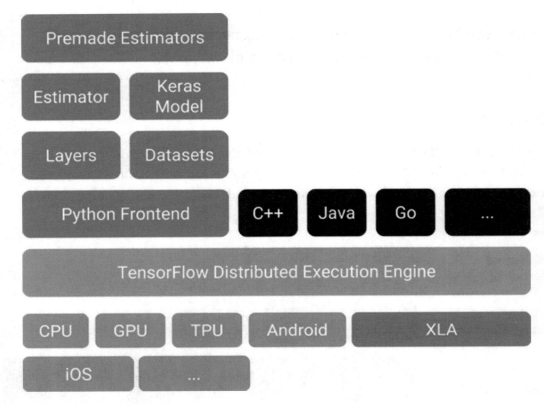

Figure 2-4. *TF 2.x Stack*

So both the Estimator API and Keras API provide a high-level API over low-level core TensorFlow API, and you can use either to train your model. But the Estimators API is better integrated with the TF ecosystem and is optimized for training and distribution and hence is sometimes preferred.

You can convert your Keras model to an Estimator object and get the best of both worlds. Go to `www.TensorFlow.org/tutorials/estimator/keras_model_to_ estimator.`

Recommendations for Best Use

There are some best practices that can be followed while using TF 2.x

1. Use higher-level APIs from `tf.keras` wherever possible and don't default to v1 for performance enhancement unless and until required.

2. Add a `tf.function` decorator to make it run efficiently in graph mode with AutoGraph.

3. Write a high performance data input pipeline using `tf.data` datasets to leverage things like shuffling, batching, and prefetching.

4. Write custom layers using Model Subclassing and use it as any other layer in a Functional or Sequential Keras Model.

Installation and Setup

In this section, you will learn about how to set your system up. By no means this is a complete guide but it gives you some ideas. I always suggest following the latest documentation from official pages.

Python Installation

I always suggest using Anaconda to set your system up. To set it up on Windows, go to `www.anaconda.com/products/individual#windows`. Depending upon your machine, choose the right installer (Figure 2-5).

Windows

Python 3.8
64-Bit Graphical Installer (457 MB)
32-Bit Graphical Installer (403 MB)

MacOS

Python 3.8
64-Bit Graphical Installer (435 MB)
64-Bit Command Line Installer (428 MB)

Linux

Python 3.8
64-Bit (x86) Installer (529 MB)
64-Bit (Power8 and Power9) Installer (279 MB)

Figure 2-5. *Anaconda Windows installation*

After you download and click the "I Agree" button, select a destination folder to install Anaconda and click the Next button (Figure 2-6).

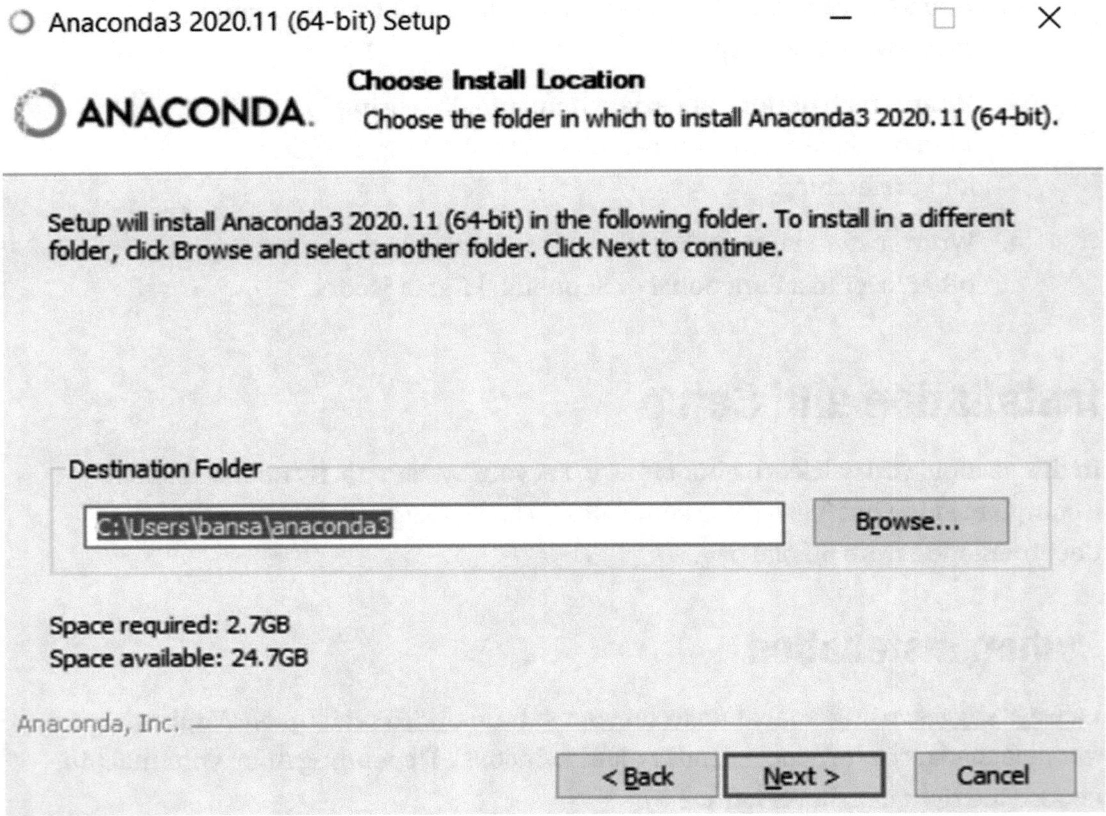

Figure 2-6. *Choosing a destination folder*

Choose whether to add Anaconda to your PATH environment variable (Figure 2-7). I don't recommend adding Anaconda to the PATH environment variable, since this can interfere with other software. Instead, use the Anaconda software by opening Anaconda Navigator or the Anaconda prompt from the Start menu.

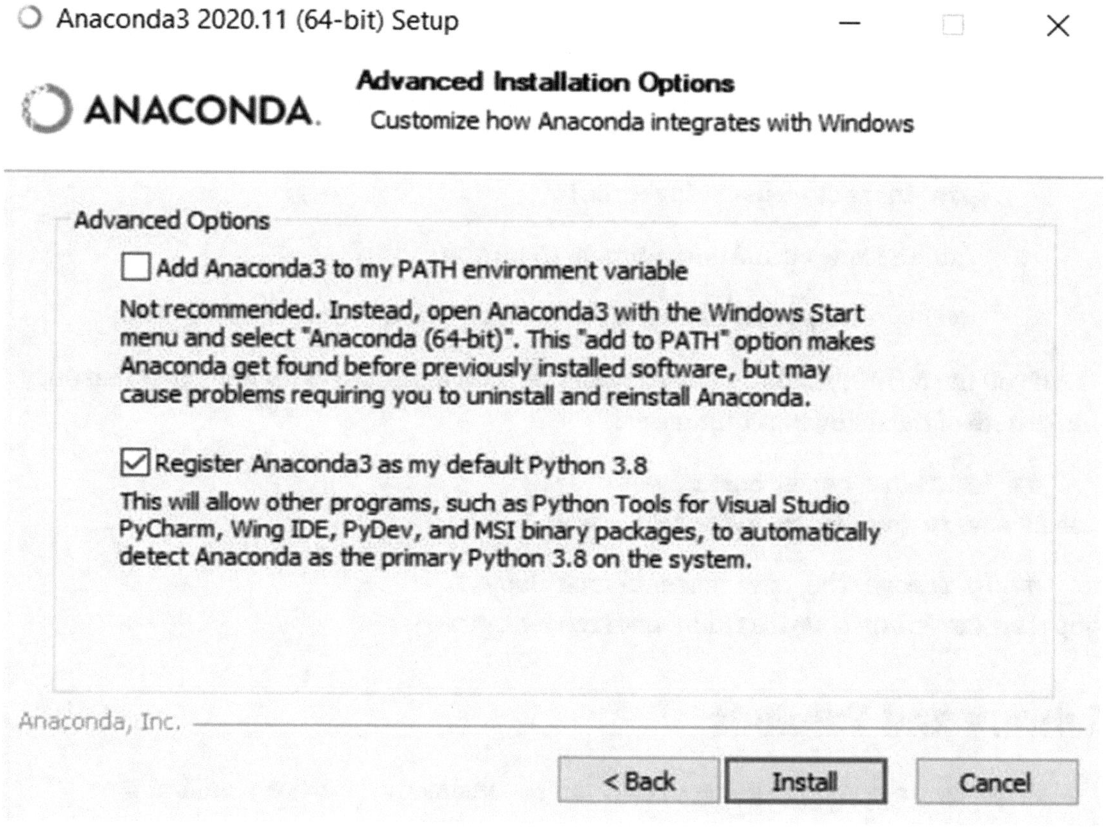

○ Anaconda3 2020.11 (64-bit) Setup   —   ☐   ✕

◯ ANACONDA.   **Advanced Installation Options**
                 Customize how Anaconda integrates with Windows

---

Advanced Options

☐ Add Anaconda3 to my PATH environment variable

Not recommended. Instead, open Anaconda3 with the Windows Start
menu and select "Anaconda (64-bit)". This "add to PATH" option makes
Anaconda get found before previously installed software, but may
cause problems requiring you to uninstall and reinstall Anaconda.

☑ Register Anaconda3 as my default Python 3.8

This will allow other programs, such as Python Tools for Visual Studio
PyCharm, Wing IDE, PyDev, and MSI binary packages, to automatically
detect Anaconda as the primary Python 3.8 on the system.

Anaconda, Inc. ───

                          [< Back] [**Install**]   [Cancel]

Figure 2-7. *Choosing the path*

Click the Install button. If you want to watch the packages Anaconda is installing,
click Show Details and then click the Next button.

Using the Virtual Environment

For each case study, it is a good practice to set up different virtual environments each
time so that different versions don't conflict with each other.

In order to create a conda environment,

1) Open the Anaconda Prompt as an Administrator.

2) In the terminal, enter

```
conda create -n virtual_env_name python=3.7 pip scikit-learn
matplotlib numpy pandas
```

3) Activate the virtual environment:

```
conda activate virtual_env_name
```

4) Make sure that ipykernel is installed:

```
pip install --user ipykernel
```

5) Add the new virtual environment to Jupyter:

```
python -m ipykernel install --user --name='environment_name'
```

If you mistakenly made an environment or want to remove it for any other reason, make note of the following commands:

```
## To remove conda environment
conda env remove -n 'environment_name'
```

```
## To remove the environment from Jupyter
jupyter kernelspec uninstall 'environment_name'
```

Library and Versions

For all the libraries you are going to use, you can install the latest version, but may be some codependencies for which you need to make sure that the correct version is maintained.

TensorFlow and GPU

Go to www.TensorFlow.org/install/source_windows to find which version of CUDA and cuDNN goes with your TensorFlow version (Figure 2-8). I personally like to work with 2.2.0 or 2.3.0 but not higher as there can be a lot of unknown bugs in the latest release and a very old release might not be suitable or might be outdated.

GPU

Version	Python version	Compiler	Build tools	cuDNN	CUDA
tensorflow_gpu-2.4.0	3.6-3.8	MSVC 2019	Bazel 3.1.0	8.0	11.0
tensorflow_gpu-2.3.0	3.5-3.8	MSVC 2019	Bazel 3.1.0	7.6	10.1
tensorflow_gpu-2.2.0	3.5-3.8	MSVC 2019	Bazel 2.0.0	7.6	10.1
tensorflow_gpu-2.1.0	3.5-3.7	MSVC 2019	Bazel 0.27.1-0.29.1	7.6	10.1

Figure 2-8. *TensorFlow and GPU version*

After you pick the TensorFlow version and the corresponding cuDNN and CUDA version, go to the Nvidia website.

The Nvidia CUDA Toolkit enables creation of GPU-accelerated applications.

The Nvidia CUDA Deep Neural Network library (cuDNN) provides efficient implementations for standard operations such as forward and backward convolution, pooling, normalization, and activation layers.

Both are necessary to enable GPUs with your TensorFlow environment.

The cuDNN library contains three files:

- `\bin\cudnn64_7.dll` (the version number may be different)

- `\include\cudnn.h`

- `\lib\x64\cudnn.lib`.

You should copy them to the following locations, respectively:

- `%CUDA_Installation_directory%\bin\cudnn64_7.dll`

- `%CUDA_Installation_directory%\include\cudnn.h`

- `%CUDA_Installation_directory%\lib\x64\cudnn.lib`

By default, `%CUDA_Installation_directory%` points to `C:\Program Files\NVIDIA GPU Computing Toolkit\CUDA\v10.1`. See Figure 2-9.

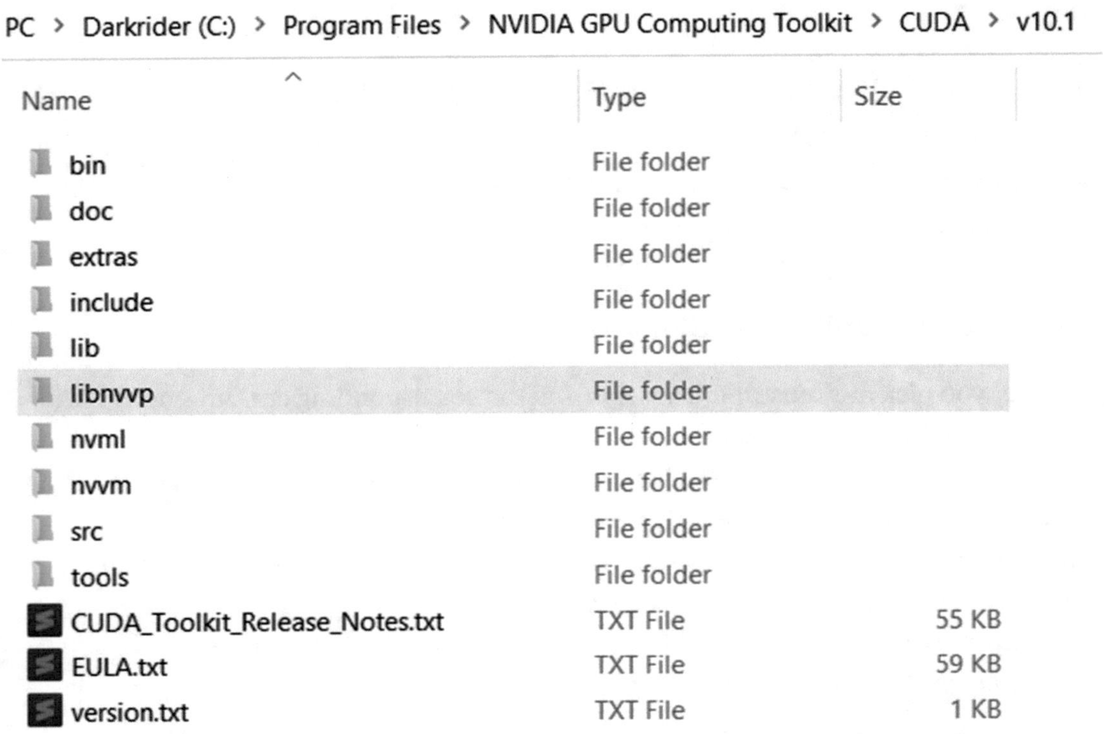

PC > Darkrider (C:) > Program Files > NVIDIA GPU Computing Toolkit > CUDA > v10.1

Name	Type	Size
bin	File folder	
doc	File folder	
extras	File folder	
include	File folder	
lib	File folder	
libnvvp	File folder	
nvml	File folder	
nvvm	File folder	
src	File folder	
tools	File folder	
CUDA_Toolkit_Release_Notes.txt	TXT File	55 KB
EULA.txt	TXT File	59 KB
version.txt	TXT File	1 KB

Figure 2-9. *CUDA installation*

Add the following paths to the Environment System variables:

- `C:\Program Files\NVIDIA GPU Computing Toolkit\CUDA\v10.1\bin`

- `C:\Program Files\NVIDIA GPU Computing Toolkit\CUDA\v10.1\libnvvp`

- `C:\Program Files\NVIDIA GPU Computing Toolkit\CUDA\v10.1\lib\x64`

For other OSes, instructions are pretty easy to follow and are mentioned on the official website.

Others

For packages like TensorFlow Federated, there is a tested TensorFlow version associated with it (Figure 2-10). If you are installing Federated using pip, it can happen that your TensorFlow version can alter so please precheck before running any code.

TensorFlow Federated	TensorFlow
0.18.0	tensorflow 2.4.0
0.17.0	tensorflow 2.3.0
0.16.1	tensorflow 2.2.0
0.16.0	tensorflow 2.2.0
0.15.0	tensorflow 2.2.0
0.14.0	tensorflow 2.2.0
0.13.1	tensorflow 2.1.0
0.13.0	tensorflow 2.1.0

Figure 2-10. *TensorFlow Federated and its compatible versions*

Also, for using packages like nltk and scispacy there are some presetups required.

For nltk, make sure you download all the prepackages required by using `nltk.download()` before you start using the package.

For scispacy models, you need to pip install on the model link you want:

```
pip install scispacy
pip install <Model URL>
```

Model links can be obtained from `https://allenai.github.io/scispacy/`.

Note   Spacy released v3.0 on Jan 31, 2021. You should use v2.0 for these case studies since it is what the code was tested on.

Conclusion

You now have a solid foundation: you know what you will be working with (Chapter 2) and the ecosystem you will enter (Chapter 1) and are ready for a deep dive in the upcoming chapters. I recommend that you follow the above steps to set up your Python environment. Most of the code associated with the case studies is available as Jupyter notebooks on the official GitHub page of the book.

CHAPTER 3

Predicting Hospital Readmission by Analyzing Patient EHR Records

A discharged patient who goes back to the hospital within a specified time frame is called *readmitted* in medical parlance. These readmission time frames can vary anywhere from 30 days to 1 year. The CMS that monitors the largest insurance programs, Medicare and Medicaid, defines a hospital readmission as "an admission to an acute care hospital within 30 days of discharge from the same or another acute care hospital."

Why it is even important to analyze this data? As evident due to a time-frame restriction, if a patient is readmitted in a short amount of time, it raises doubts about the healthcare quality. Hence it becomes imperative to analyze readmission rates as a quality benchmark. Payer programs like those of CMS have linked their reimbursement decisions on this metric as part of the Patient Protection and Affordable Care Act, which penalizes the healthcare system for an unusual and high readmission rate. This penalization can go up to 3% lower reimbursement. A patient's readmission is associated with an increase in mortality and morbidity. Hence, it becomes quite important for physicians to provide care not just for the disease the patient was admitted for but also any issues in their past medical record.

In this case study, you are going to see how readmission can be predicted by examining various factors like comorbidities, lab test values, chart events, and demographic features of the patient.

What Is EHR Data?

To understand EHR data, let's follow the journey of a patient consulting a physician.

© Anshik 2021
Anshik, *AI for Healthcare with Keras and Tensorflow 2.0*, https://doi.org/10.1007/978-1-4842-7086-8_3

Typically when a patient starts showing some symptoms of a disease in the modern world, they consult the Internet or their friends and families. If it gets worse, the patient can choose to visit a doctor.

The doctor (a.k.a. the provider) can order imaging or lab tests to diagnose the problem better, make prescriptions, and write notes about the patient's adherence and outcome from prescriptions. All of this is stored in a patient's medical record. Figure 3-1 shows how the pipeline flows. The first three steps show how a medical record can be created.

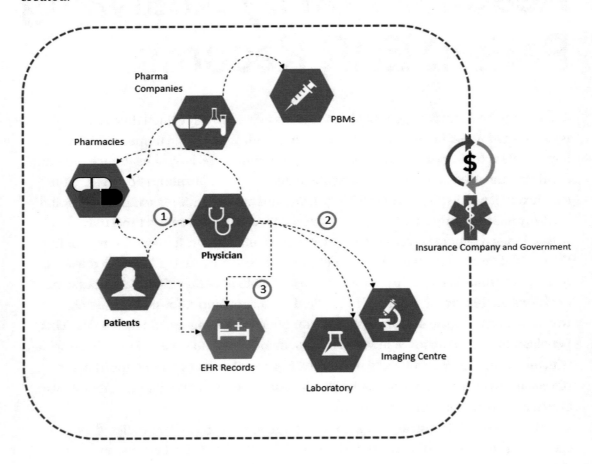

Figure 3-1. *Steps in a patient's care*

You may have noticed that I have been interchangeably using *medical* and *health records*. For our purposes, where we are just going to use clinical information for a patient, there is no difference, but actually there is a slight difference between the two.

An EMR (electronic medical record) tracks medical data over time and contains information on screenings/checkups and observations on how the patient is doing on certain parameters for which they are diagnosed.

An EHR (electronic health record) is EMR plus a lot of other patient-level data. It goes beyond standard clinical data collected at the provider's end and includes other care elements such as data from wearable devices, patient's genomic data, and signals data like ECG, respiration, etc.

Figure 3-2 shows a timeline view of different events during care for different patients.

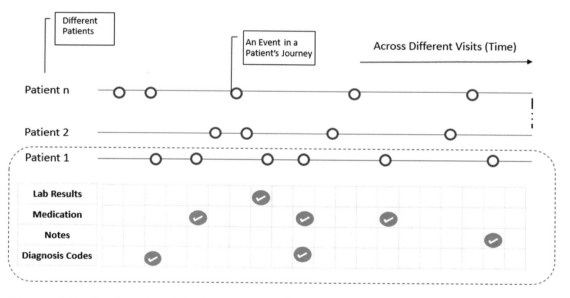

Figure 3-2. *Patients' medical events timeline view*

In your case, you will be using MIMIC 3 dataset. Here's how to obtain access to it and set it up for analysis.

I hope you have a good idea of EHR data. Let's dive deeper into the MIMIC-3 dataset, which is available after you complete a certain test, and is licensed for research purposes. It is a highly cited dataset and you will be using it for two case studies so I hope you are as excited as I am to get started.

MIMIC 3 Data: Setup and Introduction

MIMIC stands for Medical Information Mart for Intensive Care. It is part of a larger dataset called PhysioNet, which is a large open source collection of physiologic and clinical data submitted by many institutions. It comprises deidentified health-related data associated with over 40,000 patients who stayed in critical care units of the Beth Israel Deaconess Medical Center between 2001 and 2012.

The database includes information such as demographics, vital sign measurements made at the bedside (~1 data point per hour), laboratory test results, procedures, medications, caregiver notes, imaging reports, and mortality (both in and out of hospital). Figure 3-3 gives an overview of the MIMIC-3 Dataset.

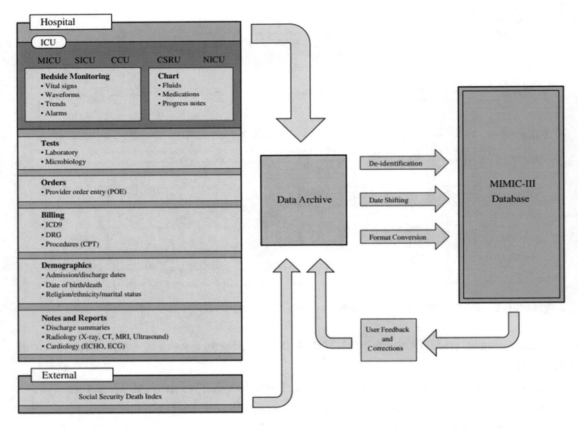

Figure 3-3. *Overview of Mimic-3 Data. Source: www.nature.com/articles/sdata201635*

Access

To obtain access, please follow the instructions at `https://mimic.physionet.org/gettingstarted/access/`.

Mainly, these are the steps to follow:

1) Create a PhysioNet account.

2) Complete the CITI Training Course.

3) Request the MIMIC 3 dataset.

4) Access MIMIC 3.

    a) Access the MIMIC 3 dataset at `https://physionet.org/content/mimiciii/1.4/` after logging in into your PhysioNet account.

    b) Go to the Files Section at the bottom of the page.

Note   You will need to enter a reference such as a colleague and clearly state your purpose for obtaining the access. The reference will be sent an email to verify. Unless and until you want to use it for commercial purposes, PhysioNet has been generous enough to give licenses without any trouble.

The instructions are quite easy to follow as detailed on the website. If you get stuck anywhere, just google it.

Introduction and Setup

If you have access to AWS or GCP, there is good news: the MIMIC 3 dataset is present in their datamart, ready to be queried.

Recently, the MIT Laboratory of Computational Physiology (LCP) started hosting the MIMIC 3 dataset on the AWS cloud through the AWS Public Dataset program. You can now use the MIMIC 3 dataset via S3 without having to download, copy, or pay to store it. Instead, you can analyze the MIMIC 3 dataset in the AWS Cloud using AWS services like Amazon EC2, Athena, AWS Lambda, or Amazon EMR.

To get access to these databases on the cloud, follow the steps detailed at `https://mimic.physionet.org/gettingstarted/cloud/`.

I will assume you don't have access to any of these cloud facilities, so you will download the zip and use it for your purpose.

Before you take a deep dive into your problem and start using MIMIC, let's understand just the basics of it. As you have seen, MIMIC 3 is available as a zip of a different CSV, which means it is a very well organized relational database. To have a look at the schema or entity relationship diagram for MIMIC 3, visit

https://cloud.githubusercontent.com/assets/26095093/23737659/454872b0-0449-11e7-987d-639b0415dca4.png

or

https://mit-lcp.github.io/mimic-schema-spy/relationships.html.

The first link is generated using DbSchema while the second one is generated using open source schema spy. I personally like DbSchema.

Some things to know about MIMIC:

1) All tables have at least one unique identifier which is the ROW_ID. See Figure 3-4.

   a) This ROW-ID is present just to make the values unique at the row level.

   b) This should never be used for the JOIN linkage variable.

   c) From a functional standpoint, there can be a single primary key for the table or a combination of multiple keys. This primary key or a set of it represents the data uniquely in that table. See Figure 3-4.

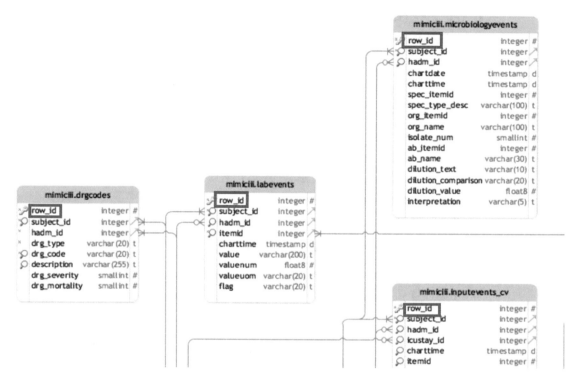

Figure 3-4. *ROW_ID column present in each MIMIC table*

2) The most important IDs are

    a) SUBJECT_ID: Refers to a unique patient

    b) HADM_ID: Refers to a hospital admission event for a patient.

    c) ICUSTAY_ID: Refers to an ICU episode for a patient

3) Dictionary Tables: MIMIC has five dictionary tables that begin
    with D_XXXX. They help convert coded information into a
    human-readable format like text.

    a) D_CPT: High-level dictionary of Current Procedural Terminology
        (CPT) codes

    b) D_ICD_DIAGNOSES: Dictionary of International Statistical
        Classification of Diseases and Related Health Problems (ICD-9)
        codes relating to diagnoses

    c) D_ICD_PROCEDURES: Dictionary of International Statistical Classification of Diseases and Related Health Problems (ICD-9) codes relating to procedures

    d) D_ITEMS: Dictionary of local codes (ITEMIDs) appearing in the MIMIC database, except those that relate to laboratory tests

        i) For example, every row of CHARTEVENTS is associated with a single ITEMID. By joining CHARTEVENTS and D_ITEMS on ITEMID you can find the concept measured like blood pressure, respiratory rate, etc.

    e) D_LABELITEMS: Dictionary of local codes (ITEMIDs) appearing in the MIMIC database that relate to laboratory tests

4) The database contains dynamic data such as patient-id, patient's demographic information, and ICU stay id, and static data such as measurement coming from lab values associated with each visit across time, etc.

5) Two different critical care information systems were in place over the data collection period: Philips CareVue and iMDsoft MetaVision ICU. With exception to data relating to fluid intake, which differed significantly in structure between the CareVue and MetaVision systems, data was merged when building the database tables. For details, please refer to https://mimic.physionet.org/mimicdata/io/.

6) Data is deidentified according to HIPAA compliance. Remember Chapter 1?

    a) Dates are shifted by a random offset. But intervals are preserved.

    b) Time of day, day of the week, and approximate seasonality were conserved during date shifting.

    c) Dates of birth for patients aged over 89 were shifted to obscure their true age and comply with HIPAA regulations. These patients appear in the database with ages of over 300 years.

    d) Protected health information was removed from free text using lookups and regex.

Data

From various studies researching the readmission problem, there are four main categories of predictors of a patient's readmission. They are

1) Social and demographic information like age, ethnicity, and payer

2) Admission-related such as discharge time, first care unit, number of transfers, length of stay

3) Lab results of important elements like urea, platelets, albumin, etc.

4) Patient's clinical data like blood pressure, heart rate, glucose, etc.

5) Comorbidities, which are preexisting chronic conditions that can affect the severity of a disease within a patient. Elixhauser codified them into 29 categories using ICD-9 codes. Finally, Quan et al proposed an enhanced ICD-9 coding methodology based on examining inconsistencies among previous definitions.

Table 3-1 details all the values you will be calculating in order to predict for readmissions.

Table 3-1. *Predictors for Readmission*

Social and Demographic	Age
	Gender
	Ethnicity
	Payor
	DOB (to get age)
Admission Related	Discharge Duration
	First Care Unit
	Discharge Location
	Number of Transfers within 24 hours (for a ICU STAY ID)

(continued)

Table 3-1. (*continued*)

Lab Results of Important Elements	Platelets (cells x 10^3 /μL)
	Hematocrit %
	Albumin (g/dL)
	Sodium (mg/dL)
	Potassium (mg/dL)
	Calcium (mg/dL)
Patient's Clinical Data	Blood Glucose Level
	Respiratory Rate
	Blood Pressure (Systolic and Diastolic)
	Heart Rate
	Body Temperature
Comorbidity Score	ELIXHAUSER-Quan Score

Social and Demographic

To get social and demographic data, you need admissions and patient data. Load the two datasets and get the features for each subject ID as laid out in the Social and Demographic tab.

```python
import pandas as pd
import numpy as np
import matplotlib.pyplot as plt
import random

# Text Processing
import re

    admissions = pd.read_csv("./Data/ADMISSIONS.csv", index_col = None)
    patients = pd.read_csv("./Data/PATIENTS.csv", index_col = None)
```

```
# Convert all the date columns
    admissions.ADMITTIME = pd.to_datetime(admissions.ADMITTIME, format =
    '%Y-%m-%d %H:%M:%S', errors = 'coerce')
    admissions.DISCHTIME = pd.to_datetime(admissions.DISCHTIME, format =
    '%Y-%m-%d %H:%M:%S', errors = 'coerce')
    admissions.DEATHTIME = pd.to_datetime(admissions.DEATHTIME, format =
    '%Y-%m-%d %H:%M:%S', errors = 'coerce')

    patients.DOB = pd.to_datetime(patients.DOB, format = '%Y-%m-%d
    %H:%M:%S', errors = 'coerce')
```

You will keep the admissions data sorted per subject to see what the post admission journey looks like.

```
    admissions = admissions.sort_values(['SUBJECT_ID','ADMITTIME'])
admissions.reset_index(drop = True, inplace = True)
```

Now, since you already have the patient's admit time and DOB from the patient's table, you can calculate a patient's age. See the result in Figure 3-5.

```
    patient_age = {row[1]: row[2] for row in patients[['SUBJECT_ID',
    'DOB']].itertuples()}
    admissions["AGE"] = [int((adm_time.date() - patient_age[subj_id].
    date()).days/365)
                        for adm_time, subj_id in zip(admissions
                        ["ADMITTIME"], admissions["SUBJECT_ID"])]
age_plot = admissions.AGE.hist()
    age_plot.set_xlabel('Age of Patients')
    age_plot.set_ylabel('Count of Patients')
```

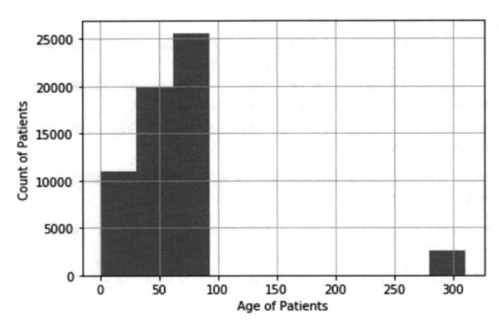

Figure 3-5. *Histogram plot of age and number of subjects withing that age bin*

This histogram shows that that more or less the age is spread up to 100, but there are a lot of patients with an age of 300. Don't be confused. This is just because patients with age of over 89 are noted as 300 in the MIMIC 3 dataset due to HIPAA compliance. There are relatively fewer patients with an age of over 89 and, based on their ICU stay and demographic pattern, it is easier to identify them so such measures were taken.

You will do two things to get the right age graph/distribution for your use case.

1) You will randomly spread the people with age 300 in your current dataset to any age between 90 and 100.

2) You will remove young patients, preferably those below the age of 18, as their chances of readmission are quite low due to rare occurrence of any existing comorbidity and general better health. This can also help correct for any imbalance between the readmission and non-readmission classes.

```
admissions.loc[admissions.AGE >= 300,"AGE"] = random.
choices(list(range(90,100)),k = sum(admissions.AGE >= 300))

admissions = admissions[admissions.AGE >18]
```

Lastly, you see that there are over 41 ethnicities in the data but the support (number of subjects) for each type is quite low. Hence you will be clubbing some of the ethnicities to get a better representation while just slightly affecting precision. See Figure 3-6.

```
admissions.ETHNICITY.value_counts().head(10).sort_values().
plot(kind = "barh")
```

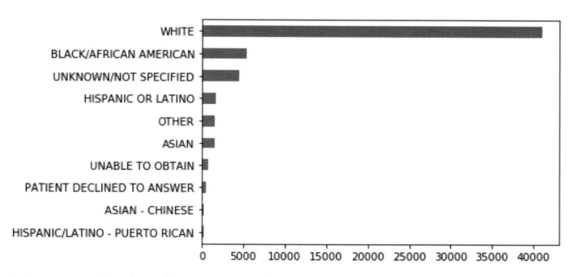

Figure 3-6. *Number of patients per ethnicity types*

```
def normalize_ethnicity(x):
    """

    Helper Function to Normalize Ethnicity into "WHITE", "HISPANIC",
    "ASIAN", "BLACK" and "OTHERS"
    """

    if "WHITE" in x:
        return "WHITE"
    elif "HISPANIC" in x:
        return "HISPANIC"
    elif "ASIAN" in x:
        return "ASIAN"
    elif "BLACK" in x:
        "BLACK"
else:
        return "OTHERS"
```

```
admissions.ETHNICITY.value_counts()
admissions.ETHNICITY = admissions.ETHNICITY.apply(lambda x: normalize_
ethnicity(x) if pd.notnull(x) else x)
```

This helps get all the patient-level characteristics that you aimed for. You will merge this data on subject ID with the admissions table. This admission table will be used to train your algorithms. Why wait? Let's quickly see how to merge the data in the admissions table and get your desired features.

Admissions Related

Similar to the reasons for the ethnicity data, you can club various discharge locations into normalized categories, which will have better support for each of them.

Let's club the discharge location into three categories: Medical Facility, Home, and Others:

```
def normalize_discharge(x):
    """
    Helper Function to Normalize Discharge Location into "HOME",
    "MEDICAL_FACILITY", and "OTHERS"
    """
    if "HOME" in x:
        return "HOME"
    elif len(re.findall("OTHER|DEAD",x)) > 0:
        return "OTHER"
    else:
        return "MEDICAL_FACILITY"
```

```
admissions.DISCHARGE_LOCATION = admissions.DISCHARGE_LOCATION.apply(lambda
x: normalize_discharge(x) if pd.notnull(x) else x)
```

The discharge location in days can easily be calculated by subtracting the discharge time from the admit time:

```
admissions["DISCHARGE_DURATION"] = (admissions["DISCHTIME"] -
admissions["ADMITTIME"]).dt.total_seconds()/(24*60*60)
```

Now, to get your train flag readmission/no-readmission, you need to get the number of days it took for each patient until the next admission. To get this, follow a two-step approach:

1) Shift the next admit time against last admit time.

2) Subtract the discharge time from the next admit time to get days until next admission.

```python
# Step 1:- Add the next Admit Time
    admissions = admissions.sort_values(['SUBJECT_ID','ADMITTIME'])
    #make sure the admittime is sorted before the shift operation
    admissions['NEXT_ADMITTIME'] = admissions.groupby('SUBJECT_ID').
    ADMITTIME.shift(-1)
# Step 2:- Subtract Discharge Time from Next Admit Time
    admissions['DAYS_NEXT_ADMIT']= (admissions.NEXT_ADMITTIME - admissions.
    DISCHTIME).dt.total_seconds()/(24*60*60)

    admissions["IS_READMISSION"] = admissions.DAYS_NEXT_ADMIT.apply
    (lambda x: 0 if pd.isnull(x) else (0 if x >30 else 1))
```

Also, you need only unplanned medical care and your patient cohort should not represent newborns, so filter out "ELECTIVE" and "NEWBORN":

```python
admissions.ADMISSION_TYPE.value_counts()
    admissions = admissions[~admissions.ADMISSION_TYPE.isin(["ELECTIVE",
    "NEWBORN"])].reset_index(drop = True)
```

```python
# Lastly we will remove those any death related admission events.
    admissions = admissions[admissions.HOSPITAL_EXPIRE_FLAG == 0].reset_
    index(drop = True)

    admissions = admissions[["SUBJECT_ID", "HADM_ID", "AGE", "ADMISSION_
    TYPE","DISCHARGE_DURATION","DISCHARGE_LOCATION","INSURANCE","ETHNICITY",
    "IS_READMISSION"]]

    admissions = pd.merge(admissions, patients[["SUBJECT_ID","GENDER"]],
    how="left", on = "SUBJECT_ID")
```

So far you have filtered the relevant events and got the discharge duration for admission-related characteristics. You have also generated your target label of readmission vs. no readmission within 30 days.

Now you can move on to get other features.

1) Prepping the data:

```
icustays = pd.read_csv("./Data/ICUSTAYS.csv", index_col = None)
transfers = pd.read_csv("./Data/TRANSFERS.csv", index_col = None)

# Convert all the date columns
icustays.INTIME = pd.to_datetime(icustays.INTIME, format = '%Y-%m-%d
%H:%M:%S', errors = 'coerce')
icustays.OUTTIME = pd.to_datetime(icustays.OUTTIME, format = '%Y-%m-%d
%H:%M:%S', errors = 'coerce')
```

```
transfers.dropna(subset=["ICUSTAY_ID"], inplace = True)
transfers.ICUSTAY_ID = transfers.ICUSTAY_ID.astype(int)
```

The number of transfers is an important determination of how critical the patient's case is and depending on comorbidities multiple ICUs can be used.

As an ICUSTAY_ID in the ICUSTAYS table groups all ICU admissions within 24 hours of each other, it is possible for a patient to be transferred from one type of ICU to another and have the same ICUSTAY_ID. To get the exact number of transfers for a particular ICUSTAYID, you can use the TRANSFERS table.

The TRANSFERS table contains EVENTTYPE, which contains two values, transfer and admit. You will sum up all the transfers for a ICUSTAY event (a unique ICUSTAY_ID) to get the transfers done within 24 hours for that patient.

```
transfers_num = transfers.groupby(["SUBJECT_ID","HADM_ID","ICUSTAY_ID"])
['EVENTTYPE'].apply(lambda x : sum(x=="transfer")).reset_index()
transfers_num.columns = ["SUBJECT_ID","HADM_ID","ICUSTAY_ID", "NUM_
TRANSFERS"]
```

```
# Updating ICU Data with number of transfer a patient undergoes once
admitted
icustays = pd.merge(icustays, transfers_num, on=["SUBJECT_ID","HADM_
ID","ICUSTAY_ID"], how="left")
```

```
# Making sure that if a key (SUBJECT_ID,HADM_ID,"ICUSTAY_ID") is not found
then number of transfers for that key automatically becomes 0
    icustays.NUM_TRANSFERS.fillna(0, inplace = True)

# ICU Transfers within 24hrs for a unique hospital admission
    icustays_transfers_num = icustays.groupby(["SUBJECT_ID","HADM_ID"])
    ["NUM_TRANSFERS"].sum().reset_index()
```

Now let's calculate the same ICU transfers for a hospital admission (a unique HADM_ID).

```
# ICU Transfers across days (>24 hours) for a unique hospital admission
    icustays_num = icustays.groupby(["SUBJECT_ID","HADM_ID"])
    ["ICUSTAY_ID"].nunique().reset_index()
    icustays_num.columns = ["SUBJECT_ID","HADM_ID","ICU_TRANSFERS"]
```

Another important determinant of patient's health during ICU STAYS can be LOS (length of stay). You get this information from ICUSTAYS table itself.

```
# Average Length of stay in ICU for a patient
    icustays_avg_los = icustays.groupby(["SUBJECT_ID","HADM_ID"])["LOS"].
    mean().reset_index()
```

You should also get the first care unit for the admission.

```
    icustays = icustays.sort_values(['SUBJECT_ID','HADM_ID','INTIME'])
    icustays_firstcare = icustays.groupby(['SUBJECT_ID','HADM_ID'])['FIRST_
    CAREUNIT'].nth(0).reset_index()
```

Merge all the different dataframes on SUBJECT_ID, HADM_ID.

```
import functools
_dfs = [icustays_num, icustays_avg_los, icustays_transfers_num, icustays_
firstcare]
    icustays_final = functools.reduce(lambda left,right: pd.merge(left,right,
    on=["SUBJECT_ID","HADM_ID"], how="inner"), _dfs)

    icustays_final["TOTAL_TRANSFERS"] = icustays_final["ICU_TRANSFERS"] +
    icustays_final["NUM_TRANSFERS"]
```

Lastly, if the first care unit relates to a newborn, it is unnecessary and insignificant for analysis, so you just drop such ICU stays.

```
icustays_final = icustays_final[~icustays_final.FIRST_CAREUNIT.isin([
"NICU","NWARD"])].reset_index(drop = True).drop(["NUM_TRANSFERS",
"ICU_TRANSFERS"], axis = 1)
```

For more information, refer to https://mimic.physionet.org/mimictables/transfers/.

Patient's Clinical Data

The clinical data for a patient is present in the CHARTEVENTS table. Historically, physicians used to maintain a complete record of a patient's key clinical data and medical history, such as demographics, vital signs, diagnoses, medication, etc.

Now both the lab events and patient's clinical data are pretty big files, almost 32GB in size, so it becomes imperative to be able to handle them seamlessly. You will adopt a smart way to read in and work with these files.

As you already know, you are working with a subset of CHARTEVENTS, the essential ones that help in understanding a patient's health. You will try to find information from such large tables only for those chart events.

For each patient's clinical event present in CHARTEVENTS there is an ITEMID associated with it, the definition for which is present in the D_ITEM table. Let's see the ITEMIDs corresponding to the clinical values.

```
dictionary_itemid = pd.read_csv("./Data/D_ITEMS.csv", index_col = None)
dictionary_itemid.dropna(subset=["LABEL"], inplace = True)
```

```
# We only need those ITEM IDs which links to chart events
dictionary_itemid = dictionary_itemid[dictionary_itemid.LINKSTO.
isin(["chartevents"])]
```

To get the ITEMIDs, follow these steps:

1) Make a combination of words you expect to show up as description.

2) Use your domain knowledge to filter down the ITEMIDs.

```
    dictionary_itemid = pd.read_csv("./Data/D_ITEMS.csv", index_col = None)
    dictionary_itemid.dropna(subset=["LABEL"], inplace = True)
```

```
# We only need those ITEM IDs which links to chart events
    dictionary_itemid = dictionary_itemid[dictionary_itemid.LINKSTO.
    isin(["chartevents"])]
```

```
    dictionary_itemid[[ True if ("sys" in x.lower() and len(re.findall(
    "bp|blood pressure|blood",x.lower()))) > 0) else False for x in
    dictionary_itemid.LABEL]]
    sys_bp_itemids = [51, 442, 6701, 220050, 220179]
```

```
    dictionary_itemid[[ True if ("dia" in x.lower() and len(re.findall(
    "bp|blood pressure|blood",x.lower()))) > 0) else False for x in
    dictionary_itemid.LABEL]]
    dia_bp_itemids = [8368, 8440, 8555, 220051, 220180]
```

```
    dictionary_itemid[[ True if ("resp" in x.lower() and len(re.
    findall("rate",x.lower()))) > 0) else False for x in dictionary_itemid.
    LABEL]]
    respr_itemids = [615, 618, 3603, 224690, 220210]
```

```
    dictionary_itemid[[ True if ("glucose" in x.lower()) else False for x
    in dictionary_itemid.LABEL]]
    glucose_itemids = [1455, 1310, 807, 811, 3744, 3745, 1529, 2338,
    225664, 220621, 226537]
```

```
# Similarly
    heartrate_itemids = [211, 220045]
    temp_itemids = [676, 678, 223761, 223762]
```

Read the CHARTEVENTS data. Keep the HADM_IDs you found in ICUSTAYs and the relevant ITEMIDs.

```
hadm_filter = icustays_final.HADM_ID.tolist()
total_itemids =
sys_bp_itemids+dia_bp_itemids+respr_itemids+glucose_itemids+temp_itemids
+heartrate_itemids
    n_rows = 100000
```

```python
# create the iterator
chartevents_iterator = pd.read_csv(
        "./Data/CHARTEVENTS.csv",
    iterator=True,
    chunksize=n_rows,
        usecols = ["SUBJECT_ID", "HADM_ID", "ICUSTAY_ID", "ITEMID",
        "VALUE", "VALUENUM", "VALUEUOM"])

# concatenate according to a filter to get our labevents data
chartevents = pd.concat(

    [chartevent_chunk[np.logical_and(chartevent_chunk['HADM_ID'].isin(hadm_
    filter),

    chartevent_chunk['ITEMID'].isin(total_itemids))] if
    str(chartevent_chunk.HADM_ID.dtype) == 'int64'
                    else
    chartevent_chunk[np.logical_and(chartevent_chunk['HADM_ID'].isin([float(x)
    for x in hadm_filter]),

    chartevent_chunk['ITEMID'].isin(total_itemids))]
    for chartevent_chunk in chartevents_iterator])

    chartevents.dropna(axis = 0, subset = ["VALUENUM"], inplace = True)
    chartevents.drop('VALUE', axis = 1, inplace = True)
```

Since the CHARTEVENTS data is collected from two different systems, it becomes important for you to check for different reporting units for your events. Let's quickly have a look.

```python
# Since the data is collected from two different systems let us check for
units for each of our patients clinical data
    print("Systolic BP :-
    ",chartevents[chartevents.ITEMID.isin(sys_bp_itemids)].VALUEUOM.unique())
    print("Diastolic BP :-
    ",chartevents[chartevents.ITEMID.isin(dia_bp_itemids)].VALUEUOM.unique())
    print("Respiratory Rate :-
    ",chartevents[chartevents.ITEMID.isin(respr_itemids)].VALUEUOM.unique())
    print("Glucose Levels :-
    ",chartevents[chartevents.ITEMID.isin(glucose_itemids)].VALUEUOM.unique())
```

```
print("Heart Rate :-
",chartevents[chartevents.ITEMID.isin(heartrate_itemids)].VALUEUOM.unique())
print("Temperature :-
",chartevents[chartevents.ITEMID.isin(temp_itemids)].VALUEUOM.unique())
```

Output

```
###############################################
Systolic BP :-   ['mmHg']
Diastolic BP :-   ['mmHg']
Respiratory Rate :-   ['insp/min' 'BPM']
Glucose Levels :-   [nan 'mg/dL']
Heart Rate :-   ['bpm' 'BPM']
Temperature :-   ['?F' '?C' 'Deg. F' 'Deg. C']
###############################################
```

There are three observations from above:

- insp/min is same as BPM, so no conversion is required here.

- You won't impute for NA in Glucose as the value is in the same range as when the unit is present.

- You need to convert Fahrenheit to Celsius.

Let's also replace the ITEMIDs by their descriptive labels to aid readability and also make them refer to a single category.

```
# Let us Replace ItemIds by their respective Chart Event Names to aid
readability
    mapping = {"Systolic_BP":sys_bp_itemids,
               "Diastolic_BP":dia_bp_itemids,
               "Resp_Rate":respr_itemids,
               "Glucose":glucose_itemids,
               "Heart_Rate":heartrate_itemids,
               "Temperature":temp_itemids}
item_id_map = {item_id: k for k,v in mapping.items() for item_id in v}
    chartevents["ITEMID"] = chartevents["ITEMID"].replace(item_id_map)
```

Let's convert Fahrenheit to Celsius:

```
cond1 = np.logical_and(np.logical_or(chartevents["VALUEUOM"] == "?F",
chartevents["VALUEUOM"] == "Deg. F"),
                pd.notnull(chartevents["VALUEUOM"])).tolist()

cond2 = np.logical_or(chartevents["VALUEUOM"] != "?F",
chartevents["VALUEUOM"] != "Deg. F").tolist()

condval1 = ((chartevents["VALUENUM"]-32)*5/9).tolist()
condval2= chartevents["VALUENUM"].tolist()
chartevents["VALUENUM"] = np.select([cond1, cond2], [condval1,condval2])
```

This brings you to standardized charts data for all the patients within your data. For analysis, you will be using two measures: one is a measure of central tendency (mean) and one is a measure of variability (standard deviation):

```
charts = chartevents.pivot_table(index=['SUBJECT_ID', 'HADM_ID'],
                        columns='ITEMID', values='VALUENUM',
                    aggfunc=[np.mean, np.std]).reset_index()

charts.columns = charts.columns.get_level_values(0)+'_'+charts.columns.
get_level_values(1)
```

There are going to be many nulls that depend on the data captured within MIMIC, and in general the number of nulls for standard deviation columns would be larger than mean columns since there are a lot of single values for a HADM_ID, but the difference is not much, as you can see:

Output

```
###############################################
SUBJECT_ID_             0
HADM_ID_                0
mean_Diastolic_BP   10988
mean_Glucose          610
mean_Heart_Rate       111
mean_Resp_Rate        134
mean_Systolic_BP    10981
mean_Temperature      241
```

```
std_Diastolic_BP     11215
std_Glucose           2557
std_Heart_Rate         121
std_Resp_Rate          173
std_Systolic_BP      11212
std_Temperature        687
##############################################
```

Some of these nulls can be corrected for by backfilling with values from the last admission visit:

```
charts = charts.groupby(['SUBJECT_ID_']).apply(lambda x: x.bfill())
```

Let's check how many null values you were able to correct. It looks like you were able to remove several nulls from the columns.

Output

```
##############################################
SUBJECT_ID_               0
HADM_ID_                  0
mean_Diastolic_BP      9053
mean_Glucose            526
mean_Heart_Rate          97
mean_Resp_Rate          116
mean_Systolic_BP       9047
mean_Temperature        210
std_Diastolic_BP       9258
std_Glucose            2131
std_Heart_Rate          107
std_Resp_Rate           150
std_Systolic_BP        9255
std_Temperature         600
##############################################
```

Lab Events

Similar to CHARTEVENTS, you will first find ITEMDs corresponding to the lab events you want to focus on and then use that to read the lab data.

```
hadm_filter = icustays_final.HADM_ID.tolist()
    total_labitems = [51265, 51221, 50862, 50983, 50971, 50893]
    n_rows = 100000

# create the iterator
labevents_iterator = pd.read_csv(
        "./Data/LABEVENTS.csv",
    iterator=True,
    chunksize=n_rows)

# concatenate according to a filter to get our labevents data
labevents = pd.concat(

    [labevent_chunk[np.logical_and(labevent_chunk['HADM_ID'].isin
    (hadm_filter),

    labevent_chunk['ITEMID'].isin(total_labitems))]if
    str(labevent_chunk.HADM_ID.dtype) == 'int64'
                else
    labevent_chunk[np.logical_and(labevent_chunk['HADM_ID'].isin([float(x)
    for x in hadm_filter]),

    labevent_chunk['ITEMID'].isin(total_labitems))]
    for labevent_chunk in labevents_iterator])
```

Let's replace ITEMIDs with actual names.

```
labevents_label =
dictionary_labitemid[dictionary_labitemid.ITEMID.isin(total_labitems)]
item_id_map = dict(zip(labevents_label.ITEMID,labevents_label.LABEL))

    labevents["ITEMID"] = labevents["ITEMID"].replace(item_id_map)
```

Let's quickly check if you need to normalize for any units.

```
    labevents.groupby(["ITEMID"])['VALUEUOM'].apply(lambda x: set(x))
```

Output

```
##############################################
Albumin              {nan, g/dL}
Calcium, Total       {nan, mg/dL}
Hematocrit               {nan, %}
```
62

```
Platelet Count       {nan, K/uL}
Potassium            {nan, mEq/L}
Sodium               {nan, mEq/L}
###############################################
```

It looks like you are good with units in case of lab events. All of the different events have a single type of unit.

Similar to CHARTEVENTS, you will calculate the mean and standard deviation on values of your lab events and then backfill any missing values.

```
labs = labevents.pivot_table(index=['SUBJECT_ID', 'HADM_ID'],
                             columns='ITEMID', values='VALUENUM',
                         aggfunc=[np.mean, np.std]).reset_index()
labs.columns = labs.columns.get_level_values(0)+'_'+labs.columns.
get_level_values(1)

labs = labs.groupby(['SUBJECT_ID_']).apply(lambda x: x.bfill())
```

```
labs.isnull().sum()
```

Output

```
###############################################
SUBJECT_ID_              0
HADM_ID_                 0
mean_Albumin         16302
mean_Calcium, Total   1849
mean_Hematocrit         17
mean_Platelet Count     30
mean_Potassium         139
mean_Sodium            153
std_Albumin          30443
std_Calcium, Total    5083
std_Hematocrit         746
std_Platelet Count     836
std_Potassium         1026
std_Sodium            1104
###############################################
```

Comorbidity Score

Comorbidities are important for predicting patient mortality, and higher comorbidities can adversely affect the mortality rate. Elixhauser and Quan's extensive research gives a numerical value to the comorbidity level of a patient. You can find more details at www.ncbi.nlm.nih.gov/pmc/articles/PMC6381763/.

Most of the ideas for creating this comorbidity score are calculated from MIMIC's original repo; see https://github.com/MIT-LCP/mimic-code/blob/master/concepts/comorbidity/elixhauser_quan.sql.

```
diagnosis_icd = pd.read_csv("./Data/DIAGNOSES_ICD.csv", index_col = None)

mapping = {'congestive_heart_failure':['39891','40201','40211','40291',
    '40401','40403','40411','40413','40491','40493','4254','4255','4257',
    '4258','4259','428'],'cardiac_arrhythmias':['42613','42610','42612',
    '99601','99604','4260','4267','4269','4270','4271','4272','4273','4274',
    '4276','4278','4279','7850','V450','V533'],'valvular_disease':['0932','7463',
    '7464','7465','7466','V422','V433','394','395','396','397','424'],
    'pulmonary_circulation_disorder':['4150','4151','4170','4178','4179',
    '416'],'peripheral_vascular_disorder':['0930','4373','4431','4432','4438',
    '4439','4471','5571','5579','V434','440','441'],'hypertension':['401',
    '402','403','404','405'],'paralysis':['3341','3440','3441','3442',
    '3443','3444','3445','3446','3449','342','343'],'other_neurological':
    ['33392','3319','3320','3321','3334','3335','3362','3481','3483','7803',
    '7843', '334','335','340','341','345'],'chronic_pulmonary_disease':
    ['4168','4169','5064','5081','5088', '490','491','492','493','494','495',
    '496','500','501','502','503','504','505'],'diabetes_w_complications':
    ['2504','2505','2506','2507','2508','2509'],'hypothyroidism':
    ['2409','2461','2468', '243','244'],'renal_failure':['40301','40311',
    '40391','40402','40403','40412','40413','40492','40493', '5880','V420',
    'V451', '585','586','V56'],'liver_disease':['07022','07023','07032',
    '07033','07044','07054','0706','0709','4560','4561','4562','5722','5723',
    '5724','5728','5733','5734','5738','5739','V427','570','571'],
```

```
'chronic_ulcer':['5317','5319','5327','5329','5337','5339','5347',
'5349'],'hiv_aids':['042','043','044'],'lymphoma':['2030','2386',
'200','201','202'],'metastasis_solid_tumor':['140','141',
'142','143','144','145','146','147','148','149','150','151','152','153',
'154','155','156','157','158','159','160','161','162','163','164','165',
'166','167','168','169','170','171','172','174','175','176','177','178',
'179' ,'180','181','182','183','184','185','186','187','188','189',
'190','191','192','193','194','195'],

'rheumatoid_arthiritis':['72889','72930',
'7010','7100','7101','7102','7103','7104','7108','7109','7112','7193',
'7285', '446','714','720','725'],

'coagulation_deficiency':['2871','2873','2874','2875', '286'],
'obesity':['2780'],
'weight_loss':['7832','7994', '260','261','262','263'],
'fluid_electrolyte_disorders':['2536','276'],
'blood_loss_anemia':['2800'],
'deficiency_anemia':['2801','2808','2809', '281'],
'alcohol_abuse':['2652','2911','2912','2913','2915','2918','2919', '3030',
'3039','3050','3575','4255','5353','5710','5711','5712','5713','V113',
'980'],
'drug_abuse':['V6542', '3052','3053','3054','3055','3056','3057','3058',
'3059', '292','304'],
'psychoses':['29604','29614','29644','29654','2938','295','297','298'],
            'depression':['2962','2963','2965','3004','309','311']}

mapping_score = pd.DataFrame({'congestive_heart_failure':9,
        'cardiac_arrhythmias':8,
        'valvular_disease':0,
        'pulmonary_circulation_disorder':3,
        'peripheral_vascular_disorder':4,
        'hypertension':-2,
        'paralysis':4,
```

```
        'other_neurological':5,
        'chronic_pulmonary_disease':3,
        'diabetes_w_complications':1,
        'hypothyroidism':0,
        'renal_failure':7,
        'liver_disease':7,
        'chronic_ulcer':0,
        'hiv_aids':0,
        'lymphoma':8,
         'metastasis_solid_tumor':17,
        'rheumatoid_arthiritis':0,
        'coagulation_deficiency':12,
        'obesity':-5,
        'weight_loss':10,
        'fluid_electrolyte_disorders':11,
        'blood_loss_anemia':-3,
        'deficiency_anemia':0,
        'alcohol_abuse':0,
        'drug_abuse':-11,
        'psychoses':-6,
        'depression':-5}, index = [0])
```

You should map the ICD_9 code to the comorbidity it represents. You will use the get_mapping function to get the comorbidity label against the ICD-9 code.

```
def get_mapping(icd_code, mapping):
    for k,v in mapping.items():
        if str(icd_code) in v:
            return k
        elif str(icd_code)[:4] in v:
            return k
        elif str(icd_code)[:3] in v:
            return k
    return None
```

```
diagnosis_icd["ICD9_CODE"] = diagnosis_icd.ICD9_CODE.apply(lambda x:
get_mapping(x, mapping) if pd.notnull(x) else None)
```

```
diagnosis_icd.dropna(subset = ['ICD9_CODE'], axis =0, inplace = True)
```

Let's pivot up the table and represent comorbidity as a column with the number of times that comorbidity has come up for that subject and hospital admission as the cell values.

```
diagnosis_icd = diagnosis_icd.drop_duplicates(['SUBJECT_ID', 'HADM_ID',
   'ICD9_CODE'])[['SUBJECT_ID', 'HADM_ID','ICD9_CODE']]
   .pivot_table(index=['SUBJECT_ID', 'HADM_ID'],columns='ICD9_CODE',
aggfunc=len, fill_value = 0).reset_index()
```

Finally, you multiply these comorbidities with the effect value given by Elixhauser and then later improved by Quan.

```
diagnosis_icd["ELIXHAUSER_SID30"] = diagnosis_icd.iloc[:,2:].multiply(
np.array(mapping_score[list(diagnosis_icd.iloc[:,2:].columns)]),
axis='columns').fillna(0).sum(axis = 1)
```

```
diagnosis_icd = diagnosis_icd[['SUBJECT_ID', 'HADM_ID','ELIXHAUSER_
SID30']]
```

As a last step, you merge all the data together for analysis and check for missing data.

```
import functools
_dfs = [admissions, diagnosis_icd, charts, labs, icustays_final]
   train_data = functools.reduce(lambda left,right: pd.merge(left,right,on=[
   "SUBJECT_ID","HADM_ID"], how="inner"), _dfs)
```

The number of nulls in the merged dataset is

Output

```
#############################################
SUBJECT_ID              0
HADM_ID                 0
AGE                     0
ADMISSION_TYPE              0
DISCHARGE_DURATION           0
DISCHARGE_LOCATION           0
INSURANCE               0
ETHNICITY             3777
IS_READMISSION             0
ADMITTIME               0
GENDER                  0
ELIXHAUSER_SID30           0
mean_Diastolic_BP      7046
mean_Glucose            185
mean_Heart_Rate          40
mean_Resp_Rate           56
mean_Systolic_BP       7042
mean_Temperature         54
std_Diastolic_BP       7200
std_Glucose            1346
std_Heart_Rate           44
std_Resp_Rate            71
std_Systolic_BP        7197
std_Temperature         153
mean_Albumin           9488
mean_Calcium, Total     611
mean_Hematocrit           5
mean_Platelet Count       8
mean_Potassium           23
mean_Sodium              32
std_Albumin           20102
std_Calcium, Total     2162
std_Hematocrit          218
```

```
std_Platelet Count      240
std_Potassium           325
std_Sodium              374
LOS               2
FIRST_CAREUNIT          0
TOTAL_TRANSFERS         0
################################################
```

There are three steps you will follow to fill in the missing values. This staggered approach is made keeping in mind at any time in imputation you are using the closest approximation possible.

1) Initially, you backfill missing lab and clinical values at the Subject ID and Hospital Visit level as this is the closest estimate. But now the closest estimate is to backfill all numeric values at the Subject ID level, assuming a single patient might have the same characteristics as their last visit.

2) Secondly, you group by `SUBJECT_ID` and impute by a measure of central tendency like mean.

3) Lastly, you group on ethnicity, age, and gender and impute on mean. This will fill all missing values for you.

More details are in the official GitHub repo for the chapter.

Modeling for Patient Representation

Machine learning models developed for clinical prediction tasks have the ability to aid care staff in deciding appropriate treatments. However, these clinical decision-making tools typically are not developed with specific subpopulations in mind, or they are developed for a single subpopulation and can suffer from data scarcity. The existence of these different subpopulations gives rise to a multifaceted problem:

- A single model built for the entire patient population in aggregate does not imply equally good performance across distinct patient subpopulations.

- Separate models learned on each of the distinct patient subpopulations do not take advantage of the shared knowledge that is common across patient subgroups.

In your dataset, you are dealing with a diverse set of individuals, so having one model for the whole population can give you a lower performance. Also, having different models for each population will inhibit across population learning and hence can lead to an overall lower performance.

The idea of addressing such heterogeneous populations for patients in ICU was first handled by H. Suresh, J. Gong, et al in their paper "Learning Multitask Learning: Heterogeneous Patient Populations in the ICU." The authors used mortality prediction as a problem for ICU patients and showed how a multitask learning setup can help account for the diverse population set in the MIMIC data.

You are going to try to address this problem but with slight modifications:

- Patient representation

- Cohort discovery

A Brief Introduction to Autoencoders

Autoencoders are feed-forward neural networks that learn via an unsupervised or semi-supervised training technique. Generally, the way autoencoders learn is by recreating the input, which utilizes an encoder and a decoder. In essence, an autoencoder works on minimizing the reconstruction error. This reconstruction is done by the decoder from the compressed representation of the encoder.

Any kind of data panel data, text data, or even image data can be used in the autoencoder. This just means that the cascaded network of the encoder and decoder can thus be constructed by different types of neural network layers: dense, rnn/lstm, and convolutional.

Depending on the various factors listed below, there can be different types of autoencoders. Some of these factors are

- Dimension of bottleneck layers: Undercomplete (like vanilla autoencoder, sparse autoencoder, etc.) and overcomplete (like denoising autoencoders)

- Number of neurons that are used for training: Sparse autoencoder

- Method of training: Stacked autoencoder, denoising autoencoder, etc.

- Expected output: Variational autoencoder (generative) vs. traditional (non-generative like denoising and vanilla autoencoders)

Figure 3-7 shows a vanilla autoencoder. Every autoencoder contains a bottleneck layer which limits the number of dimensions for latent representation for the input.

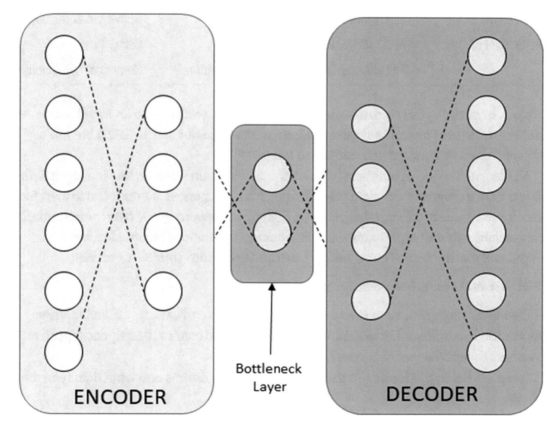

Figure 3-7. *Vanilla autoencoder*

Feature Columns in TensorFlow

To accomplish your task, first you need to select the columns that pertain to patient characteristics and can help in a better representation of them. Table 3-2 shows different columns that reflect different aspects of patient characteristics.

Table 3-2. *Features Representing Patients*

Demographics	AGE	Numerical/Continuous
	INSURANCE	Categorical
	ETHNICITY	Categorical
	GENDER	Categorical
Comorbidities	ELIXHAUSER_SID30	Numerical/Continuous
Patients Clinical Data	FIRST_CAREUNIT	Categorical
	All Labs and ChartEvents related features	Numerical/Continuous

Now, to encode your features into a neural network, you will use an excellent feature provided in TensorFlow called feature columns. They are not new to TF2.0 but are relatively new as a concept (introduced in late 2017).

All deep nets work on numbers (tf.float32) but as you can see even for your input data you can have a range of input data types ranging from categorical to numerical to even free text columns. Feature columns helps bridge this gap of converting raw data into a numerical format seamlessly and experiment with different representations of input features.

You will use the DenseFeatures layer to input them into your Keras model:

`tf.keras.layers.DenseFeatures()`

It's a layer that produces a dense tensor based on given feature_columns. More information can be found at `www.tensorflow.org/versions/r2.0/api_docs/python/tf/keras/layers/DenseFeatures`.

Table 3-3 helps you figure out the different feature columns and what data type they work on.

Table 3-3. *Feature Columns in TF 2.0*

Feature Column Type	Description	Data Type
Numeric Columns	Represents real valued features. The data remains unchanged.	Numerical
Bucketized Columns	Buckets real value features into categories and one-hot encodes them. The buckets are decided by boundaries/cuts.	Numerical
Categorical Column with Vocabulary	One-hot encodes a fixed set of categorical values.	Categorical

(continued)

Table 3-3. (*continued*)

Feature Column Type	Description	Data Type
Embedding Column	Generally used in cases where categorical values are really large in number and hence a lower-dimensional representation is generated instead of a one-hot encoding, which will be sparse.	Categorical
Categorical Column with Hash Bucket	Hashes different categorical values and fits into one of the hash buckets. Number of buckets can be optimized. Note: As hashing is applied, it can lead to collision.	Categorical
Crossed Feature	Used in cases where you want feature interaction. Note: Not all combinations are created. Rather, a hashed approach is used.	Categorical

Creating an Input Pipeline Using tf.data

The tf.data API enables you to build custom input pipelines and handle large amounts of data read from different formats. It provides an abstraction td.data.Dataset which holds sequences of elements. These elements can be of any type.

For your case, you will be using `tf.data.Dataset.from_tensor_slices`. It's a static method that combines different elements into one dataset, such as combining predictor and target variables into one dataset. More information can be found at `www.tensorflow.org/api_docs/python/tf/data/Dataset#from_tensor_slices`.

```
import os
import tensorflow as tf
from tensorflow import feature_column
from tensorflow.keras import layers

    tf.keras.backend.set_floatx('float32')
    tf.random.set_seed(123)
    np.random.seed(123)
    random.seed(123)
    os.environ['PYTHONHASHSEED']=str(123)
```

```python
def df_to_dataset(dataframe, target_col_name, shuffle=True, batch_
size=32, autoenc=True):
    """
    A utility method to create a tf.data dataset from a Pandas Dataframe
    """
    dataframe = dataframe.copy()
    labels = dataframe.pop(target_col_name)

    if autoenc:
        ds = tf.data.Dataset.from_tensor_slices((dict(dataframe), feature_
        layer(dict(dataframe)).numpy()))
    else:
        ds = tf.data.Dataset.from_tensor_slices((dict(dataframe), labels))
    if shuffle:
        ds = ds.shuffle(buffer_size=len(dataframe))
    ds = ds.batch(batch_size)
    return ds
```

One thing to note in the df_to_dataset function is how easy it is to create training labels using the tensor_slices function, even for a dataframe as an output!

Note   Although the target column doesn't make sense for autoencoders, the function is kept generic for later use.

Before moving onto creating your feature columns, you must make sure that the variable names in your dataframe adhere to the variable_scope of TensorFlow. You can find more info here:

https://github.com/tensorflow/tensorflow/blob/r1.2/tensorflow/python/framework/ops.py#L2993.

```python
import pandas as pd
import numpy as np
import random
import re
```

```
data =pd.read_csv("./train.csv", index_col = None)
data.columns = [re.sub(r"[,.;@#?!&$]+\ *", " ",x).replace('/\s\s+/g',
' ').replace(" ","_") for x in data.columns]
```

After defining the feature columns, you will create a layer to input them into your Keras model. You will use the DenseFeatures layer for this. Also, since you have just numerical and categorical columns, you will let the numerical columns remain as is and do one-hot encoding on categorical variables.

But before that, let's make sure you have scaled your numerical columns before ingesting them into a neural network. This is a very important step before training your autoencoder as all neural networks work on is on a gradient descent. Having a non-scaled data can make your loss really huge and the network won't actually converge properly as it can lead to weights of some features having more representation.

```
num_cols = ['AGE', 'ELIXHAUSER_SID30', 'mean_Diastolic_BP', 'mean_
    Glucose',
            'mean_Heart_Rate', 'mean_Resp_Rate', 'mean_Systolic_BP',
            'mean_Temperature', 'std_Diastolic_BP', 'std_Glucose',
            'std_Heart_Rate',
            'std_Resp_Rate', 'std_Systolic_BP', 'std_Temperature',
            'mean_Albumin',
            'mean_Calcium_Total', 'mean_Hematocrit', 'mean_Platelet_Count',
            'mean_Potassium', 'mean_Sodium', 'std_Albumin',
            'std_Calcium_Total',
            'std_Hematocrit', 'std_Platelet_Count', 'std_Potassium', 'std_
            Sodium']

from sklearn import preprocessing
min_max_scaler = preprocessing.MinMaxScaler()
data_minmax = min_max_scaler.fit(data[num_cols])
data_num = data_minmax.transform(data[num_cols])

data_scaled = pd.concat([pd.DataFrame(data_num, columns = num_cols),
                    data[['INSURANCE', 'ETHNICITY', 'GENDER',
                    'FIRST_CAREUNIT','IS_READMISSION']]],
                axis = 1)
```

You will also split your data into train and validation sets to test the performance of your autoencoder later.

```
from sklearn.model_selection import train_test_split
    train, val = train_test_split(data_scaled, test_size=0.2)
```

Creating Feature Columns

You are finally ready to create your feature columns. In the following code you see how numeric and categorical columns can be handled:

```
feature_columns = []
# numeric cols
for numeric_cols in num_cols:
    feature_columns.append(feature_column.numeric_column(numeric_cols))

# categorical cols
    for cat_cols in ['INSURANCE', 'ETHNICITY', 'GENDER', 'FIRST_CAREUNIT']:
    categorical_column = feature_column.categorical_column_with_vocabulary_
    list(
      cat_cols, train[cat_cols].unique())
    indicator_column = feature_column.indicator_column(categorical_column)
    feature_columns.append(indicator_column)

feature_layer = layers.DenseFeatures(feature_columns)
```

Building a Stacked Autoencoder

Now you will convert the train and validation pandas dataframe to TensorFlow's Dataset class. Please note in the code below, besides having train and validation data, you are also keeping a full unshuffled data for the next task, which is cohort discovery.

```
    batch_size = 32
train_ds = df_to_dataset(train,
                            target_col_name='IS_READMISSION',
                        batch_size=batch_size)
```

```
val_ds = df_to_dataset(val,
                            target_col_name='IS_READMISSION',
                       batch_size=batch_size)

full_ds = df_to_dataset(data_scaled,
                            target_col_name='IS_READMISSION',
                       batch_size=batch_size,
                       shuffle = False)

# To modularize the shape of output layer in the autoencoder
    output_shape = feature_layer(next(iter(train_ds))[0]).numpy().shape[1]
```

Creating an autoencoder is very simple. You just need to keep a couple of things in mind:

- There are two different submodels representing the encoder and decoder.

- Try to reduce the DenseLayer size stepwise.

- Make sure the input and output tensor shapes match.

- Since it is a regression problem, you can use mse as your loss function. If all your features were 0 or 1, as in the case of a black and white image, you could also use binary cross entropy loss to converge the network faster.

- No overfitting is observed on the train set. This can happen unknowingly since you are using a very small data with over 2k parameters.

```
encoder = tf.keras.Sequential([
    feature_layer,
        layers.Dense(32, activation = "selu", kernel_initializer="lecun_normal"),
        layers.Dense(16, activation = "selu", kernel_initializer="lecun_normal"),
        layers.Dense(8, activation = "selu", kernel_initializer="lecun_normal"),
        layers.Dense(4, activation = "selu", kernel_initializer="lecun_normal"),
        layers.Dense(2, activation = "selu", kernel_initializer="lecun_normal")
])
```

```
decoder = tf.keras.Sequential([
        layers.Dense(4, activation = "selu", kernel_initializer="lecun_
        normal", input_shape=[2]),
        layers.Dense(8, activation = "selu",kernel_initializer="lecun_normal"),
        layers.Dense(16, activation = "selu",kernel_initializer="lecun_
        normal"),
        layers.Dense(32, activation = "selu",kernel_initializer="lecun_
        normal"),
        layers.Dense(output_shape, activation = "selu", kernel_initializer=
        "lecun_normal"),
])

stacked_ae = tf.keras.Sequential([encoder, decoder])
    stacked_ae.compile(loss='mse', metrics = "mean_absolute_error",
                        optimizer= tf.keras.optimizers.Adam(learning_
                        rate=0.01))

history = stacked_ae.fit(train_ds,
                        validation_data = val_ds,
                            epochs=15)
```

A couple of things about what's happening in the code above:

1) Note the use of the feature layer as an input layer to the encoder submodel.

2) All dense layer sizes (32, 16, 8) reduce in a staggered fashion and are less than the maximum dimension, which is 41 in your case, equal to output_shape. This forces the network to learn more condensed representation of the features.

3) Note the use of selu as an activation function. SELU, or scaled exponential linear unit, is a relatively new activation function with many advantages like internal normalization of weights and biases, which centers the mean of weights to zero and guarantees that vanishing and exploding gradient problems can't happen, which intuitively makes sense as the weights follow a

standard normal distribution. The activation function is shown in Figure 3-8. The image is adapted from the paper "SNDCNN: Self-Normalizing Deep CNNs with Scaled Exponential Linear Units for Speech Recognition" by Z. Huang et al.

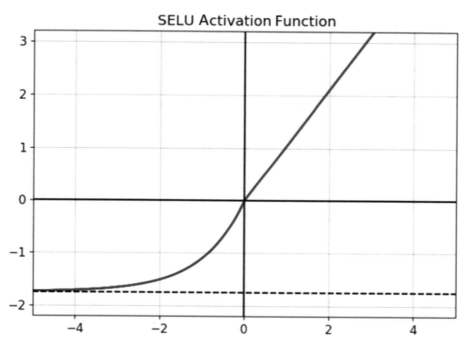

Figure 3-8. *SELU activation function*

Let's also see how the performance metric and loss charts look for the validation chart over different epochs. Divergence in charts means either underfitting or overfitting. In your case, you observe no such issues. See Figure 3-9.

```python
# Plotting libraries and parameters
import matplotlib.pyplot as plt
    plt.figure(figsize=(12,8))
import seaborn as sns

    mae = history.history['mean_absolute_error']
    val_mae = history.history['val_mean_absolute_error']

    loss = history.history['loss']
    val_loss = history.history['val_loss']
```

```
epochs_range = range(15)

plt.subplot(1, 2, 1)
plt.plot(epochs_range, mae, label='Training MAE')
plt.plot(epochs_range, val_mae, label='Validation MAE')
plt.legend(loc='upper right')
plt.title('Training and Validation MAE')

plt.subplot(1, 2, 2)
plt.plot(epochs_range, loss, label='Training Loss')
plt.plot(epochs_range, val_loss, label='Validation Loss')
plt.legend(loc='upper right')
plt.title('Training and Validation Loss')
plt.show()
```

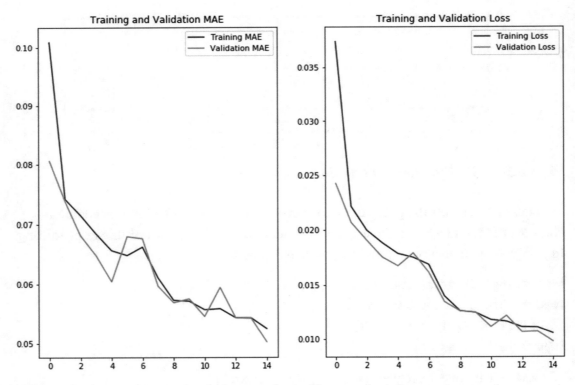

Figure 3-9. *Training and validation plots of loss and performance metric*

Let's also save your model for future reference.

```
stacked_ae.save('trained_model')
```

Cohort Discovery

Now let's use a condensed representation of patient-level features from the autoencoder trained in the previous section. You'll shift the focus to see how many patient clusters exist in your data for which you will the multitask learning.

What Is an Ideal Cohort Set?

Before diving into different techniques, here's how the clustering algorithm should behave:

1) Able to use the full data for clustering

2) Noise-aware so that a small patient group with different characteristics doesn't distort the clustering

3) Healthy cluster size and similar prevalence. The clusters formed from the algorithm should have a decent n-size and the same prevalence, which basically means the number of readmission and non-readmission patients should be similar.

4) No prior assumption over distribution of points belonging to a cluster like that in the case of GMMs.

5) You are also not that concerned with finding embedded structures in your data. Nor are you too focused on finding just dense clusters and rendering everything else as noise. For these reasons, a hierarchical clustering or density-based clustering is out of scope.

This means you can go for a centroid-based clustering algorithm like k-means. Now k-means doesn't fit the bill for all the expected behaviors listed above but you can still mitigate some of these issues by changing the initialization strategy and number of clusters. Also, you will keep an extra eye on boundary points. If there are a lot of boundary points, then maybe you will have to choose another clustering algorithm, such as GMM.

Optimizing K-Means Performance

K-means is present in the sklearn library and offers a variety of options to cluster data. A lot of information regarding this on the official page documentation at `https://scikit-learn.org/stable/modules/generated/sklearn.cluster.KMeans.html`.

Key parameters to note here are

- `n_clusters`: Number of clusters. As it is a centroid-based clustering algorithm, you need to provide the number of clusters beforehand.

- `init`: The parameter to select the initial centroids.

- `n_init`: The number of times a centroid is initialized (with different seeds).

- `max_iter`: The number of times k-means is run

- `algorithm`: Which algorithm to use, eklan or auto. You will not touch this parameter because based on the data (dense or sparse) the algorithm is auto-selected.

Let's take each of the parameters one by one and discuss each in length.

The `init` parameter tells the algorithm a way to decide on the initial centroids. The default method is to select randomly but based on a 2006 paper by David Arthur et al titled "K-means++: The Advantages of Careful Seeding," there is a smarter way to initialize these clusters. In summary, k-means++ tries to select centroids in a way that all centroids are far away from each other. It starts with selecting a random point as a centroid and then the next centroid is selected such that the probability of its selection is proportional to its distance from the nearest centroid. This is iteratively done until the total number of centroids matches the `n_clusters` parameter value.

`n_init,` a parameter closely tied to the `init` parameter, is used to choose the clustering with best inertia while also stabilizing the results of the `init` parameter, so you are not going to experiment a lot with this parameter. Keep it a fixed value of 10.

Next, let's move on to `max_iter.` This parameter helps k-means converge and find the optimum distribution of points around the centroids. This can play an important role in determining the overall health of your clusters, such as the total number of datapoints, overall silhouette score or inertia, and also prevalence of datapoints.

Lastly, the most important parameter is n_clusters. It helps you see how many clusters are present in your data. You will try to determine this number by two methods:

1) Inertia (a.k.a. the Elbow Method): The sum of within (intra) cluster variances

2) Silhouette Score: This takes both intra and inter cluster distances into account. It varies from -1 to 1, where a value close to 1 indicates that the data points align well to the cluster it is present in and less to neighboring clusters (so it tells both the things as compared to inertia), while for values far away from 1 show that the data points are misclustered.

Since you are deciding how to deal with init and n_init parameters, let's have a quick look at the max_iter and n_clusters parameters.

```python
from sklearn.cluster import KMeans
import matplotlib.pyplot as plt
    plt.figure(figsize=(12,8))
import seaborn as sns

codings = encoder.predict(full_ds)

    k_means_data = pd.concat([data[["SUBJECT_ID","IS_READMISSION"]],
                        pd.DataFrame(codings, columns =
                        ["val1","val2"])],
                        axis = 1)

    kmeans_iter1 = KMeans(n_clusters=4, init="k-means++", n_init=5,
                        max_iter=1, random_state=123)
    kmeans_iter2 = KMeans(n_clusters=4, init="k-means++", n_init=5,
                        max_iter=2, random_state=123)
    kmeans_iter3 = KMeans(n_clusters=4, init="k-means++", n_init=5,
                        max_iter=3, random_state=123)
kmeans_iter1.fit(codings)
kmeans_iter2.fit(codings)
kmeans_iter3.fit(codings)
```

If you plot the centroid and labels for these three different versions, the plot will look something like Figure 3-10.

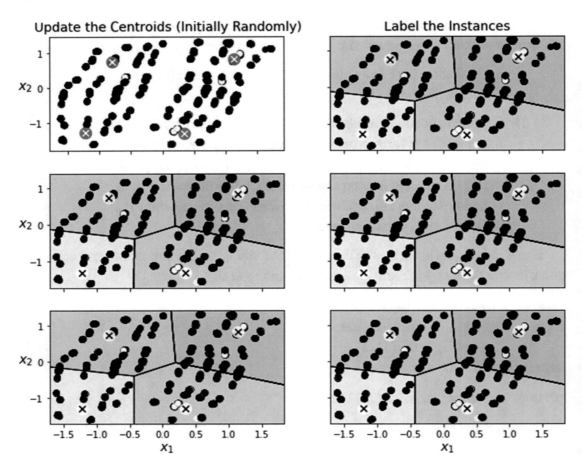

Figure 3-10. *Clustering with different numbers of iterations*

You can see that `max_iter` doesn't have a big effect on the clustering performance and hence here as well you keep the `max_iter` fixed to 3.

Deciding the Number of Clusters by Inertia and Silhouette Score Analysis

Now the only thing you must decide on is the number of clusters. For this you will see both the inertia values and the silhouette score. If they mutually agree on a number, you will take it.

```
kmeans__ncluster = [KMeans(n_clusters=x, init="k-means++",
                          max_iter = 3,
```

```
                             n_init = 5,
                             random_state=123).fit(codings)
                  for x in range(1, 10)]
inertias = [kmeans_model.inertia_ for kmeans_model in kmeans__ncluster]

from sklearn.metrics import silhouette_score
silhouette_scores = [silhouette_score(codings, kmeans_model.labels_)
                       for kmeans_model in kmeans__ncluster[1:]]

    plt.figure(figsize=(12, 6))

    plt.subplot(121)
    plt.plot(range(1, 10), inertias, "ro-")
    plt.xlabel("Number of Clusters", fontsize=15)
    plt.ylabel("Inertia", fontsize=15)

    plt.subplot(122)
    plt.plot(range(2, 10), silhouette_scores, "ro-")
    plt.xlabel("Number of Clusters", fontsize=15)
    plt.ylabel("Silhouette score", fontsize=15)
plt.show()
```

Figure 3-11 shows that a cluster size of 4 gives the best clustering performance.

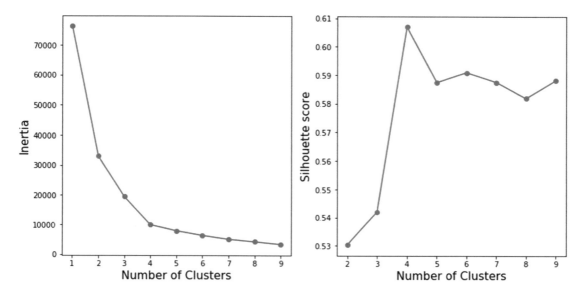

Figure 3-11. *Inertia and silhouette scores over different cluster numbers*

Checking Cluster Health

Let's quickly check for the sample size in each cluster as well as prevalence of readmission patients.

```
k = 4
kmeans = KMeans(n_clusters=k, init="k-means++", n_init=5, max_iter = 3,
random_state=123)
cluster_predictions = kmeans.fit_predict(codings)
    k_means_data["cluster_label"] = cluster_predictions
# Appending the cluster prediction to the main data
    data["cluster_label"] = cluster_predictions

    count_labels = k_means_data.groupby(['cluster_label','IS_READMISSION'])
    ['SUBJECT_ID'].count().reset_index()

    sample_count = pd.pivot_table(count_labels, index="cluster_label",
    columns=['IS_READMISSION'], values="SUBJECT_ID").reset_index()

    sample_count.columns = [sample_count.columns.name + "_" +str(x) if
    type(x)!=str else x for x in list(sample_count.columns)]

sample_count.reset_index(drop = True, inplace = True)
    sample_count["Total_Samples"] = sample_count[["IS_READMISSION_0",
    "IS_READMISSION_1"]].apply(sum, axis =1)
    sample_count["Readmission_Percentage"] = (sample_count
    ["IS_READMISSION_1"]/sample_count["Total_Samples"])*100
```

Figure 3-12 shows the sample size and readmission percentage across the four patient cohorts.

cluster_label	IS_READMISSION_0	IS_READMISSION_1	Total_Samples	Readmission_Percentage
0	9357	918	10275	8.93431
1	5098	380	5478	6.93684
2	8892	743	9635	7.71147
3	8149	562	8711	6.45161

Figure 3-12. *Distribution of samples and of positive class in each cluster*

Now you have four patient cohorts to work with. The final prediction model should perform well overall but also on these distinct patient cohorts. You'll see how to do this in the next section.

Multitask Learning Model
What Is Multitask Learning ?

Imagine building an image classification system and you want to detect people in the images. If you just had a single label depicting whether the image has people in it or not, then you could very well create a classification model. But what if you had the chance to make the model more robust by optimizing your model for other objectives as well to help generalize your solution of people detection?

A multitask model helps you further improve your learning metric by cotraining certain auxiliary but relevant tasks. In the case of the image classification example above, an auxiliary class can be for bounding box identification. This can help it learn features such as a person's box, which has low width but longer height. If a bbox of such a nature occurs, then the image is more likely to be an image with people. Figure 3-13 shows how the bounding box can help you further improve on your image classifying capability by sharing info on the dimensions of bboxes.

Figure 3-13. *An image that can be classified as "people"*

Different Ways to Train a MTL Model

There are various ways to train a MTL model. Some of the prominent ones are

- **Hard parameter sharing**: It involves sharing hidden layers parameters while having a separate output layer for each task. Figure 3-14 is an abstract figure adapted from Sebastian Ruder's blog on MTL.

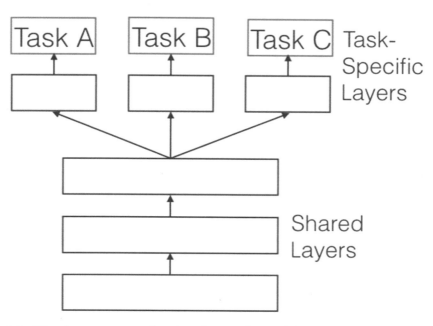

Figure 3-14. *Hard parameter sharing for multi-task learning in deep neural networks*

- **Soft parameter sharing**: This is a little different. Here all tasks have their own model, and then all the parameters of this distinct model are regularized using trace norm to allow reuse of learned information. You can understand a trace norm as something that measures complexity. If you have a more complex model vs. a simpler one where both are able to understand the data well, which one would you choose? The simpler one, right? That's what happens in soft parameter sharing. See Figure 3-15.

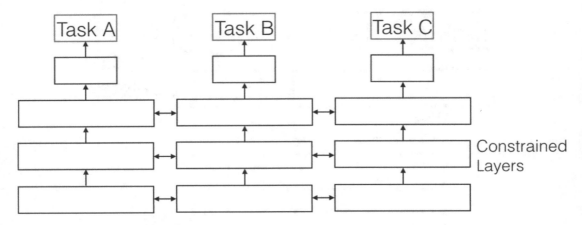

Figure 3-15. *Soft parameter sharing for multi-task learning in deep neural networks*

- **Continual incremental learning**: This is a relatively new approach and you can think of it as a form of hard parameter sharing but with a new way of looking at MTL. It was proposed fairly recently at AAAI '20 by Yu Sun et al in a paper titled "Ernie 2.0: A Continual Pre-Training Framework for Language Understanding." The approach is represented in Figure 3-16.

All the shared layers parameters are transferred from the last task combination and updated with next training task

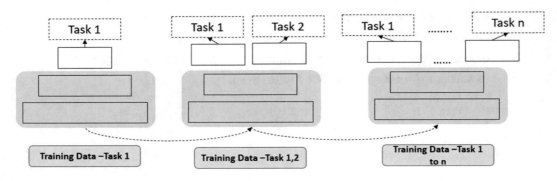

Figure 3-16. *Continual incremental learning*

For simplicity, you are going to try the hard parameter sharing approach as it is most widely used and is good enough to introduce MTL.

Training Your MTL Model

You start by aligning the cluster prediction of each sample to the original data.

```python
import pandas as pd
import numpy as np
    data["cluster_labels"] = cluster_predictions
    data.columns = [re.sub(r"[,.;@#?!&$]+\ *", " ",x).replace('/\s\s+/g',
    ' ').replace(" ","_") for x in data.columns]
```

Next, you include all the numeric and categorical columns for the final model
training.

```python
# Updating the num_cols and categorical_cols
    num_cols = ['AGE', 'DISCHARGE_DURATION', 'ELIXHAUSER_SID30',
    'mean_Diastolic_BP', 'mean_Glucose',
            'mean_Heart_Rate', 'mean_Resp_Rate', 'mean_Systolic_BP',
            'mean_Temperature', 'std_Diastolic_BP', 'std_Glucose',
            'std_Heart_Rate',
            'std_Resp_Rate', 'std_Systolic_BP', 'std_Temperature',
            'mean_Albumin',
            'mean_Calcium_Total', 'mean_Hematocrit', 'mean_Platelet_Count',
            'mean_Potassium', 'mean_Sodium', 'std_Albumin', 'std_Calcium_Total',
            'std_Hematocrit', 'std_Platelet_Count', 'std_Potassium',
            'std_Sodium','LOS','TOTAL_TRANSFERS']
    target_col = ['IS_READMISSION']
    categorical_col = ['ADMISSION_TYPE','DISCHARGE_LOCATION','INSURANCE',
    'ETHNICITY', 'GENDER', 'FIRST_CAREUNIT']
```

Now you scale and split the data into training and validation sets.

```python
# Updating Scaling with new numerical columns
from sklearn import preprocessing
min_max_scaler = preprocessing.MinMaxScaler()
data_minmax = min_max_scaler.fit(data[num_cols])

data_num = data_minmax.transform(data[num_cols])
```

```
data_scaled = pd.concat([pd.DataFrame(data_num, columns = num_cols),
                        data[categorical_col + target_col + ["cluster_
                        labels"]]],
                    axis = 1)

from sklearn.model_selection import train_test_split
    train, val = train_test_split(data_scaled, test_size=0.2)
```

The next set of functions help you create a multi-output label:

- gen_labels: Creates an output of 1 or 0 for each output (or cluster)

- df_to_dataset_multio: Returns a tuple of features used for training and mapping of each output layer to the output cluster

- get_data_generator: A generator function that yields a batch of training samples

```
def gen_labels(readm_val, cluster_val):
    """
    Helper function to generate labels for multi-output system
    """
    res = [0,0,0,0]
if readm_val:
        res[cluster_val] = 1
return res

def df_to_dataset_multio(dataframe, target_col_name = 'IS_READMISSION'):
    """
    A utility method to create a Input data for the MTL NN
    """
dataframe = dataframe.copy()
    labels = [gen_labels(row[1], row[2]) for row in dataframe[[
    target_col_name, 'cluster_labels']].itertuples()]

assert np.sum(labels) == dataframe[target_col_name].sum()
    dataframe.drop([target_col_name, 'cluster_labels'], axis = 1,
    inplace = True)
```

```python
# Generating Tensorflow Dataset
train_ds = feature_layer(dict(dataframe)).numpy()
    y_train_ds = {'cluster_0':np.array([x[0] for x in labels]),
                  'cluster_1':np.array([x[1] for x in labels]),
                  'cluster_2':np.array([x[2] for x in labels]),
                  'cluster_3':np.array([x[3] for x in labels])}
    return train_ds, y_train_ds

train_ds, train_col_map = df_to_dataset_multio(train)
val_ds, val_col_map = df_to_dataset_multio(val)

def get_data_generator(df, cluster_map, batch_size=32):
    """
    Generator function which yields the input data and output for
    different clusters
    """
    feats, cluster_0, cluster_1, cluster_2, cluster_3 = [], [], [], [], []
    while True:
        for i in range(len(df)):
            feats.append(df[i])
            cluster_0.append(cluster_map['cluster_0'][i])
            cluster_1.append(cluster_map['cluster_1'][i])
            cluster_2.append(cluster_map['cluster_2'][i])
            cluster_3.append(cluster_map['cluster_3'][i])
            if len(feats) >= batch_size:
                yield np.array(feats), [np.array(cluster_0),
                np.array(cluster_1), np.array(cluster_2),
                np.array(cluster_3)]
                feats, cluster_0, cluster_1, cluster_2, cluster_3 = [], [],
                [], [], []
```

Finally, you create a model as shown in Figure 3-17, which shows the architecture you are going to build for your MTL task.

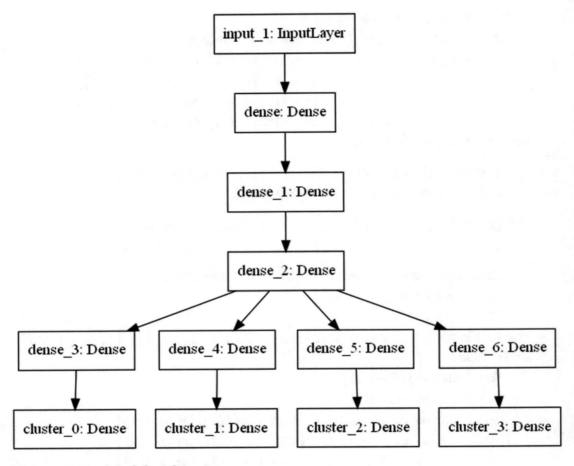

Figure 3-17. *Model architecture*

```
input_layer = layers.Input(shape = (train_ds.shape[1]))
_ = layers.Dense(32, activation = "selu", kernel_initializer=
"lecun_normal")(input_layer)
_ = layers.Dense(16, activation = "selu", kernel_initializer=
"lecun_normal")(_)
last_shared_layer = layers.Dense(8, activation = "selu", kernel_
initializer="lecun_normal")(_)

_ = layers.Dense(4, activation = "selu", kernel_initializer="lecun_
normal")(last_shared_layer)
cluster_0 = layers.Dense(1, activation = "sigmoid", name='cluster_0')(_)
```

```
    _ = layers.Dense(4, activation = "selu", kernel_initializer="lecun_
    normal")(last_shared_layer)
    cluster_1 = layers.Dense(1, activation = "sigmoid", name='cluster_1')(_)

    _ = layers.Dense(4, activation = "selu", kernel_initializer="lecun_
    normal")(last_shared_layer)
    cluster_2 = layers.Dense(1, activation = "sigmoid", name='cluster_2')(_)

    _ = layers.Dense(4, activation = "selu", kernel_initializer="lecun_
    normal")(last_shared_layer)
    cluster_3 = layers.Dense(1, activation = "sigmoid", name='cluster_3')(_)

mtl_model = tf.keras.Model(inputs = input_layer,
                           outputs = [cluster_0, cluster_1, cluster_2,
                           cluster_3])

    mtl_model.compile (optimizer=tf.keras.optimizers.Adam(learning_rate=0.01),
                loss={'cluster_0': 'binary_crossentropy',
                      'cluster_1': 'binary_crossentropy',
                      'cluster_2': 'binary_crossentropy',
                      'cluster_3': 'binary_crossentropy'},
                loss_weights={'cluster_0': 0.25,
                      'cluster_1': 0.25,
                      'cluster_2': 0.25,
                      'cluster_3': 0.25},
                metrics={'cluster_0': 'AUC',
                      'cluster_1': 'AUC',
                      'cluster_2': 'AUC',
                      'cluster_3': 'AUC'})

    batch_size = 32
    valid_batch_size = 32
train_gen = get_data_generator(train_ds, train_col_map,  batch_size=
batch_size)
valid_gen = get_data_generator(val_ds, val_col_map, batch_size=
valid_batch_size)
```

```
history = mtl_model.fit_generator(train_gen,
                    steps_per_epoch=len(train)//batch_size,
                       epochs=10,
                    validation_data=valid_gen,
                    validation_steps=len(val)//valid_batch_size)
```

One clear takeaway from the code above is how versatile constructing a neural net is. In case of multioutput, you can use different loss and loss_weights metrics for each output.

Finally, please see the performance and loss charts in Figure 3-18. Some clusters learn really well, like clusters 1 and 3, while there is mild overfitting in cluster 2 as the loss chart for cluster 2 shows that validation loss is generally higher than the train loss.

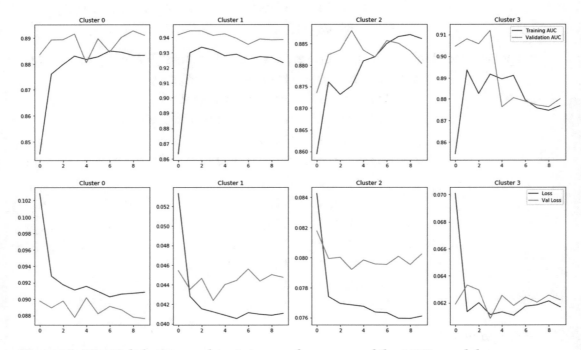

Figure 3-18.   *Validation and training performance of the MTL model*

Conclusion

Firstly, congratulations on working through and understanding one of the most complex data within pharma. The EHR data contains all kinds of data like tabular and text, and some EHR systems also contain images.

Secondly, we covered many topics and TensorFlow-specific features in this chapter. You learned about the use of feature columns and how to build an input pipeline. You also explored autoencoders and clustering in detail. Lastly, you were introduced to multitask learning and its types. Multi-task learning is an emerging field especially in NLP where tasks are generally complex and a single global model can't learn all the complexities, hence a multi-task model is useful. I hope you learned a lot and are looking forward to more.

CHAPTER 4

Predicting Medical Billing Codes from Clinical Notes

Clinical notes contain information on prescribed procedures and diagnosis from doctors and are used for accurate billing in the current medical system, but they are not readily available. We must extract them manually or use some assistive technology for the process to be carried out seamlessly.

This adds to the administrative costs for both the payers and providers. Providers alone spend roughly $282 billion on just the insurance and medical billing costs. Good record keeping and quality tracking is an added cost. Compared to the professional revenue associated with each type of visit, the emergency department visit generates the greatest billing costs, equal to 25.2 percent of revenue.

In this chapter, you will explore the latest transformer models with a deep-dive on BERT and the transformer architecture in depth. You will also learn how different fine-tuning techniques can be applied to transformer models. Finally, you will learn to use concepts of transfer learning in NLP with multi-label classification as a downstream task.

Prediction of diagnosis and procedures from unstructured clinical notes saves time, eliminates errors, and minimizes costs, so let's get started.

Introduction

First things first: what are these ICD codes I am talking about? Those familiar with ICD codes might be confused with the difference between ICD-9 and ICD-10 codes.

ICD stands for International Classification of Disease, and it is a set of standard codes regulated and maintained by the Department of Health and Human Services (remember HHS from Chapter 1?). These codes are used to accurately measure outcomes and care provided to patients while also providing a structured way to report disease and symptoms for research and clinical decision-making.

© Anshik 2021
Anshik, *AI for Healthcare with Keras and Tensorflow 2.0*, https://doi.org/10.1007/978-1-4842-7086-8_4

HHS mandated that all entities under the HIPAA act must transition their ICD codes to the ICD-10 format. This was done to various reasons but the key ones are

- **Tracking new diseases and health conditions**: The old system contained roughly 17.8K distinct ICD codes but ICD-10 maps more than 150,000 conditions and diseases to distinct codes.

- More space allows for better and more accurately defined ICD codes and supports epidemiological research such as comorbidity or severity of disease, etc.

- Prevents reimbursement fraud

Since MIMIC 3 contains EHR data from before a new system of codes was mandated, you can comfortably proceed with using the ICD data present there, but keep this in mind in case you see a new EHR data. Don't worry. You can get your hands dirty and apply your learning from here to the new ICD convention.

Since there are a lot of ICD-9 codes, for all practical purposes you will just try to identify the top 15 ICD-9 codes, which is decided by how many admitted patients were tagged with that particular ICD-9 code.

I already covered MIMIC 3 data in depth, so let's just focus on picking the right tables and outlining steps to prepare the data. Let's dive deeper into it.

Figure 4-1 shows the difference in ICD-9 and ICD-10 CM codes. Note that there are two variations of the type of ICD codes.

- CM (clinical modifications): Diagnosis coding on inpatient and outpatient data

- PCS (procedure coding systems): Procedure coding on inpatient data

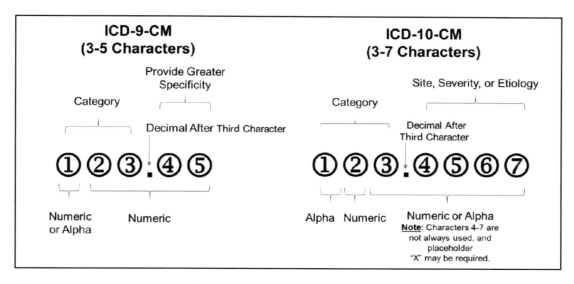

Figure 4-1. *ICD-9-CM and ICD-10-CM diagnosis coding systems*

Data

I covered the MIMIC 3 dataset in depth in the last chapter, so let's jump right into creating the data.

NOTEEVENTS

This table contains the text pertaining to all the clinical notes recorded after a patient's admission. Two important columns to look at in the NOTEEVENTS table are CATEGORY and DESCRIPTION. While CATEGORY contains the anonymized clinical notes, DESCRIPTION tells us whether these are full reports or addendum.

Since the use case centers around making admin costs for providers and payers lower, the best source of this information is present in the "Discharge summary - Reports".

```
    n_rows = 100000

# create the iterator
noteevents_iterator = pd.read_csv(
        "./Data/NOTEEVENTS.csv",
    iterator=True,
    chunksize=n_rows)
```

```
# concatenate according to a filter to get our noteevents data
    noteevents = pd.concat( [noteevents_chunk[np.logical_and(noteevents_
    chunk.CATEGORY.isin(["Discharge summary"]), noteevents_chunk.
    DESCRIPTION.isin(["Report"]))]
    for noteevents_chunk in noteevents_iterator])
```

```
noteevents.HADM_ID = noteevents.HADM_ID.astype(int)
```

Now that you have your dataset in place, let's explore it a little.

Duplicates on primary keys: There are duplicates within the NOTEEVENTS dataset although there should be a unique record for a SUBJECT_ID and HADM_ID pair.

On further investigation, it looks like the records have different discharge summary text at different dates for the same Admission ID. This looks like an impossible event and hence is a more data issue. For now, you will sort your data on the CHARTDATE column and keep the first entry.

```
try:
        assert len(noteevents.drop_duplicates(["SUBJECT_ID","HADM_ID"])) ==
        len(noteevents)
except AssertionError as e:
        print("There are duplicates on Primary Key Set")

    noteevents.CHARTDATE  = pd.to_datetime(noteevents.CHARTDATE , format =
    '%Y-%m-%d %H:%M:%S', errors = 'coerce')
    pd.set_option('display.max_colwidth',50)
    noteevents.sort_values(["SUBJECT_ID","HADM_ID","CHARTDATE"], inplace
    =True)
    noteevents.drop_duplicates(["SUBJECT_ID","HADM_ID"], inplace = True)

noteevents.reset_index(drop = True, inplace = True)
```

One more thing to do before you move onto the next datasource to look at the text data. You can see a sample abstract of the text below:

```
    Admission Date: [**2118-6-2**] Discharge Date: [**2118-6-14**]

Date of Birth: Sex: F

Service: MICU and then to [**Doctor Last Name **] Medicine
```

HISTORY OF PRESENT ILLNESS: This **is** an 81-year-old female
with a history of emphysema (**not** on home O2), who presents
with three days of shortness of breath thought by her primary
care doctor to be a COPD flare. Two days prior to admission,
she was started on a prednisone taper **and** one day prior to
admission she required oxygen at home **in** order to maintain
    oxygen saturation greater than 90%. She has also been on
levofloxacin **and** nebulizers, **and** was **not** getting better, **and**
    presented to the [**Hospital1 18**] Emergency Room.

You can see certain patterns that can be used to clean the text:

1) **Anonymized** dates, patient name, hospital and physician's name

2) **Use of a pattern** like "Topic: Text" such as "Admission Date:
   [**2118-6-2**]:, "HISTORY OF PRESENT ILLNESS: This is an
   81-year-old female....

3) **Use of newline character** ("\n")

You will leverage all of these patterns to clean the data and make sure that each unique sentence gets recorded correctly.

There are two things that you will do. First, you will make sure that all the irrelevant topics are removed from the discharge summary. For this, you will find the most frequent topics.

```
import re
import itertools

    def clean_text(text):
        return [x for x in list(itertools.chain.from_iterable([t.split("<>")
        for t in text.replace("\n"," ").split("|")])) if len(x) > 0]

most_frequent_tags = [re.match("^(.*?):",x).group() for text in
noteevents.TEXT for x in text.split("\n\n") if pd.notnull(
re.match("^(.*?):",x))]
pd.Series(most_frequent_tags).value_counts().head(10)
```

An extract of the most frequent topic tags is shown in Figure 4-2.

```
|:----------------------------------------------|------:|
| Admission Date:                                | 51704 |
| Date of Birth:                                 | 44491 |
| Service:                                       | 44219 |
| Allergies:                                     | 38198 |
| Attending:                                     | 38060 |
| Discharge Diagnosis:                           | 37863 |
| Major Surgical or Invasive Procedure:          | 34285 |
| Physical Exam:                                 | 28767 |
| Followup Instructions:                         | 28401 |
| Facility:                                      | 24265 |
| Medications on Admission:                      | 23856 |
| Discharge Medications:                         | 20354 |
| Brief Hospital Course:                         | 20167 |
| Past Medical History:                          | 19100 |
| Social History:                               | 19004 |
| Family History:                                | 18847 |
| Pertinent Results:                             | 17994 |
| Completed by:                                  | 17724 |
| History of Present Illness:                    | 15511 |
| Dictated By:                                   | 14046 |
| IMPRESSION:                                    | 12051 |
```

Figure. 4-2. *Most frequent topics from the discharge summary*

```
irrelevant_tags = ["Admission Date:", "Date of Birth:", "Service:",
"Attending:", "Facility:", "Medications on Admission:", "Discharge
Medications:", "Completed by:", "Dictated By:" , "Department:" , "Provider:"]

updated_text = ["<>".join(["|".join(re.split("\n\d|\n\s+",re.sub(
"^(.*?):","",x).strip()))) for x in text.split("\n\n") if pd.notnull(
re.match("^(.*?):",x)) and re.match("^(.*?):",x).group() not in
irrelevant_tags ]) for text in noteevents.TEXT]
updated_text = [re.sub("(\[.*?\])", "", text) for text in updated_text]

updated_text = ["|".join(clean_text(x)) for x in updated_text]
noteevents["CLEAN_TEXT"] = updated_text
```

For the above sample, the following is the cleaned text. Pretty neat, right?

'This is an 81-year-old female with a history of emphysema (not on home O2), who presents with three days of shortness of breath thought by her primary care doctor to be a COPD flare. Two days prior to admission, she was started on a prednisone taper and one day prior to admission she required oxygen at home in order to maintain oxygen saturation greater than 90%. She has also been on levofloxacin and nebulizers, and was not getting better, and presented to the Emergency Room.',

'Fevers, chills, nausea, vomiting, night sweats, change in weight, gastrointestinal complaints, neurologic changes, rashes, palpitations, orthopnea. Is positive for the following: Chest pressure occasionally with shortness of breath with exertion, some shortness of breath that is positionally related, but is improved with nebulizer treatment.'

DIAGNOSES_ICD

This is the ICD-9 code table. It contains all of the ICD-9 codes relevant to a subject's admission events. As discussed in the introduction, you are looking for the top 15 most frequent ICD-9 codes for the problem at hand.

```
top_values = (icd9_code.groupby('ICD9_CODE').
              agg({"SUBJECT_ID": "nunique"}).
              reset_index().sort_values(['SUBJECT_ID'], ascending =
              False).ICD9_CODE.tolist()[:15])

icd9_code = icd9_code[icd9_code.ICD9_CODE.isin(top_values)]
```

Understanding How Language Modeling Works

Before you jump into using BERT directly, let's first understand how it works, what the building blocks are, why it's required, etc.

The paper titled "BERT: Pre-training of Deep Bidirectional Transformers for Language Understanding" released by the Google AI Language Team in 2018 was when the non-research community got really excited about the new form of language modeling and the application of transformer model. **Transformer** models were introduced in 2017 by the Google Brain Team in a paper titled "Attention Is All You Need."

Interesting thus far, right? **Attention** was introduced to learn language in a more human way, such as by correlating words in a sentence. Attention helped better model sentences for transduction problems within NLP, thereby improving the encoder-decoder architecture.

The encoder-decoder architecture was in turn built on **RNNs, LSTMs, and Bi-LSTMs**, which were at some stage the state of the art for sequence modeling. They all fall under the recurrent networks class. Since a sentence is a sequence of words, you need a sequence modeling network in which the current inputs reoccur in the second element of the sequence to understand the word better. This chain of information then helps in encoding a meaningful representation of a sentence.

The point that I am trying to make here is that to actually understand BERT or any other transformer-based architecture models, you need a deep understanding of many interconnected concepts. To keep the discussion focused on BERT, I will restrict it to mostly discussing attention and BERT architecture.

Paying Attention

Let's start with an example. If I ask you to tell me the sentiment for the following sentences, what would you say?

1) Dogs are very cute. I love spending my time with them.

2) Dogs ~~are very cute~~. I love ~~spending my time with~~ them.

For both sentences it's very easy for a human to understand that the speaker has a positive sentiment for dogs. But what about the following sentence?

3) Dogs are very cute. I ~~love spending my time~~ with them.

For this sentence as well, although not conclusively, we can say that the sentence should be something positive about dogs. This is called *attention*. To understand a sentence, we anchor on certain words only, while all others are just garbage (from understanding perspective).

The recurrent net family, although helpful in modeling sequences, fails for very large sentences because a fixed-length representation that encodes the contextual information can only capture so much of these correlations. But what if we picked only the important ones from a large sentence? Then we don't have to worry about the vestiges.

I like to understand this from the information theory perspective. We can model all the whole numbers by just using different combinations of the powers of 2, as shown in Figure 4-3.

1	0	0	0	0	1
2	0	0	0	1	0
3	0	0	0	1	1
4	0	0	1	0	0
5	0	0	1	0	1

Figure 4-3. *Whole numbers as power of 2*

So to get any number, what we are essential doing is taking a dot-product of two vectors:

Any whole number x,

$$x = [\ldots, 32, 16, 8, 4, 2, 1] \odot [\ldots, 0, 0, 0, 0, 1]$$

Attention works in a very similar manner. It takes the context vector or the encoded vector of a sequence and weighs only the important aspects. Although in our case, we shift from whole numbers to real numbers. See Figure 4-4.

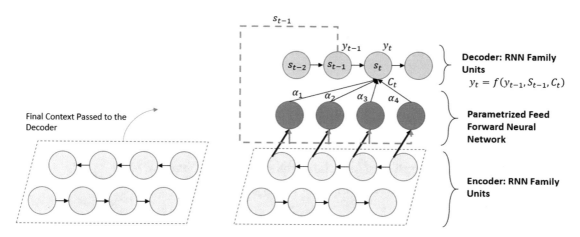

Figure 4-4. *Shows how adding a feed-forward layer can help us learn attention weights*

The concept of attention was first discussed in the paper by Dzmitry Bahdanau et al in 2014 called "Neural Machine Translation by Jointly Learning to Align and Translate."

In Figure 4-4, notice the green arrow coming from the last decoder unit. This is the decoder state represented by S_{t-1}. The way we combine the hidden state and the output of the last hidden layer can provide various kinds of attention, as shown in Table 4-1. This is also called the score or the energy of the encoder output. This combination function or scoring function is designed to maximize similarity between the decoder's hidden state and the encoder output. This way more coherent words are generated, giving more power to MTL (multilanguage translation) systems.

Table 4-1. *Different Scoring Functions for Computing Similarity Between Decoder and Encoder States*

Attention Name	Paper
Additive or Concat: Last decoder unit's hidden state is added to the encoder unit hidden state. Say the dimension is d, then the concatenated dimension becomes 2d.	Bahdanau et al, 2014, "Neural Machine Translation by Jointly Learning to Align and Translate"
Dot-Product: Last decoder unit's hidden state is multiplied by the encoder unit's hidden state. Say the dimension is d, then the concatenated dimension becomes d.	Luong et al, 2015, "Effective Approaches to Attention-based Neural Machine Translation"
Scaled Dot Product: Same as above, just a scaling factor is added to normalize the value and be in a differentiable range of the Softmax function.	Vaswani et al, 2017, "Attention Is All You Need"
General (Dot Product): The encoder hidden state is passed through a feed-forward net before calculating the scores.	Luong et al, 2015, "Effective Approaches to Attention-based Neural Machine Translation"

Some details you should keep in mind:

- To make this process faster, you leverage Keras' TimeDistributedLayer, which makes sure that the feed-forward happens faster for each time unit. (It is just a dense layer.)

- The last consolidated encoder hidden state is fed as input to the first decoder cell. The output of this decoder cell is called the first decoder hidden state.

- All the scores are passed through a Softmax layer to give the attention weights, which are then multiplied with the encoder's hidden state to get the context vector C_t from each encoder unit.

Lastly, there are many classes of attention:

- Local and global attention

- Self-attention

- Multi-head attention

I will discuss them briefly for completeness as each one deserves a write-up of its own and hence I am including only definitions for an overall understanding. I will discuss multi-head attention in detail in the transformer architecture discussion. Please refer to Table 4-2 for an overview of different types of attention.

Table 4-2. *Different Types of Attention*

Attention	Description	Paper
Local and Global Attention	**Global**: All encoder units are given importance. **Local**: Only a part of the input is considered for context vector generation. This input is centered at a position p_t and has a width of p_t-2L to p_t+2L, where L is the window length.	Inspired from Xu et al, 2015, "Show, Attend and Tell: Neural Image Caption Generation with Visual Attention"
Self-Attention	Works similarly to the attention explained in the encoder-decoder architecture above; we just replace the target sequence with the input sequence itself.	Cheng et al, 2016, "Long Short-Term Memory-Networks for Machine Reading"
Multi-Head Attention	Multi-head attention is a way of implementing self-attention but with multiple keys. More on this later.	Vaswani et al, 2017, "Attention Is All You Need"

Transforming the NLP Space: Transformer Architecture

Transformer models can be said to have brought the ImageNet movement for NLP transfer learning tasks. Until now, this required a large dataset to capture context, huge amounts of compute resources, and even greater time. But as soon as transformer architecture came into picture, it could capture context much better, have shorter training time because they can be parallelized, and also set the SOTA for many tasks. Figure 4-5 shows the transformer architecture from the paper by Vaswani et al titled "Attention Is All You Need."

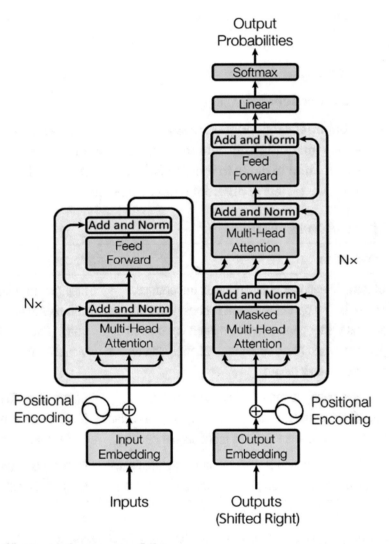

Figure 4-5. *The transformer model*

For the uninitiated, the model can be quite daunting at first, but it is very easy to understand if different concepts are understood in silos.

To understand transformers, you need to understand

- Encoder-decoder frameworks

- Multi-head attention

- Positional encoding

- Residual connections

The encoder and decoder modules were discussed along with the attention topic above and the residual connection just serves the purpose of making sure that residuals from the target loss can easily help in changing the weights accurately as sometimes due to non-linearities the gradient doesn't produce the desired effect.

Positional Encoding

Transformers are able to parallelize and achieve faster training with bigger data and even bigger numbers of parameters. But how is it possible? It is possible by removing all the stateful cells like RNN, GRU, or LSTM.

But then how do we make sure that syntactic grammar of the sentence is not disrupted and there is some sense of ordering in the words of a sentence? We do so by using a dense vector that encodes the position of a word within a sequence.

One very simple way of thinking about this is to label each word a positive integer (unbounded). But what if we get a very long sentence or sentences with different lengths? In both cases, having an unbounded number representation doesn't work.

Ok, then can a bounded representation work? Let's order everything between [a to b] where a represents the first word and b represents the last and everything else lies in between. Since it is range bound to model a 10-word sentence, you must increment the index by $\left\lceil \frac{(b-a)}{10} \right\rceil$ and for a 20-word sentence the delta is $\left\lceil \frac{(b-a)}{20} \right\rceil$. Hence the increment doesn't have the same meaning. The author proposed the formulas in Figure 4-6 for the positional encoding vector.

$$PE_{(pos,2i)} = sin(pos/10000^{2i/d_{model}})$$
$$PE_{(pos,2i+1)} = cos(pos/10000^{2i/d_{model}})$$

Figure 4-6. *Positional encoding*

A good way to understand this, without going into much of the math, is

- The positional encoder is a vector of d-dimension. This vector is added to the word-vector representation of the word and hence dpe = dmodel.

- It is a matrix of size (n, d) where n is the number of words in the sequence and d is the dimension of word embedding.

- It is a unique vector for each position.

- A combination of sin and cos functions allows the model to learn relative positions well. Since any offset k, PEpos+k can be represented as a linear function of PEpos.

- This positional information is preserved in the deeper layers as well due to presence of residual blocks.

Multi-Head Attention

Multi-head attention is the main innovation of the transformer architecture. Let's understand it in detail. The paper is used a general framework to define attention.

It introduced three terms:

1) Key (K)

2) Query (Q)

3) Value (V)

Each embedding of the word should have these three vectors. They are obtained by using matrix multiplications. This captures a certain subspace of information from the embedding vector.

An abstract understanding is something like this: you are trying to identify certain key,value pairs by the use of a query. The word for which you are trying to identify the attention score is the query.

Example: There is traffic congestion due to bad weather.

Say your query is **traffic**. The query vector captures some semantic meaning of the word traffic, maybe its pos tag or that is related to travel/commute, etc. Similarly for the key and value vectors, some nuances are captured.

Now you reach the word **weather** and similarly you capture K, Q, and V. If the query of *traffic has a high similarity with the key of weather*, then the value of the weather contributes highly to the self-attention vector of the word **traffic.** See Figure 4-7.

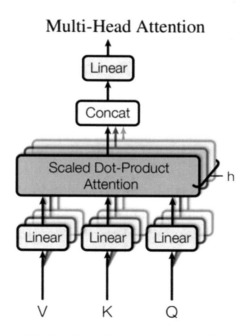

Word	Vectors			Scale (Paper had a 64 dimension vector)	SoftMax	Z
	Q	K	V			
Traffic	q_1	k1	v1	$(q_1 * k1)/8$	a_{11}	$v_1 * a_{11}$
congestion		k2	v2	$(q_1 * k2)/8$	a_{12}	$v_2 * a_{12}$
due		k3	v3	$(q_1 * k3)/8$	a_{13}	$v_3 * a_{13}$
to		k4	v4	$(q_1 * k4)/8$	a_{14}	$v_4 * a_{14}$
bad		k5	v5	$(q_1 * k5)/8$	a_{15}	$v_5 * a_{15}$
weather		k6	v6	$(q_1 * k6)/8$	a_{16}	$v_6 * a_{16}$

$$\Sigma(\uparrow \cdots)$$

Figure 4-7. *Self-attention. Image adapted from "Attention Is All You Need"*

In multi-headed attention, there are multiple such matrix multiplications, which allow you to capture different subspaces each time. They are all done in parallel. See Figure 4-8.

Figure 4-8. *Multi-head self-attention. Image adapted from "Attention Is all You Need"*

The above two were the main innovations in the transformer model. No doubt it is able to capture sentence semantics so well. Here are some other details that deserve mention:

- The decoder model contains a masked multi-head attention model. It masks out all the words after the query word. The value vector is masked, which then carries on to the self-attention vector.

- The self-attention vector from the masked attention block serves as the value vector to the multi-head attention block above it.

- Skip connections (inspired from ResNet, introduced by He et al in "Deep Residual Learning for Image Recognition") are used to prevent signal loss.

- There are multiple encoder-decoder blocks stacked on top of each other, Figure 4-5 shows the last of such pairs. Softmax is added to just the last decoder block.

Note   The output from the last encoder is passed to all the decoder units and not just the last one.

BERT: Bidirectional Encoder Representations from Transformers

BERT laid the foundation for bringing the ImageNet movement for NLP to reality. Now we have a BERT model zoo, which basically means there is a BERT model for almost every kind of application.

From the standpoint of architecture, BERT is nothing but just stacked transformers (only the encoder block). But it brought some new innovations in handling the input data and training. Let's discuss them briefly before we deep-dive into the code.

Input

BERT authors shared some innovative ways to input text. I already discussed position embedding in length so let's quickly jump to token and segment embeddings. See Figure 4-9.

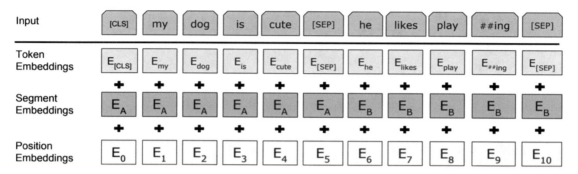

Figure 4-9. *BERT input representation. Image adapted from "BERT: Pre-training of Deep Bidirectional Transformers for Language Understanding"*

Token Embeddings

Token embeddings are just a way to represent each token in a numerical form. In BERT, this is a 768-dimensional vector. What's interesting here is the workpiece tokenization technique. It helps BERT maintain a decent sized library, which is 30,522 and yet not compromised on the out-of-vocabulary words.

Let's understand it by example. Say initially you have a dictionary of just five words and their respective count from the corpus are known:

1) Church</w>, 5

2) Child</w>, 3

3) Return</w>, 8

4) Earn</w>, 10

5) Lift</w>, 5

The </w> at the end represents the word boundary. The WordPiece algorithm looks through each character in the text and tries to find the highest frequency character pairing.

Say the system encounters an out-of-vocabulary word like **Churn**. For this word, BERT would do the following:

1) $c : 5 + 3 = 8$ <- count of alphabet c in the start of a word.

2) $c + h : 5+3 = 8$ <- count of c and h alphabet pair.

3) ~~$c + h + u : 5$~~, Rejected as the overall sum has come down

4)   n</w> : 10

5)   ~~r + n</w> : 8,~~ Rejected as it brings down the count for n</w> as well.

6)   u + r :8, count of u +r

Hence the tokens that get created are
[ch,ur,n</w>]

What I discussed above is BPE or binary pair encoding. As you can observe, it works in a greedy manner to merge individual characters based on frequency. The WordPiece algorithm is slightly different, in a way that the character merging is still based on frequency but the final decision is taken based on the likelihood of occurrence (seeing which wordpieces are more likely to occur).

Segment Embeddings

BERT is trained on two distinct kinds of training tasks:

1.   **Classification**: Determines the category of the input sentence

2.   **Next-sentence prediction**: Predicts the next sentence or a sentence that ideally/coherently follows the previous one (as present in the training corpora)

To do a next-sentence prediction, BERT needs a way to distinguish between the two sentences, hence a special token [SEP] is introduced at the end of each sentence.

Since I have already talked about positional embeddings, I will not be taking it up again here.

Training

The BERT model is pretrained on two tasks:

1.   Masked language mModeling

2.   Next-sentence prediction

Masked Language Modeling

Masked language mModeling was mainly introduced to allow models to learn in a bidirectional manner and enable the model to capture context for any random word within the sequence.

A classification layer is added on top of the encoder output. These outputs are passed through a time-distributed dense layer to convert them to a dimension size of the vocabulary and the probability is then calculated for each word. See Figure 4-10.

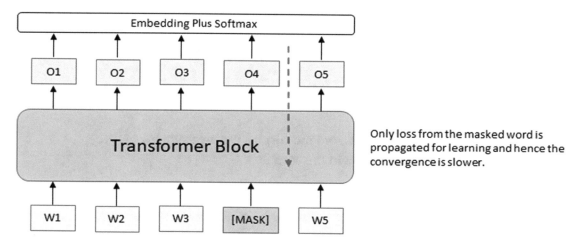

Figure 4-10. *Masked language mModeling*

- In order to make the model position-agnostic and yet give enough context, only **15%** of the words in **each sequence** were **randomly** masked.

- Not all masked words were replaced by [MASK] tokens as shown in Figure 4-10. Rather the following approach was chosen:

  - 80% of the time the [MASK] token was used.

  - 10% of the time the words were replaced with random words.

  - The remaining 10% of the time words were left unchanged.

Now if you're thinking deeply, there are many questions that would come to your mind about the choice of these percentages. No ablation study was done to support these empirical numbers; however, there are some intuitions.

- **Can using random words make BERT learn wrong embeddings?**
  Ideally not, as it is corrected by the correct label during
  backpropagation. It is also done to introduce variance.

- **Why not keep 100% [MASK] token?** It is done to avoid any confusion
  during fine-tuning where if the [MASK] token is not found it will give
  some random output depending on the task.

Next-Sentence Prediction

According to the authors, learning how to relate two sentences can have significant
performance improvements for tasks like question answering and natural language
inference.

Here as well they proposed certain ratios with which they created a training data for
the NSP:

- For 50% of the sentences from the corpus, the next sentence is the
  same sentence as present in the corpus.

- For the remaining 50%, the next sentence is picked randomly.

This gives us a binary classifier to train. The [CLS] token is used for binary
classification, the final state of which is passed to a FFN plus Softmax Layer.

I hope you now have a deeper understanding of transformer-based models and
BERT in particular. I think this should be sufficient for you to apply BERT to the case and
learn how to fine-tune it.

Modeling

Let's deep dive into modeling now. You already prepared your data in the "Data" section
above. You are trying to do multi-label classification. You will have to prepare your data
in such a way.

For your task, you will use the BERT large model from the DMIS (Data Mining and
Information Systems) Lab, Korea University. You are doing so because it is one of the few
pretrained models that offers a custom vocabulary for BERT. Most of the free pretrained
models keep the same vocabulary, which in my opinion is a bad practice.

Secondly, you are also going to leverage a transformers library by the Hugging Face group which provides general-purpose architectures (BERT, GPT-2, RoBERTa, XLM, DistilBert, XLNet) for language understanding (NLU) and natural language generation (NLG) tasks.

But before that, let's a sense of how the vocabulary for a BERT model looks. Post that, you will form your data and do the multi-label classification.

BERT Deep-Dive

One of the benefits of having a custom vocabulary, besides just better performance, is the ability to see what concepts are getting captured. You are going to use a UMLs database to identify which concepts are getting captured in the vocabulary; for this, you are going to see subword tokens (without "##") and pick up all tokens with a length greater than 3.

For this, you must set up the **scispacy** library. Built on spacy, it is an extremely fast and useful library for applied NLP work. Please see the installation steps in Chapter 2.

Scispacy provides a way to link knowledge bases. The concept extraction works on string overlap. It covers most of the major biomedical DBs available openly like UMLs, Mesh, RxNorm, etc.

Also, you are going to use a large spacy model based on biomedical data. Make sure that you have already set up the model by downloading and linking it to spacy. Keep the default parameters for the match because it is just an exploratory exercise and your modeling is not directly affected by this choice. The official documentation is at `https://github.com/allenai/scispacy.`

What Does the Vocabulary Actually Contain?

Before you deep-dive into training the classification model or further improving it using fine-tuning, you should have a closer look at the vocabulary you have. Does it even cover biomedical concepts? What is the average token length? (Biomedical words generally have decent token length of >5 characters in general.)

Let's have a look at these questions one by one.

1) Finding any biomedical concepts

To find biomedical concepts, you will make use of an extensive UMLs KB. It comes linked with scispacy through an easy interface.

For the first run, linking can take some time depending on your PC configuration. Firstly, you start by importing the libraries and loading the relevant model.

```
# Load Hugging-face transformers
from transformers import TFBertModel, BertConfig, BertTokenizerFast
import tensorflow as tf

# For data processing
import pandas as pd
from sklearn.model_selection import train_test_split

# Load pre-trained model tokenizer (vocabulary)
    tokenizer = BertTokenizerFast.from_pretrained('dmis-lab/biobert-large-
    cased-v1.1')
```

Let's next find total number of unique tokens.

```
vocab = tokenizer.vocab.keys()
# Total Length
    print("Total Length of Vocabulary words are : ", len(vocab))
```

The total length of vocabulary words are 58996, which is almost twice as long as the first BERT model shared by the team at Google. Any guesses why?

Well, the vocabulary size is something that's decided on the basis of how distinctly you are able to encode each word present in the corpus with the subword of the vocabulary. Google didn't share the code so the exact reason is unknown, but I place my bet on the hypothesis that the above size is sufficient to represent different words in the corpus in an optimized manner. You can read more about it from Google's official repo at https://github.com/google-research/bert#learning-a-new-wordpiece-vocabulary.

Let's link the UMLs database.

```
import spacy
import scispacy

from scispacy.linking import EntityLinker
    nlp = spacy.load('en_core_sci_lg')
    linker = EntityLinker(resolve_abbreviations=False, name="umls")
# keeping default thresholds for match percentage.
nlp.add_pipe(linker)
```

```python
# subword vs whole word selection based on length
    target_vocab = [word[2:] for word in vocab if "##" in word and
    (len(word[2:]) > 3)] + [word[2:] for word in vocab if "##" not in word
    and (len(word) > 3)]

umls_concept_extracted = [[umls_ent for entity in doc.ents for umls_ent in
entity._.umls_ents] for doc in nlp.pipe(target_vocab)]

    umls_concept_cui = [linker.kb.cui_to_entity[concepts[0][0]] for
    concepts in umls_concept_extracted if len(concepts) > 0]
# Capturing all the information shared from the UMLS DB in a dataframe
umls_concept_df = pd.DataFrame(umls_concept_cui)
```

UMLs provides a class name to each of its TXXX identifiers. TXXX is code for parents for each of the CUI numbers, a unique concept identifier used by UMLs KB. Let's next map the TXXX ids to human-readable labels.

```python
# To obtain this file please login to https://www.nlm.nih.gov/research/
umls/index.html
# Shared in Github Repo of the book :)
    type2namemap = pd.read_csv("SRDEF", sep ="|", header = None)
    type2namemap = type2namemap.iloc[:,:3]
    type2namemap.columns = ["ClassType","TypeID","TypeName"]
    typenamemap = {row["TypeID"]:row["TypeName"] for i,row in type2namemap.
    iterrows()}
```

Create the count for each Type ID.

```python
concept_df = pd.Series([typenamemap[typeid] for types in umls_concept_
df.types for typeid in types]).value_counts().reset_index()
    concept_df.columns = ["concept","count"]
```

Let's visualize the top 20 concepts. See Figure 4-11.

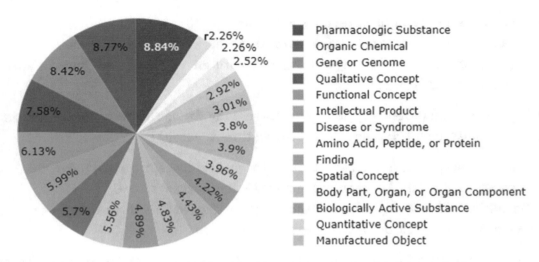

Figure 4-11. *Distribution of biomedical concepts in the BERT vocabulary*

Wow, the vocabulary actually does capture a variety of biomedical concepts like disease, body parts, organic chemicals (compounds), and pharmacologic substances (used in treatment of pathologic disorders). It looks like you have the right model for your task. All of these concepts are quite a common occurrence in EHR notes as well.

Next, let's also look at the token lengths you observe in the dataset for both the subword and the actual tokens.

```
subword_len = [len(x.replace("##","")) for x in vocab]
token_len = [len(x) for x in vocab]

import seaborn as sns
import matplotlib.pyplot as plt
import matplotlib.ticker as ticker

    with sns.plotting_context(font_scale=2):
        fig, axes = plt.subplots(1,2, figsize=(10, 6))
        sns.countplot(subword_len, palette="Set2", ax=axes[0])
    sns.despine()
        axes[0].set_title("Subword length distribution")
        axes[0].set_xlabel("Length in characters")
        axes[0].set_ylabel("Frequency")
```

```
    sns.countplot(token_len, palette="Set2", ax=axes[1])
sns.despine()
    axes[1].set_title("Token length distribution")
    axes[1].set_xlabel("Length in characters")
    axes[1].set_ylabel("Frequency")
```

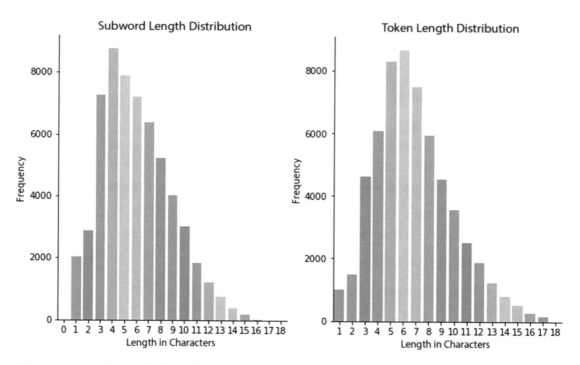

Figure 4-12. *Length distribution of vocabulary tokens*

In Figure 4-12, you indeed see the mean of the distribution in between [5-8], which is a good indicator that you are using a right pretrained model.

If you want to peruse through different words present in the vocabulary, you can visit the following link:

https://huggingface.co/dmis-lab/biobert-large-cased-v1.1/blob/main/vocab.txt.

Training

BERT can be used for fine-tuning in multiple ways:

- **Fine-tuning:** You add a another set of layers on top of the last pretrained layer of the BERT model and then train the whole model with a task-specific dataset, although in this process you must make sure that the weights of the pretrained model are not disrupted, so you freeze them for some epochs and then resume the full backpropagation into BERT layers for another set of epochs. This is also called warm-up.

- **Extracting weights from the last set of layers:** The extracted contextual embeddings are used as input to the downstream task. They are fixed vectors and hence are non-trainable. There are four different types of methods discussed in the original paper to do so (Table 7).

  - Weighted sum of the 12 layers. Weighing can be empirical.

  - Use the last hidden layer.

  - Extract the penultimate hidden layer (second to last).

  - Concat the last four hidden layers.

- **Word embeddings:** Take word embeddings from the encoder layer of BERT. The wrapper is present in Hugging Face's transformer library.

Fine-tuning is argued to be the best approach with better control on model performance, so you will be going with that approach.

Since you are going to train a multi-label classification, let's prepare your final dataset for the same. You are making a practical decision of not keeping shorter sentences where there are just three tokens or less.

```
# Making icd9_code unique at SUBJECT ID and HADM_ID level by clubbing
different ICD9_CODE
    icd9_code = icd9_code.groupby(["SUBJECT_ID","HADM_ID"])["ICD9_CODE"].
    apply(list).reset_index()

    full_data = pd.merge(noteevents, icd9_code, how="left", on =
    ["SUBJECT_ID","HADM_ID"])
```

```
# Removing any SUBJECT_ID and HADM_ID pair not having the top 15 ICD9 Codes
    full_data = full_data.dropna(subset = ["ICD9_CODE"]).reset_index(drop = True)

# Make sure we have text of considerable length
    full_data.CLEAN_TEXT = [" ".join([y for y in x.split("|") if len(
    y.split()) > 3]) for x in full_data.CLEAN_TEXT]
```

You will also create the training and validation set with the full_data variable. Also, your target will be a one-hot matrix with each sample having one label for the ICD-9 code it belongs to and zero for the remaining one.

```
# Binarizing the multi- labels
from sklearn.preprocessing import MultiLabelBinarizer
from sklearn.model_selection import train_test_split

mlb = MultiLabelBinarizer()
mlb_fit = mlb.fit(full_data.ICD9_CODE.tolist())

    train_X,val_X,train_y,val_y = train_test_split(full_data[["SUBJECT_ID"," ",
    "CLEAN_TEXT"]],full_data.ICD9_CODE.values, test_size=0.2, random_state=42)
```

You are finally ready to load the Hugging Face transformer library and get the BERT model from DMIS Labs.

```
# Load Huggingface transformers
from transformers import TFBertModel, BertConfig, BertTokenizerFast
import tensorflow as tf
import numpy as np

# For data processing
import pandas as pd
from sklearn.model_selection import train_test_split

# Load pre-trained model tokenizer (vocabulary)
    tokenizer = BertTokenizerFast.from_pretrained('dmis-lab/biobert-large-
    cased-v1.1')

# Import BERT Model
from transformers import BertModel, BertConfig, TFBertModel
    bert = TFBertModel.from_pretrained("./dmis-lab/biobert-large-cased-v1.1",
                          from_pt = True)
```

The model shared by the DMIS team is a pytorch model and hence can't be directly used for your task. You are going to use a wrapper function provided in the transformers library to convert the pytorch model to a TensorFlow BERT model.

You must make sure you pass the parameter `from_pt = True` which signifies that you are trying to create a TFBertModel from a Python pretrained file.

Next, decide on the model parameters you are going to use.

```
EPOCHS = 5
BATCH_SIZE = 32
MAX_LEN = 510
LR = 2e-5
NUM_LABELS = 15 # Since we have 15 classes to predict for
```

Ideally, you decide on `MAX_LEN`. You can draw a histogram plot of the sentence length present in your corpus, but since the text is generally long, you have taken the maximum length possible for a sentence in terms of number of tokens.

For now, the learning rate is kept static with no warm-up. The design parameters used, like the choice of activation functions, batch size, etc., are just empirical design choices, so you can explore and experiment with different design choices.

Just like in Chapter 3, you will create a generator function which will yield the input data in batch size dimension.

```
X = (BATCH_SIZE, {'input_ids':[0 to VOCAB LENGTH],'token_type_ids':
[1/0],'attention_mask':[1/0]}
```

BERT takes a dictionary as input:

- **input ids** represent the index of tokenized words as per the BERT model vocabulary

- **token type ids** is also called the segment ID. Since you are training a sequence classification problem, all the token type ids are all zero.

- **attention mask** is a 1/0 vector, which tells which word to focus on. Generally all words are considered important but this can be easily changed as per the design decisions.

Note that you are also padding the sentences to a maximum length of tokens possible.

```python
def df_to_dataset(dataframe,
                  dataframe_labels,
                  batch_size = BATCH_SIZE,
                  max_length = MAX_LEN,
                  tokenizer  = tokenizer):
    """

    Loads data into a tf.data.Dataset for finetuning a given model.
    """

while True:
    for i in range(len(dataframe)):
        if (i+1) % batch_size == 0:
            multiplier = int((i+1)/batch_size)
        print(multiplier)
            _df = dataframe.iloc[(multiplier-1)*batch_size:
            multiplier*batch_size,:]
        input_df_dict = tokenizer(
            _df.CLEAN_TEXT.tolist(),
            add_special_tokens=True,
            max_length=max_length, # TO truncate larger sentences,
            similar to truncation = True
            truncation=True,
            return_token_type_ids=True,
            return_attention_mask=True,
                padding='max_length', # right padded
        )
        input_df_dict = {k:np.array(v) for k,v in input_df_dict.
        items()}
            yield input_df_dict, mlb_fit.transform(dataframe_
            labels[(multiplier-1)*batch_size:multiplier*batch_size])

train_gen = df_to_dataset(train_X.reset_index(drop = True),train_y)
val_gen = df_to_dataset(val_X.reset_index(drop = True),val_y)
```

```python
from tensorflow.keras import layers
    def create_final_model(bert_model = bert):

        input_ids = layers.Input(shape=(MAX_LEN,), dtype=tf.int32,
        name='input_ids')
        token_type_ids = layers.Input((MAX_LEN,), dtype=tf.int32,
        name='token_type_ids')
        attention_mask = layers.Input((MAX_LEN,), dtype=tf.int32,
        name='attention_mask')

    # Use pooled_output(hidden states of [CLS]) as sentence level embedding
        cls_output = bert_model({'input_ids': input_ids, 'attention_mask':
        attention_mask, 'token_type_ids': token_type_ids})[1]
        x = layers.Dense(512, activation='selu')(cls_output)
        x = layers.Dense(256, activation='selu')(x)
        x = layers.Dropout(rate=0.1)(x)
        x = layers.Dense(NUM_LABELS, activation='sigmoid')(x)
        model = tf.keras.models.Model(inputs={'input_ids': input_ids,
        'attention_mask': attention_mask, 'token_type_ids': token_type_ids},
        outputs=x)
    return model

model = create_final_model(bert_model = bert)
```

Also, make sure that you are only learning the custom layers at least for the few first epochs; then you can learn the whole network. For this, you freeze the BERT layers and only train the custom layers.

```python
for layers in bert.layers:
    print(layers.name)
    layers.trainable= False
```

Let's check how the model looks; see Figure 4-13. Take a special note of the number of trainable and non-trainable parameters.

```python
model.summary()
```

```
Model: "model"
```

Layer (type)	Output Shape	Param #	Connected to
attention_mask (InputLayer)	[(None, 510)]	0	
input_ids (InputLayer)	[(None, 510)]	0	
token_type_ids (InputLayer)	[(None, 510)]	0	
tf_bert_model (TFBertModel)	TFBaseModelOutputWit	364299264	attention_mask[0][0] input_ids[0][0] token_type_ids[0][0]
dense (Dense)	(None, 512)	524800	tf_bert_model[0][1]
dense_1 (Dense)	(None, 256)	131328	dense[0][0]
dropout_73 (Dropout)	(None, 256)	0	dense_1[0][0]
dense_2 (Dense)	(None, 15)	3855	dropout_73[0][0]

```
Total params: 364,959,247
Trainable params: 659,983
Non-trainable params: 364,299,264
```

Figure 4-13. *Model summary*

One thing to note here is that you are using a sigmoid function and not a Softmax function since you are trying to identify whether a particular ICD-Code exists or not and hence Softmax is suffice for the same.

```
model.compile(optimizer= tf.keras.optimizers.Adam(learning_rate=LR),
              loss='binary_crossentropy',
              metrics=['AUC'])
```

Since this is a big model and can take a lot of time to train, it would be good to set up a TensorBoard to keep track of the loss and AUC.

```
# You can change the directory name
    LOG_DIR = 'tb_logs'

import os
if not os.path.exists(LOG_DIR):
    os.makedirs(LOG_DIR)

    tensorboard_callback = tf.keras.callbacks.TensorBoard(log_dir=LOG_DIR,
    histogram_freq=1)
```

```
with tf.device('/device:GPU:0'):
history = model.fit(train_gen,
                    steps_per_epoch=len(train_X)//BATCH_SIZE,
                    epochs=EPOCHS,
                    validation_data=val_gen,
                      callbacks=[tensorboard_callback])
```

You can train the model with or without a GPU but make sure that the hardware you are using has the GPU enabled. If you don't have it set up, please revisit Chapter 2 for the notes.

To know if you have a GPU available, run the following command:

```
tf.test.gpu_device_name()
```

The training of this model can take a lot of time on a CPU and little lesser on the GPU for NVIDIA GeForce GTX 1660Ti. It takes roughly four hours for one epoch whereas it takes almost five times longer on a CPU machine. Hence I will not be discussing the results from the model here.

Here are a couple of ideas to enhance training:

1) For a couple of epochs, you can keep the BERT layer frozen, but eventually to achieve slightly better performance on the downstream task you can unfreeze and train the parameters of the BERT layer as well.

2) Try using a more distilled model. Distilled models are less parameter-hungry models, achieving almost equal performance on many downstream tasks. This makes overall training really fast.

3) Another modification can be made in the dataset generation. `input_token_dict` can be made on the whole data and subsetted for each batch.

Conclusion

Well, with those thoughts I would like to end this chapter. In this chapter, you learned about the transformer, multiple attention concepts, and BERT in length. You applied all of these learned concepts to train a multi-label classification model with the use of the Hugging Face library.

The foundations of transformers you learned in this chapter is going to be really important for the coming years as there are multiple papers trying to leverage transformers for a variety of tasks. They being used for image problems, drug prediction, graph networks, and more.

Although there is a developing interest in making inference from such models faster without much loss of performance, papers such as "When BERT Plays the Lottery, All Tickets Are Winning" by Rogers et al show that you can prune away many of BERT's components and it still works. This paper analyzes BERT pruning in light of the Lottery Ticket Hypothesis and finds that even the "bad" lottery tickets can be fine-tuned to good accuracy. It still remains a very important milestone in pushing the boundary for NLU. I urge you to read about XLNext, Longformer and Reformer, Roberta, etc. They are other transformer-based or inspired architectures and they perform better than BERT on certain tasks. You will be using the BERT model to develop the Question and Answering system. Until then, keep reading and learning.

## CHAPTER 5

Extracting Structured Data from Receipt Images Using a Graph Convolutional Network

Just like any other sales job, the sales rep of a pharma firm is always in the field. Being in the field means generating lots of receipts for reimbursement on food and travel. It becomes difficult to keep track of bills that don't follow company guidelines. In this case study, you will explore how to extract information from receipt images and structure this various information.

You are also going to learn how to use different information extraction techniques on templatic documents (documents following a standard template or set of entities). You are going to build upon the use case of information extraction from out-of-the-box OCR to a graph convolutional network (GCR). GCRs are relatively new and belong to the class of graph neural networks, an idea that is being actively researched and applied.

Data

The data you are going to use for this case is the ICDAR 2019 Robust Reading Challenge on Scanned Receipts OCR and Information Extraction Dataset. The website link is `https://rrc.cvc.uab.es/?ch=13.` It can be obtained easily from the Downloads section after you register on the website. You may find blogs/articles that mention data issues in the original data because some data was incorrectly labeled, but this has been corrected by the team.

© Anshik 2021
Anshik, *AI for Healthcare with Keras and Tensorflow 2.0*, https://doi.org/10.1007/978-1-4842-7086-8_5

What you are trying to do is identify certain entities, namely company, date, address, and total. Figure 5-1 shows some of the image samples with labels and their values.

Company	BOOK TA .K (TAMAN DAYA) SDN BHD	UNIHAKKA INTERNATIONAL SDN BHD	SOON HUAT MACHINERY ENTERPRISE
Date	25/12/2018	12 MAR 2018	11/01/2019
Address	NO.53 55,57 & 59, JALAN SAGU 18, TAMAN DAYA, 81100 JOHOR BAHRU, JOHOR	12, JALAN TAMPOI 7/4,KAWASAN PERINDUSTRIAN TAMPOI,81200 JOHOR BAHRU,JOHOR	NO.53 JALAN PUTRA 1, TAMAN SRI PUTRA, 81200 JOHOR BAHRU JOHOR
Total	9.00	$8.20	327.00

Figure 5-1. *Sample images and their labels*

The dataset is split into a training/validation set (trainval) and a test set (test). The trainval set consists of 626 receipt images whereas the test set contains roughly 361 images.

There are two kinds of labeled data available:

1) OCR output: Each image in the dataset is annotated with text bounding boxes (bboxes) and the transcript of each text bbox. Locations are annotated as rectangles with four vertices, which are in clockwise order starting from the top.

a) You can simplify this representation. What you effectively need is (x_{min},y_{min}) and (x_{max},y_{max}), which is the top right and bottom left corner, respectively, of the rectangle.

2) Node labels: Each image in the dataset is annotated with a text file.

Now there are no labels present at the OCR output level so you must find a way to model each text bbox to any of the four labels.

Mapping Node Labels to OCR Output

If you carefully peruse through the labels and the text, you can observe certain things such as:

1) The OCR text is broken into multiple lines, whereas the label output contains a concatenated version of the same. Hence you can do a substring search both ways because sometimes label text is short compared to the output, especially for date labels.

2) The total is sometimes reported with currency and sometimes not, so this is a little inconsistent but it should be ok because you will be just focusing on the numerical part of the total label.

Let's start by loading the data. Download the data from the competition website, unzipped it, changed the folder name to ICDAR_SROIE, and then place the folder in a Data folder for better organization.

You are also going to create a folder named processed inside your directory to store the bounding box of the text along with its label, but it is not as simple as there are several nuances to it, which I will discuss further into the chapter.

```python
import pandas as pd
import numpy as np

import glob
import os

    PROCESSED_PATH = "./Data/ICDAR_SROIE/processed/"

# Loading ocr and label data
    receipt_train_img = {os.path.split(x)[-1].replace(".jpg",""):x for x in
    glob.glob("./Data/ICDAR_SROIE/0325updated.task1train(626p)/*.jpg") if
    not os.path.split(x)[-1].replace(".jpg","").endswith(")")}

    ocr_data = {os.path.split(x)[-1].replace(".txt",""):x for x in
    glob.glob("./Data/ICDAR_SROIE/0325updated.task1train(626p)/*.txt") if
    not os.path.split(x)[-1].replace(".txt","").endswith(")")}
    label_data = {os.path.split(x)[-1].replace(".txt",""):x for x in
    glob.glob("./Data/ICDAR_SROIE/0325updated.task2train(626p)/*.txt") if
    not os.path.split(x)[-1].replace(".txt","").endswith(")")}
```

```
# Checking if all the sets have the same number of labeled data
assert len(receipt_train_img) == len(ocr_data) == len(label_data)
```

Next, create three functions:

1) Read the OCR output and just keep (x_{min}, y_{min}) and (x_{max}, y_{max}), i.e. (x_1, y_1) and (x_3, y_3).

2) Read the label data as a dictionary.

3) Map the OCR output to the labels.

```python
import json
    def extract_ocr_data_fromtxt(file_path, key, save = False):
        """

        Extract the bounding box coordinates from txt and returns a pandas
        dataframe
        """

        with open(file_path, 'r') as in_file:
        stripped = (line.strip() for line in in_file)
            lines = [line.split(",")[:2] + line.split(",")[4:6] +
            [",".join(line.split(",")[8:])] for line in stripped if line]

            df = pd.DataFrame(lines, columns = ['xmin', 'ymin','xmax',
            'ymax','text'])
        # Option to save as a csv
        if save:
            if not os.path.exists(PROCESSED_PATH):
                os.mkdir(PROCESSED_PATH)
                df.to_csv(os.path.join(PROCESSED_PATH,key + '.csv'), index
                =None)
        return df

    def extract_label_data_fromtxt(file_path):
        """

        Read the label json and return as a dictionary
        """

    with open(file_path) as f:
        json_data = json.load(f)
        return json_data
```

```python
def map_labels(text,k):
    """

    Maps label to ocr output using certain heuristics and logic
    """

    text_n = None
    k_n = None
    try:
        text_n = float(text)
    except Exception as e:
        pass

    try:
        k_n = float(k)
    except Exception as e:
        pass
    # if both are text then we are doing a substring match
    if (pd.isnull(text_n) and pd.isnull(k_n)):
        if (text in k) or (k in text):
            return True
    # if both are numerical then we just check for complete match
    elif (text_n is not None) and (k_n is not None):
        return text == k
    # special case to handle total, using endswith
    # as sometimes symbols are attached to ocr output
    elif (k_n is not None) and (text_n is None):
        return text.endswith(k)

    return False
```

Note that the mapping function map_labels is not a perfect way to create labels. There can be many false positives for the total tag, as shown in Figure 5-2 where the total gets mismatched. But it is not a frequent occurrence and hence can be either manually corrected or labeled as is. Let's keep the label as is.

Finally, you make a wrapper function to save the mapped data in a separate folder.

```python
def mapped_label_ocr(key):
    """
    Wrapper function to yield result of mapping in desired format
    """
    data = extract_ocr_data_fromtxt(ocr_data[key],key)
    label_dict = extract_label_data_fromtxt(label_data[key])

    data['labels'] = ["".join([k for k,v in label_dict.items() if
    map_labels(text, v)]) for text in data.text]

    if not os.path.exists(PROCESSED_PATH):
        os.mkdir(PROCESSED_PATH)
        data.to_csv(os.path.join(PROCESSED_PATH,key + '.csv'), index =None)

    return data

# save the data
mapped_data = {key: mapped_label_ocr(key) for key in ocr_data.keys()}
```

Let's quickly check if the heuristic you applied even works. Figures 5-2 and 5-3 show two examples for comparison.

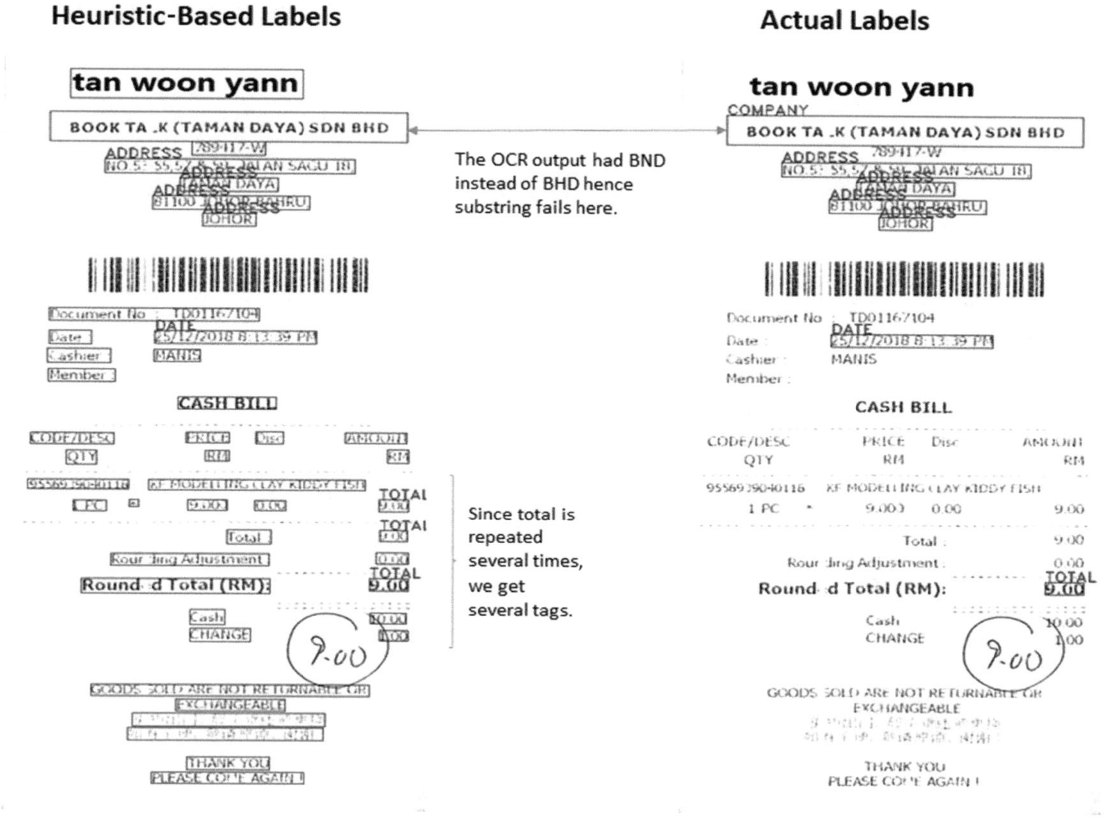

Heuristic-Based Labels

Actual Labels

Figure 5-2. Example 1: Heuristic lLabeling

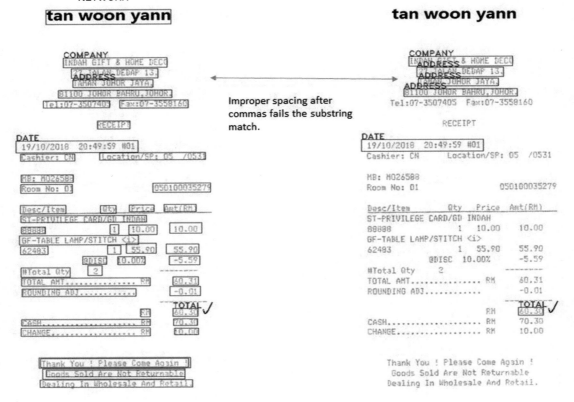

Figure 5-3. *Example 2: Heuristic lLabeling*

Both examples show that a simple substring search can't be used due to data
inconsistencies. Hence you are going to go the fuzzy route and try to fuzzy search for text
with a very high cutoff in place.

For this you are going to use the fuzzywuzzy package, a very effective package that
provides access to various types of fuzzy matches (Levenstein, phonetic, etc.) applied in
various ways (token, character level, etc.).

```python
import json
from fuzzywuzzy import fuzz
    def extract_ocr_data_fromtxt(file_path, key, save = False):
        """

        Extract the bounding box coordinates from txt and returns a pandas
        dataframe
        """

    .....
```

```
def extract_label_data_fromtxt(file_path):
    """

    Read the label json and return as a dictionary
    """

....

def map_labels(text,k):
    """

    Maps label to ocr output using certain heuristics and logic
    """

.....
# if both are text then we are doing a fuzzy match
if (pd.isnull(text_n) and pd.isnull(k_n)):
        if fuzz.token_set_ratio(text,k) > 90:
        return True

.....
```

Also, sometimes the company name becomes part of the address. For this, you modify your wrapper function and give preference to the address.

Node Features

In order to model these receipts with a GCN, you need to transform them into a graph. Each word that gets extracted as part of the OCR process can be considered an individual node.

These nodes can be of the following types:

1) Company

2) Address

3) Date

4) Total

5) Undefined

Each node will have a feature vector associated with it, which will tell about the data that the node carries. Ideally you can use any advanced LM models to extract information from text, but in this particular case the text doesn't entail a lot of semantic

context, so using any LM model can be overkill. Instead, you can go with a trivial feature
generation pipeline for text. You will be generating the following features:

- `SpecialCharacterCount`: Total number of special character count

- `isFloat`: If the text represents a floating point number, then the
  column has a value of 1.

- `isDate`: See if a text represents a date or not.

- `TotalDistinctNumber`: How many distinct digits are present in the
  text. The idea is that an address generally contains a lot of digits (such
  as house number, street number, and Pin/ZIP code) compared to
  other entities and hence it can be a useful feature.

- `BigNumLength`: Length of the biggest number. Pin/ZIP codes will have
  a higher length than house and row number. Also, the total of the bill
  could be the highest number.

- `IsContainsNum`: Whether the text contains a numerical entity or not.

- `POSTagDistribution`: See the distribution (total counts) of the
  following pos tags for each text. You will use the spacy pos tagger for
  this purpose (`https://spacy.io/api/annotation#pos-tagging`)

  - SYM: Currency symbol (total value of the bill can have currency
    symbols)

  - NUM: Cardinal number

  - CCONJ: Conjunctions (addresses can have a lot of conjunctions)

  - PROPN: Proper nouns

So you have a total of 10 features for each node.

You will maintain an in-memory object for the processed dataframe but let's also
save it for later reference in a separate directory

```
      PROCESSED_TEXT_PATH = "./Data/ICDAR_SROIE/processed_text_features"
if not os.path.exists(PROCESSED_TEXT_PATH):
    os.mkdir(PROCESSED_TEXT_PATH)
```

```python
import spacy
import string
import collections
import re
from dateutil.parser import parse
from itertools import groupby

import en_core_web_sm
nlp = en_core_web_sm.load()

    def get_text_features(text):

    # SpecialCharacterCount
    special_chars = string.punctuation
    SpecialCharacterCount = np.sum([v for k, v in collections.
    Counter(text).items() \
                if k in special_chars])

    # isFloat
    try:
        float(text)
            isFloat = 1
    except Exception as e:
            isFloat = 0

    # isDate
    try:
        parse(text, fuzzy=True)
            isDate = int(True and len(text) > 5)
    except Exception as e:
            isDate = 0

    # TotalDistinctNumber
        num_list = re.findall(r"(\d+)", text)
    num_list = [float(x) for x in num_list]

    TotalDistinctNumber = len(num_list)
```

```
# BigNumLength
    BigNumLength = np.max(num_list) if TotalDistinctNumber > 0 else 0

# DoesContainsNum
    DoesContainsNum = 1 if TotalDistinctNumber > 0 else 0

# POSTagDistribution
spacy_text = nlp(text)
pos_list = [token.pos_ for token in spacy_text]

POSTagDistribution = {}
    for k in ['SYM','NUM','CCONJ','PROPN']:
        POSTagDistribution['POSTagDistribution' + k] = [0]

    POSTagDistribution.update({'POSTagDistribution'+ value:
[len(list(freq))] for value, freq in groupby(sorted(pos_list)) if
    value in ['SYM','NUM','CCONJ','PROPN']})

pos_features = pd.DataFrame.from_dict(POSTagDistribution)
other_features = pd.DataFrame([[SpecialCharacterCount, isFloat, isDate,
                                TotalDistinctNumber, BigNumLength,
                                DoesContainsNum]],
                                    columns = ["SpecialCharacterCount",
                                    "isFloat","isDate",
                                    "TotalDistinctNumber",
                                    "BigNumLength", "DoesContainsNum"])

    df = pd.concat([other_features, pos_features], axis = 1)
return df
```

As explained, you will be creating 10 features with the text values. Although the code is self-explanatory, there are some points to be discussed.

- You're using the dateutil package to extract and identify date values, but it's not perfect and led to many false positives, so now there's another condition that the length of the text should be at least 5. This removes the false positives that got captured.

- iertools is a phenomenal package when it comes to performance, so
  you should always try to leverage it for your applications. There are
  other ways to get the frequency of list elements, but this method is
  really good and optimal.

Store the results in a separate dataframe.

```
mapped_data_text_features = {}
for k, v in mapped_data.items():
    _df = pd.concat([get_text_features(x) for x in v.text], axis = 0)
    final_df = pd.concat([v.reset_index(drop = True), _df.reset_index(
    drop = True)], axis = 1)
    final_df.to_csv(os.path.join(PROCESSED_TEXT_PATH,k+".csv"),
    index = None)
    mapped_data_text_features[k] = final_df
```

There are two more things that need to be seen before you move further in this
chapter.

1. In the datasets you have there, are no connections given between
   words and nodes.

2. How is the input data decided for training? Is it in batches of
   nodes or a single node matrix?

Hierarchical Layout

Lohani et al in their paper titled "An Invoice Reading System Using a Graph
Convolutional Network" discussed how to model relationships for the nodes/words for
an invoice system. These relations are formed on the concept of nearest neighbor. See
Figure 5-4.

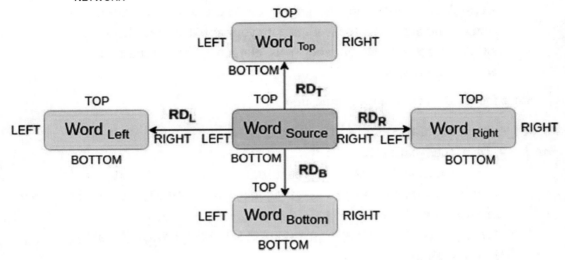

Figure 5-4. *Creating edges based on the nearest neighbor concept. Image source: Lohani et al paper titled "An Invoice Reading System Using a Graph Convolutional Network"*

Each word node has only one neighbor in each direction. This can be generalized to any semi-structured document graph modeling problem beyond this case study.

The authors propose two main steps to create this hierarchical layout in their paper.

Line Formation

1. **Sort words based on the top coordinate.**

2. **Form lines as group of words,** which obeys the following:

    Two words (Wa and Wb) are in same line if Top(Wa) ≤ Bottom(Wb) and Bottom(Wa) ≥ Top(Wb)

3. **Sort words in each line based on the left coordinate**

This gives a direction to the link formation. You start from the top left and end at the right bottom. This also ensures that you are seeing a word/node only once.

```
import itertools
    def get_line_numbers(key):
        """

        Get line number for each word.
        """
```

################ 1 ##################

```python
df = mapped_data_text_features[key]
    df.sort_values(by=['ymin'], inplace=True)
df.reset_index(drop=True, inplace=True)

# To avoid spacing issue, lets reduce ymax by some small value
    df["ymax"] = df["ymax"].apply(lambda x: int(x) - 0.5)
```

################ 2 ##################

```python
# In order to get line number we start with left most word/phrase/node
# and then check all non-matching words and store their indices from L->R
word_idx = []
for i, row in df.iterrows():
    flattened_word_idx = list(itertools.chain(*word_idx))
    #print(flat_master)
    # check if the word has not already been checked
    if i not in flattened_word_idx:
            top_wa = int(row['ymin'])
            bottom_wa = int(row['ymax'])

        # Store the word
        idx = [i]

        for j, row_dash in df.iterrows():
            if j not in flattened_word_idx:
            # check a different word, double check
                if not i == j:
                        top_wb = int(row_dash['ymin'])
                        bottom_wb = int(row_dash['ymax'] )
                    # Valid for all the words next to Wax
                    if (top_wa <= bottom_wb) and (bottom_wa >= top_wb):
                        idx.append(j)
                        #print(line)
        word_idx.append(idx)
```

```
    # Create line number for each node

        word_df = pd.DataFrame([[j,i+1] for i,x in enumerate(word_idx) for j
        in x], columns= ["word_index","line_num"])

    # put the line numbers back to the list
        final_df = df.merge(word_df, left_on=df.index, right_on='word_index')
        final_df.drop('word_index', axis=1, inplace=True)

    ################ 3 ##################
        final_df = final_df.sort_values(by=['line_num','xmin'],ascending=True)\
                .groupby('line_num').head(len(final_df))\
            .reset_index(drop=True)
        final_df['word_id'] = list(range(len(final_df)))

    return final_df
```

Since the axes are inverted,

1) The top coordinate is Ymin (leftmost coordinate).

2) You need to run two for loops comparing each word with others in the dataframe with respect to their position vertically.

3) The output of the final dataframe is sorted by its line number.

Note   The above strategy can fail in case of lots of overlapping bounding boxes, which is not the case right now, so we are fine with it.

Finally, you store the results in a separate variable.

```
mapped_data_text_features_line = {key:get_line_numbers(key) for key,_ in
mapped_data_text_features.items()}
```

Next, the authors discuss the graph formation where actual linkages are formed.

Graph Modeling Algorithm

1. Read words from each line starting from the topmost line going towards the bottom most line.

2. For each word, perform the following:

2.1 Check words that are in the vertical projection with it.

2.2 Calculate RDL and RDR for each of them.

2.3 Select the nearest neighbor words in the horizontal direction
     that have the least magnitude of RDL and RDR, provided that
     those words do not have an edge in that direction.

    2.3.1 If two words have same RDL or RDR, the word having the
           higher top coordinate is chosen.

2.4 Repeat steps from 2.1 to 2.3 similarly for retrieving nearest
     neighbor words in the vertical direction by taking the horizontal
     projection, calculating RDT and RDB, and choosing words
     having the higher left coordinate in case of ambiguity.

2.5 Draw edges between a word and its four nearest neighbors if
     they are available.

First, let's create a directory to save the graph of connected nodes.

```
GRAPH_IMAGE_PATH = "./Data/ICDAR_SROIE/processed_graph_images"

if not os.path.exists(GRAPH_IMAGE_PATH):
    os.mkdir(GRAPH_IMAGE_PATH)
```

Then, create a class that holds different information for you, namely:

– **Connection list**: Nested list containing information on connected
  nodes

– **G**: Networkx graph object. Networkx is a Python library used for
  handling network objects.

– **Processed dataframe**: Pandas dataframe containing connections of
  a node.

```
class NetworkData():
    def __init__(self, final_connections, G, df):
    self.final_connections = final_connections
    self.G = G
    self.df = df
```

```
def get_connection_list():
return self.final_connections
def get_networkx_graph():
return self.G
def get_processed_data():
return self.df
```

Note   Here you can either use the getter functions or just reference the class
object.

```
import networkx as nx
from sklearn.preprocessing import MinMaxScaler
    def graph_modelling(key, save_graph =False):

    # Horizontal edge formation

    df = mapped_data_text_features_line[key]
        df_grouped = df.groupby('line_num')

    # for directed graph
    left_connections = {}
    right_connections = {}

    for _,group in df_grouped:
            wa = group['word_id'].tolist()
        #2
        # In case of a single word in a line this will be an empty dictionary
            _right_dict = {wa[i]:{'right':wa[i+1]} for i in range(len(wa)-1) }
            _left_dict = {wa[i+1]:{'left':wa[i]} for i in range(len(wa)-1) }

        #add the indices in the dataframes
            for i in range(len(wa)-1):
                df.loc[df['word_id'] == wa[i], 'right'] = int(wa[i+1])
                df.loc[df['word_id'] == wa[i+1], 'left'] = int(wa[i])

    left_connections.update(_left_dict)
    right_connections.update(_right_dict)
```

```python
# Vertical edge formation
bottom_connections = {}
top_connections = {}

for i, row in df.iterrows():
    if i not in bottom_connections.keys():
        for j, row_dash in df.iterrows():

            # since our dataframe is sorted by line number and we are
            looking for vertical connections
            # we will make sure that we are only searching for a word/
            phrase next in row.
            if j not in bottom_connections.values() and i < j:
                if row_dash['line_num'] > row['line_num']:
                    bottom_connections[i] = j

                    top_connections[j] = i

                    #add it to the dataframe
                    df.loc[df['word_id'] == i , 'bottom'] = j
                    df.loc[df['word_id'] == j, 'top'] = i

                    # break once the condition is met
                    break

# Merging Neighbours from all 4 directions
final_connections = {}

# Taking all the keys that have a connection in either horizontal or
vertical direction
# Note : Since these are undirected graphs we can take either of
(right, left) OR (top, bottom)
for word_ids in (right_connections.keys() | bottom_connections.keys()):
        if word_ids in right_connections: final_connections.setdefault(
        word_ids, []).append(right_connections[word_ids]['right'])
    if word_ids in bottom_connections: final_connections.setdefault(
    word_ids, []).append(bottom_connections[word_ids])
```

```python
    # Create a networkx graph for ingestion into stellar graph model
    G = nx.from_dict_of_lists(final_connections)

    # Adding node features
    scaler = MinMaxScaler()
        scaled_features = scaler.fit_transform(df[['SpecialCharacterCount',
        'isFloat', 'isDate', 'TotalDistinctNumber',
            'BigNumLength', 'DoesContainsNum', 'POSTagDistributionSYM',
            'POSTagDistributionNUM', 'POSTagDistributionCCONJ',
            'POSTagDistributionPROPN', 'line_num']])
    node_feature_map = {y:x for x,y in zip(scaled_features, df.word_id)}

    for node_id, node_data in G.nodes(data=True):
            node_data["feature"] = node_feature_map[node_id]

    if save_graph:
        # There are multiple layouts but KKL is most suitable for
        # non-centric layout
        layout = nx.kamada_kawai_layout(G)

        # Plotting the Graphs
            plt.figure(figsize=(10,5))
        # Get current axes
        ax = plt.gca()
            ax.set_title(f'Graph form of {key}')
        nx.draw(G, layout, with_labels=True)
            plt.savefig(os.path.join(GRAPH_IMAGE_PATH, key +".jpg"),
            format="JPG")
        plt.close()

    networkobject = NetworkData(final_connections, G, df)
    return networkobject
```

The code is quite intuitive. These are the high-level things happening in the code:

1) Horizontal connections

   a) They can only be formed between words in the same line and
      hence you group your processed data on a line number.

   b) You maintain right and left connections for better clarity, but for
      the undirected graph a right connection dictionary is sufficient.

2) Vertical connections

   a) They can never be formed between words belonging to the
      same line.

   b) Two for loops are used because you must traverse along
      different lines.

   c) Again, direction is not relevant but is maintained for clarity.

3) Both the right and bottom dictionaries are used to create
   adjacency lists for the networkx graph.

4) Finally, you scale and normalize node features. You also include
   line numbers as one of the features because it is a templatic
   document with address/company number, etc. coming on the top
   and total coming in the bottom.

Calling the above code, you get the results in Figure 5-5.

```
mapped_net_obj = {key: graph_modelling(key, save_graph=True) for key,_ in
mapped_data_text_features_line.items()}
```

Graph Form of X51005675095

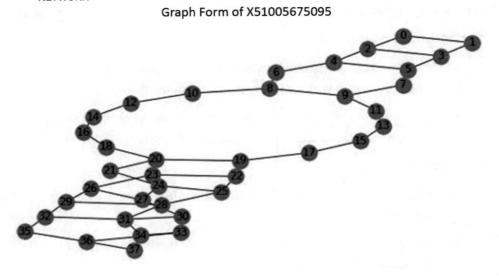

Graph Form of X51005711404

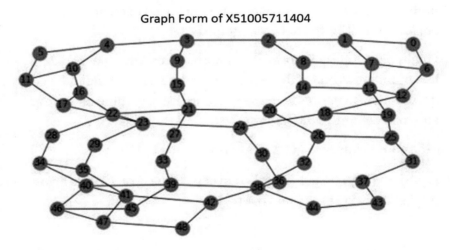

Figure 5-5. *Examples of Network layout for different Bills*

Input Data Pipeline

In the stellar graph library you are using, you can't train different networks but a union
of all can be used. What this will lead to is a big graph with a large adjacency matrix. See
Figure 5-6.

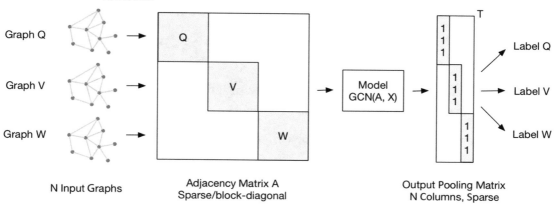

Figure 5-6. *Union of multiple graphs and training process. Source:* `https://`
`github.com/tkipf/gcn`

You will leverage a built-in function in Networkx.

```
U = nx.union_all([obj.G for k,obj in mapped_net_obj.items()],
rename=[k+"-" for k in mapped_net_obj.keys()])
```

Now, since you finally have the desired data, it's time to learn a bit about graphs and
the graph convolutional network in detail.

What Are Graphs and Why Do We Need Them?

In computer science theory, we define graphs as a data structure that consists of a finite
set of vertices (a.k.a. nodes) and a set of edges that connect these nodes. The edges of the
graph can be ordered or unordered depending upon whether the graph is directed or
undirected.

$$G = (V, E)$$

$$V, set\ of\ vertices\ or\ nodes$$

$$E, set\ of\ edges$$

Besides the direction of edges, there are other distinctions between types of graphs:

- A graph maybe be weighted or unweighted. In weighted graphs, each edge is given a weight.

- An undirected graph G is called *connected* if there is a path between every pair of distinct vertices of G.

- A simple graph has no self-loops, meaning there are no edges connecting a vertex to itself.

So there can be multiple terminologies and ways to differentiate graphs. Now the question arises, why do we even care about graphs in machine learning?

Most of the readers of this book would generally be familiar with four types of data, namely

1) Text

2) Structured/tabular

3) Audio

4) Images

All of this data can be represented by well-known neural network architectures, but there are is a special class of data that can't and it's called a *non-Euclidean dataset*. Such datasets can represent much more complex items and concepts with more accuracy than a 1D or a 2D dataset like those mentioned above.

Let's understand this.

Say you want to classify a sentence:

1) John is a nice guy.

In Case 1, you have just the pos tag and you can very well model it in GRU/LSTM/RNN cells to classify capturing the linear and non-hierarchical connections between words.

In Case 2, though, you are also given information on the dependencies between them. How do you plan to model them? See Figure 5-7.

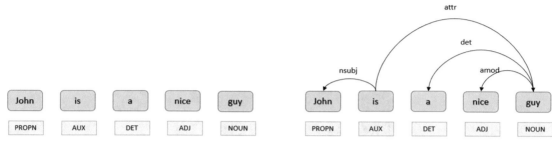

A sequential data can be classified using any sequence based
architectures or even CNNs (1D).

How can we model hierarchies for each word?
Does a **longer** arrow from is -> guy represent something?
Can we model the hierarchies and node-specific features
together?
How about the type of relationship between words. If I change
'attr' to 'amod' how does it affect the downstream task?

Figure 5-7. *Modeling connected data, case in point*

This is where graphs come in. They can help you model such hierarchies naturally
and effectively, more so than for other datasets like social network data, chemical
molecular data, trees/ontologies, and manifolds, which preserve rich information
through hierarchies, interconnectedness, and across multiple dimensions. In these
cases, graphs are more naturally suited.

Graphs help in modeling such non-Euclidean databases. It also allows us to
represent intrinsic features of the node, while also providing information regarding
relationships and structure, and is very easy to represent as a neural network for
learning.

Most of the neural networks can be classified into something called a multipartite
graph, which is basically graph that can be separated into different sets of nodes. These
sets of nodes do not share edges with nodes of the same set. See Figure 5-8.

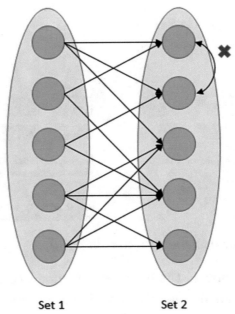

Set 1   Set 2

Figure 5-8. *Neural networks as multipartite graphs*

Graphs are represented using something called an adjacency matrix in the computer
system. An adjacency matrix is made up of the edge weights between connected entities.
It shows the three most important properties of a graph:

- Relation

- Relation strength (edge weight)

- Direction of the relation

Adjacency matrices of directed graphs will not be symmetrical along the diagonal
line, since directed graphs have edges that go in only one direction. For an undirected
graph, the adjacency matrix is always symmetrical.

Also, a degree shows the complexity of the graph. The degree of a vertex represents
the total number of vertices connected to it. In undirected graphs, it's a simple sum of
connected components whereas for directed graphs, the degree is further segmented into
inbound and outbound degrees, based on the direction of the relation. See Figure 5-9.

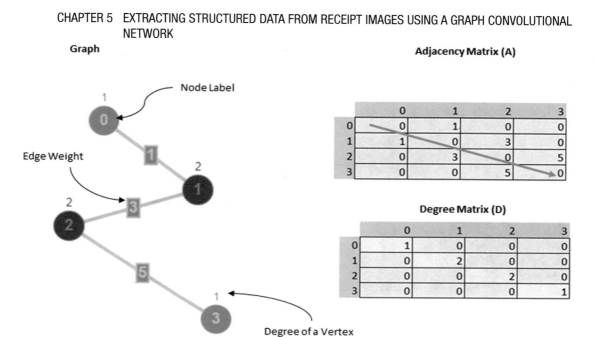

Figure 5-9. *Undirected graph with adjacency matrix*

Another matrix that captures the graph information is a Laplacian matrix.

$$L = D - A$$

Each value in the degree matrix is subtracted by its respective value in the adjacency matrix. A Laplacian matrix basically helps determine how smooth the graph function is. In other words, when shifting from one vertex to the next, the change in value shouldn't be abrupt. This is more true for a densely connected cluster. With isolated nodes, however, the smoothness reduces and also the performance of various tasks, which can be done using graph, so the more connected the graph is, the more information it will contain.

Graph Convolutional Networks

Convolutions over Graph

Graph convolutional networks work on the principle of applying convolutions to the graph networks. But what does this mean? Let's see.

You understand convolutions traditionally where given an input image representation you try to learn a kernel matrix, which helps you aggregate information from the neighboring pixels. See Figure 5-10 for an illustration.

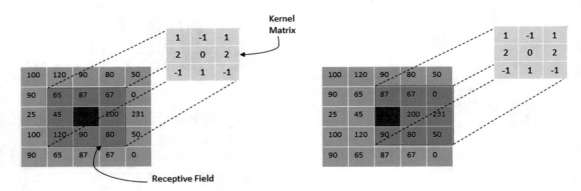

Figure 5-10. *Convolution operation over images*

The main thing that happens here is that you can aggregate information from neighboring pixels. This is the concept that gets borrowed when modeling graph data for various tasks, such as

1) **Node classification**: Predict the type of node.

2) **Link prediction**: Predict if new connections/links are getting formed between any two nodes

3) **Community detection**: Identify if there are any definite clusters getting formed in the graph, largely similar to densely linked clusters but in a more statistical sense. (Imagine PageRank.)

4) **Network similarity**: If the graph or its subnetwork resembles another graph or its subnetwork.

There are certain subtle differences in the way convolution works over graph data.

1) Images have a **rigid** (there is a strong sense of direction such that shifting one pixel value to from the left to the right of a central pixel changes the meaning) and **regular** (pixels are equidistant geometrically) connectivity structure. But graphs certainly don't.

2) Graph learning should work irrespective of the size of the input data.

Just like pixels are there for image representation, there are things known as node features and edge features in graphs.

Node features semantically identify what the node is all about, whereas edge features can help identify different relations shared between the two nodes.

The network that I will be talking about is the GCN network conceptualized by Kipf and Wellling in a paper titled "Semi-Supervised Classification with Graph Convolutional Networks" from 2017. This network does not take into account the edge features but you won't be using them for your application. Edge features are required for most complex networks. As in molecular chemistry where a double bond is much stronger than a single bond, so both can't be treated in the same manner; they have to be used differently. In your case however, an edge represents a connection between different text entities present in the invoice and hence carry the same meaning, so you can do away with networks that can model edge features.

But for the curious lot, here are two papers which are improvements over the GCN architecture shared by Kipf and Welling:

- "MPNN" by Gilmer et al in ICML 2017

- "Graph Attention Network" by Veličković et al in ICLR 2018

A good overview is also present in the paper by Zhou, Cui, Zhang et al in "Graph Neural Networks: A Review of Methods and Applications"

Understanding GCNs

Figure 5-11 explains how convolutions work over graph data, given an undirected graph $G = (V,E)$ with nodes $v_i \in V$, edges $(v_i, v_j) \in E$ and an adjacency matrix (A) of size NXN where N represents the number of nodes and a feature matrix (H) of size NXK where K is the dimension of a feature vector. To find the feature values from the neighbors for each node, you multiply the matrix A and H.

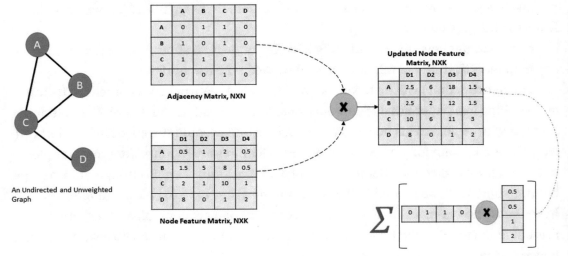

Figure 5-11. *Convolution operation over graphs*

As you can see in the updated node feature matrix, there are two things that can be improved:

1) You can prevent scale issues due to differences in connectivity degree of a node. Certain nodes are highly connected while some are not, so naturally a highly connected node will have a higher feature value as compared to a sparsely connected node.

2) Each node has completely forgotten its own features and learned all from the label, so you need to make sure that the current information is not completely lost.

First, you make sure that each node is able to retain information from itself as well. For this, you update the graph by adding a connection to itself, which basically means the adjacency matrix will now have all ones along the diagonal.

Since the scale can be corrected by normalizing with the degree of a node, you multiply the values with D^{-1}. Since D is a diagonal matrix, D^{-1} just reciprocates all the diagonal elements. Note that this D matrix is the updated matrix post the self-loop created above.

Kipf and Welling in their proposed idea note that a lower degree node will exert more influence on its neighbors as compared to a highly connected layer. Basically a node that passes information to all nodes doesn't provide any "distinct" info about the nodes. To do so, the authors suggest multiplying the resultant matrix of D⁻¹ AH with D⁻¹. Since you are normalizing twice, you just make sure to divide by $\sqrt{D\,D}$. This way, when computing the aggregate feature representation of the ith node, you not only take into consideration the degree of the ith node, but also the degree of the jth node. This is also known as the spectral rule.

One thing to note in this idea is that Kipf et al proposed it keeping in mind that edge doesn't have a role to play here. If you have different edge features for connections of even a highly connected node, then the above assumption doesn't always hold.

Finally, the updated feature matrix for a node looks like this:

$H_{updated} = f(A, D, H)$

A complete equation looks something like this:

$$H_{updated} = Relu\left(\frac{1}{\sqrt{DD}}AHW\right)$$

Relu or any other non-linear activation can be applied for that matter. Here W is a trainable weight matrix of size (KxK') where K' is the dimension of the feature vector for the next layer. This can basically help address overfitting by reducing dimensions with depth.

Layer Stacking in GCNs

All the neighbors of the graphs are updated this way. Once all the nodes are updated with their immediate neighbor, you have what is called as an output from the first layer.

The second layer is something that captures information from secondary connections as well, which basically means, since in the first step each node has modeled information from its children, if you run the same steps again in the next layer, these features of children of children get added to the parent node. Basically, the deeper the network, the larger the local neighborhood. See Figure 5-12.

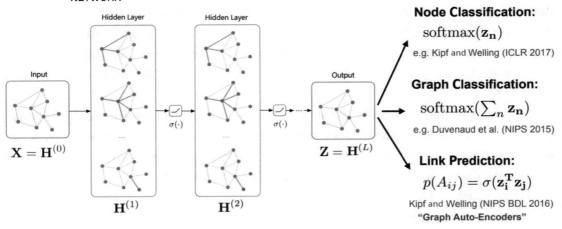

Figure 5-12. Layers in a GCN. Image source `http://helper.ipam.ucla.edu/`
`publications/glws4/glws4_15546.pdf`

Training

For a node classification problem like yours, the training largely involves the following steps.

1. Perform forward propagation through the GCN layers.

2. Apply the sigmoid function row-wise (i.e. for each node on the last layer in the GCN).

3. Compute the cross entropy loss on the known node labels.

4. Backpropagate the loss and update the weight matrices W in each layer.

Note that there is a final weight matrix that maps the final hidden state representation of each node with the number of classes expected for the node classification task. So, if you call the number of classes as C, this weight matrix is of shape (K,'C). Assuming the last feature representation of the nodes has a dimension of K,' the total number of weight matrices = L+1, where L is the number of GCN layers.

Modeling

Although constructing your own GCN layer in TensorFlow isn't that difficult, there are some libraries that make doing graph deep learning easier with Keras and TF 2.0 by providing prebuilt APIs. One such library is StellarGraph. It has over 1.7K stars on its

official GitHub and has an active community. StellarGraph can ingest data from various
data sources networkx graphs, pandas, or even numpy arrays.

Since you have already prepared a union of all graphs, let's load your data directly
from networkx.

```
G_sg = sg.from_networkx(U, node_features="feature")
print(G_sg.info())

###################### Output ###############
StellarGraph: Undirected multigraph
    Nodes: 33626, Edges: 46820

 Node types:
     default: [33626]
        Features: float32 vector, length 11
    Edge types: default-default->default

 Edge types:
     default-default->default: [46820]
         Weights: all 1 (default)
      Features: none
```

As you can see, in total you have 33626 nodes and 46820 edges. It is still a small graph
but it's quite useful for training purposes.

Train-Test Split and Target Encoding

Next, make sure you have a one-to-one mapping between the node id and the target. For
this, you will create this data from the processed data and replace all empty labels with
"others."

```
labelled_data = pd.DataFrame([[k+"-"+str(node_idx), label]
            for k,obj in mapped_net_obj.items()\
          for node_idx,label in zip(obj.df.word_id,obj.df.labels)],
                         columns = ["node_id","node_target"])

labelled_data = labelled_data.replace(r'^\s*$', "others", regex=True)
```

The distribution of target class is shown below.

	index	node_target
0	others	28861
1	address	1692
2	total	1562
3	date	764
4	company	747

The other class is most represented, which is expected. There is some class imbalance in the node prediction. I urge you to try to correct the imbalance and then retrain the model.

Finally, before creating the model, let's also create your train and validation data.

You will also binarize the multi-class output and set the model for a multiclass classification problem.

```
train,val = model_selection.train_test_split(labelled_data,
    random_state = 42,train_size = 0.8, stratify = labelled_data.node_target)
```

```
# Encoding the targets
target_encoding = preprocessing.LabelBinarizer()
train_targets = target_encoding.fit_transform(train.node_target)
val_targets = target_encoding.fit_transform(val.node_target)
```

Creating Flow for Training in StellarGraph

Next, you will use an built-in generator function to generate batches of nodes given the Stellar Network Graph.

```
generator = FullBatchNodeGenerator(G_sg)
```

Once the generator object is created, you call the flow function and pass the target label and the nodes to get an object that can be used as a Keras data generator.

```
train_flow = generator.flow(train.node_id, train_targets)
val_flow = generator.flow(val.node_id, val_targets)
```

Training and Model Performance Plots

You form a very basic Keras model. You add two GCN layers of size 8 and 4. The two layers also imply that you are going to the second degree neighbors of each node. For each of the activations (node embeddings), you use a SELU activation function to prevent vanishing gradient issues.

You also introduce a dropout to prevent overfitting.

Since your input and output gets created using the generator object, you will get the input and output tensor from the GCN layer to know about the input and output.

Lastly, the output is fed into a dense layer with a shape equal to the number of target labels. Basically, each node embedding is multiplied with a final weight matrix and then activations are applied to see which class is most probable for the node. See Figure 5-13.

```
# Model Formation
# two layers of GCN
    gcn = GCN(layer_sizes=[8, 4], activations=["selu", "selu"],
    generator=generator, dropout=0.5)
# expose in and out to create keras model
x_inp, x_out = gcn.in_out_tensors()

# usual output layer
    predictions = layers.Dense(units=train_targets.shape[1],
    activation="softmax")(x_out)

# define model
model = Model(inputs=x_inp, outputs=predictions)
# compile model
model.compile(
        optimizer=optimizers.Adam(lr=0.01),
    loss=losses.categorical_crossentropy,
        metrics=["AUC"])
```

Layer (type)	Output Shape	Param #	Connected to
input_9 (InputLayer)	[(1, 33626, 11)]	0	
input_11 (InputLayer)	[(1, None, 2)]	0	
input_12 (InputLayer)	[(1, None)]	0	
dropout_4 (Dropout)	(1, 33626, 11)	0	input_9[0][0]
squeezed_sparse_conversion_2 (S	(33626, 33626)	0	input_11[0][0] input_12[0][0]
graph_convolution_4 (GraphConvo	(1, 33626, 8)	96	dropout_4[0][0] squeezed_sparse_conversion_2[0][0
dropout_5 (Dropout)	(1, 33626, 8)	0	graph_convolution_4[0][0]
graph_convolution_5 (GraphConvo	(1, 33626, 4)	36	dropout_5[0][0] squeezed_sparse_conversion_2[0][0
input_10 (InputLayer)	[(1, None)]	0	
gather_indices_2 (GatherIndices	(1, None, 4)	0	graph_convolution_5[0][0] input_10[0][0]
dense_2 (Dense)	(1, None, 5)	25	gather_indices_2[0][0]

```
Total params: 157
Trainable params: 157
Non-trainable params: 0
```

Figure 5-13. *GCN model summary*

As you can see, you can introduce many more parameters and make an even more effective model. But for now the model performance is decent for your task.

Now fit the model and check the result.

```
from tensorflow.keras.callbacks import EarlyStopping
    es_callback = EarlyStopping(monitor="val_auc", patience=10,
    restore_best_weights=True)

history = model.fit(
    train_flow,
        epochs=10,
    validation_data=val_flow,
        verbose=2,
    callbacks=[es_callback])
```

```
Epoch 1/10
1/1 - 1s - loss: 1.7024 - auc: 0.4687 - val_loss: 1.5375 - val_auc: 0.7021
Epoch 2/10
1/1 - 0s - loss: 1.5910 - auc: 0.5962 - val_loss: 1.4360 - val_auc: 0.8740
Epoch 3/10
1/1 - 0s - loss: 1.4832 - auc: 0.7261 - val_loss: 1.3445 - val_auc: 0.9170
Epoch 4/10
1/1 - 0s - loss: 1.3891 - auc: 0.8178 - val_loss: 1.2588 - val_auc: 0.9189
Epoch 5/10
1/1 - 0s - loss: 1.2993 - auc: 0.8753 - val_loss: 1.1768 - val_auc: 0.9175
Epoch 6/10
1/1 - 0s - loss: 1.2219 - auc: 0.8958 - val_loss: 1.0977 - val_auc: 0.9160
Epoch 7/10
1/1 - 0s - loss: 1.1405 - auc: 0.9068 - val_loss: 1.0210 - val_auc: 0.9146
Epoch 8/10
1/1 - 0s - loss: 1.0638 - auc: 0.9120 - val_loss: 0.9469 - val_auc: 0.9134
Epoch 9/10
1/1 - 0s - loss: 0.9890 - auc: 0.9131 - val_loss: 0.8767 - val_auc: 0.9129
Epoch 10/10
1/1 - 0s - loss: 0.9191 - auc: 0.9140 - val_loss: 0.8121 - val_auc: 0.9120
```

Training for a higher epoch hits the early stop criteria at the 18th epoch and yields the train and validation curves shown in Figure 5-14.

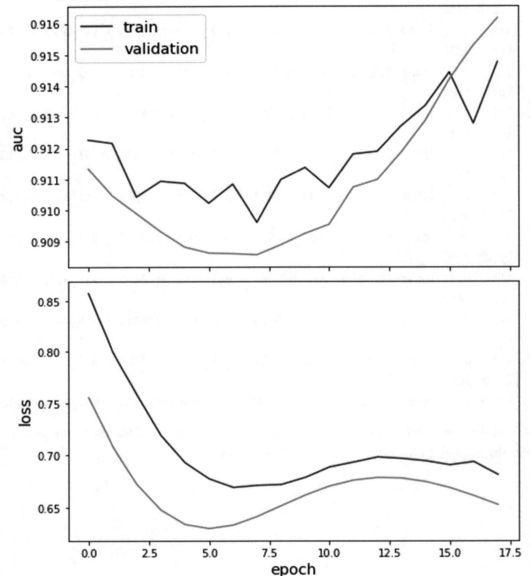

Figure 5-14. *Train and validation performance curves*

Looks like there is no case of overfitting but you can definitely use more parameters
and try to improve the performance. The following changes can be made:

1) Include more features for the node.

2) Experiment with different normalization techniques except
   min-max scaler.

3)   A more dense prediction model can help in capturing the nuances
     better.

     a) Note that after you get the inputs and outputs from the GCN layer,
        the model can be built like any normal Keras model.

4)   Handle class imbalance.

Conclusion

I hope you were excited about being introduced to this new class of neural networks. It
opens so many doors for handling real-world data. Well, don't just restrict yourself to the
GCN model discussed here. There is a big ocean of knowledge out there!

You learned a stellar technique but there are shortcomings for GCN:

- It doesn't consider node edges.

- It's mostly useful for homogeneous graphs (graphs with a single type
  of nodes/edges).

- Node locality still plays a good role in its classification. Try doing
  some ablation modeling by removing the line number parameter
  from the feature set and remodeling.

The world we live in is deeply connected and will be even more so as we move ahead
in this century. Arming yourself with the knowledge of how to model such data will be a
revered skill and will definitely help further your career and interests.

## CHAPTER 6

Handling Availability of Low-Training Data in Healthcare

The availability of training data is a critical bottleneck in machine learning applications. This is further augmented by working in a specialized domain like healthcare where one needs to be highly skilled to understand the data and then tag or label it for machine learning to use. In addition to finding a skill steward, there is a heavy investment in terms of time and cost for the organization.

You have already learned one way of handling availability of limited information, which is by transfer learning. Unlike transfer learning, which is an algorithmic approach to handling low-training data, in this chapter you will use a data-first approach where you try to understand and model the data in order to create training labels.

You will be learning about different ways of handling low-training data and the challenges in applying them. Finally, you will take a hands-on case exploring how to augment training data for biomedical relation extraction using Snorkel.

Introduction

Creating datasets with high quality training labels involves significant investment of time and money and sometimes even domain experts for highly specialized domains. Hence, it becomes imperative for us to find smarter ways to leverage the data patterns of our unlabeled data in one way or another that can help us create training labels over unseen data.

Anshik, *AI for Healthcare with Keras and Tensorflow 2.0*, https://doi.org/10.1007/978-1-4842-7086-8_6

Semi-Supervised Learning

Semi-supervised learning involves using a small gold-label dataset and unlabeled data. There are four key steps to semi-supervised learning:

1) You use the small amount of gold-label data to train a model of choice, much like standard supervised learning.

2) Then you use the unlabeled data to predict the outputs using the trained model labels. Since the model is trained only on a handful of samples, it's difficult to say that the predictions are highly accurate and hence the label outputs from such a model are called pseudo labels.

3) You then collect the gold-label data and a chunk of pseudo-labeled data and create a new training set.

4) You retrain your model using this new set.

5) You repeat the process until the performance metric chart (across epochs) flattens out.

In Chapter 5, you worked on the node classification problem, where you had to predict for company name, address, date, and total cost of the bill. You had less training data available, yet you were able to predict with reasonable accuracy on the training labels because the model was not only learning on the node features but also its edge connection and hence a powerful graph neural network could learn well over this small dataset.

Although any model can be used to train on a small gold-label dataset plus pseudo labels, there are two main model strategies that have been leveraged extensively.

GANs

Generator adversarial networks (GANs) include two networks that are adversaries and hence compete with each other until a state of desirable equilibrium is reached. These two networks are the generator and the discriminator. See Figure 6-1.

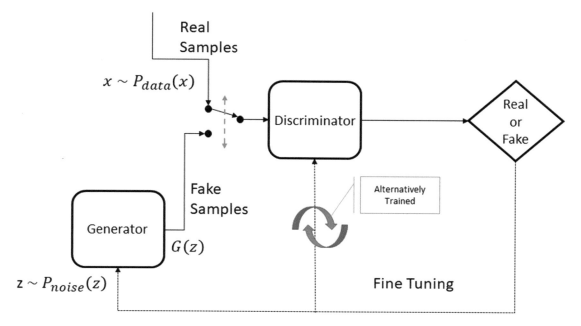

Figure 6-1. *A generator adversarial network*

Generator: Learns to generate real data

Discriminator: Learns to discriminate between the generator's fake data and real data

The key steps involved in training a GAN are

- Samples from both real data and fake data are used to train discriminators alone. Here, fake data is generated from a noisy distribution.

- Then the weights for the discriminator are frozen and the generator is trained.

- Alternatively, these networks are trained, competing with each other until they reach a state of equilibrium (gradient flow normalizes).

The loss function involved in training both networks is based on the real vs. fake prediction of the discriminator network. In semi-supervised learning with GANs, the discriminator network not only outputs distribution for real or fake but for all the labels involved.

An input is classified as real if it is classified as any class label, as shown in Figure 6-2.

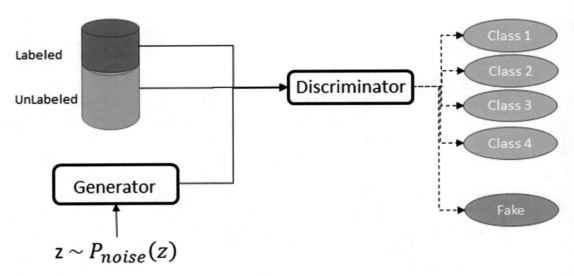

Figure 6-2. *Semi-supervised GAN architecture*

The discriminator now has a dual objective of first distinguishing real from fake images (also called an unsupervised task) and secondly classifying real images to their respective classes (the supervised task).

For each iteration, you do the following:

- Train the supervised discriminator. Take a batch of training labels and train the multiclass network.

- Train the unsupervised discriminator. Take a batch of unlabeled data and a batch of fake samples and train the binary classifier and backpropagate the binary loss.

- Train the generator (just like a simple GAN).

Read the paper by Odena titled "Semi-Supervised Learning with Generative Adversarial Networks" to further deep dive and understand the use of semi-supervised learning with GANs.

Autoencoders

I introduced autoencoders in Chapter 3, where you used them to encode your training features to get a lower dimensional, dense representation so that it could be used for clustering. See Figure 6-3.

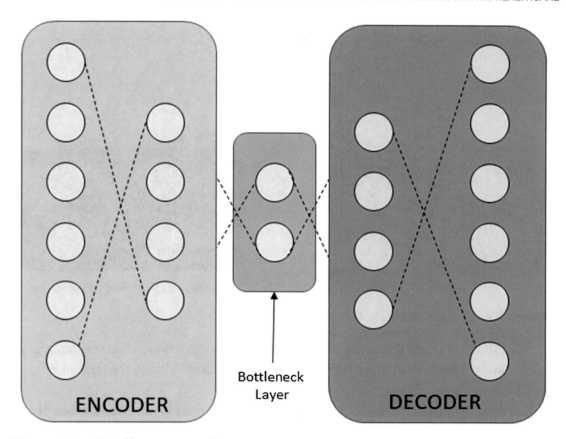

Figure 6-3. *Vanilla autoencoder*

Well, the idea is still the same, but this time rather than just optimizing on the reconstruction loss, you will also be using the lower-dimensional dense vector for predicting the output. See Figure 6-4.

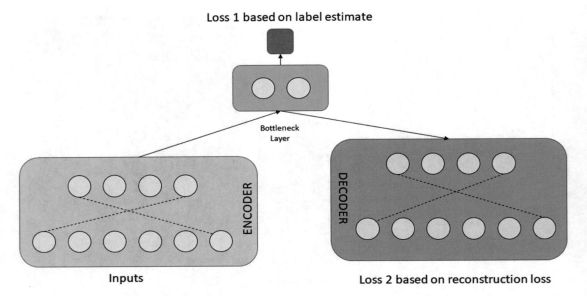

Figure 6-4. *Autoencoder for semi-supervised learning*

Now, many of you might be thinking that these reconstruction losses are sometimes not that low and hence you might get a suboptimal representation in the bottleneck layer. Well, that's not entirely true.

You don't need to capture all of the semantics of the input to predict the label. You can work with representations that capture a part of the meaning such that Loss 1 is minimized.

Although, having said that, the best results are achieved when the general representation (Loss 2) also helps in predicting the class labels.

People have gone a step ahead and experimented with different ways to minimize both Loss 1 and 2. Some of the papers you can read are

- "Semi-Supervised Learning with Ladder Networks" by Valpola et al

- "Exploring Semi-supervised Variational Autoencoders for Biomedical Relation Extraction" by Zhang et al

Transfer Learning

You explored transfer learning and why it works in natural language tasks in detail in Chapter 4. Transfer learning works on the principle of using large labeled data in a similar domain to train neural networks such that it can learn lower-level features really well and then you can use that architecture to fine-tune the task at hand using the few labeled data you have.

It is a really powerful technique, but it has some limitations:

- Input data for your task can be widely different from the training set for such pretrained networks.

- The pretrained tasks and the new task are vastly different, such as classification vs. span extraction.

- **Overfitting and unnecessary use of large models**: Sometimes your task doesn't require the use of complex multi-million parameters, so in these cases transfer learning might be overkill.

Transfer learning can also be used in a completely unsupervised setting where it is not necessary to require large training labels. This is also called self-supervision. For example, when you train a good language model, you try to do the following:

1) Masked language modeling

2) Next sentence prediction

Both of these techniques don't require a labeled dataset but yet give a really good network capable of doing a variety of tasks.

Weak Supervised Learning

Weak supervised learning is another way of working with limited data. The idea here is to harness patterns in the current data using noisy, heuristical, and limited sources to label the data.

Like the techniques discussed above, it effectively alleviates the problem of having a large amount of training data prehand to do your ML task. Read "Snorkel: Rapid Training Data Creation with Weak Supervision," a paper by the Stanford AI Lab team, that explores how well weak supervision works. See Figure 6-5.

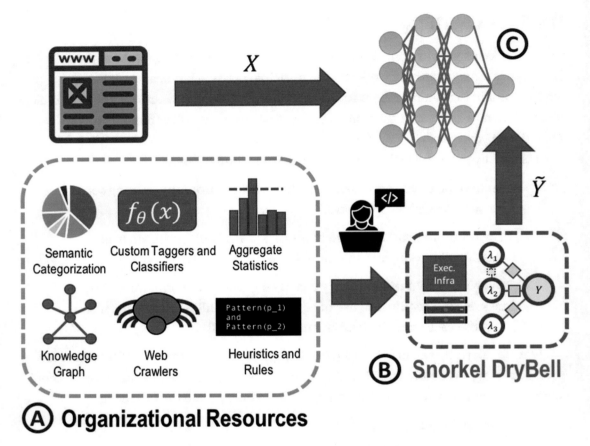

Figure 6-5. *Diverse knowledge sources as weak supervision.*
Source: `ai.googleblog.com`

In this chapter, you will be using this concept of weak learning. You will also exploring the Snorkel library, which was developed by the Stanford AI Lab.

Exploring Snorkel

Snorkel is a programming library that facilitates creating, modeling, and managing training datasets without manually labeling. Its workflow is designed around data programming and is made up of three stages:

1) **Writing labeling functions/weak supervision**

This includes use of hand-designed features, distant supervision functions leveraging external databases, etc. These labeling functions don't have a good recall but are quite precise. If you choose a subprecise function, its recall is generally higher. Hence your labeling function set should be a mix of both kinds.

Labeling functions in Snorkel are created with the @labeling_ function decorator. The decorator can be applied to any Python function that returns a label for a single data point.

Each LF function outputs three values (binary class):

$$L_i(x) = \begin{cases} -1, & if \; not \; enough \; evidence \\ 0, & if \; no \; evidence \\ 1, & if \; evidence \end{cases}$$

2) **Combine LF outputs**

Based on the quality of the labeling functions and their agreements and disagreements, Snorkel's generative model combines the labeling functions to output labels. For example, if two labeling functions have a high correlation in their output, then the generative model tries to avoid double counting of such functions. This also shows why a generative model is better than max counting. Snorkel also provides an immense number of analysis parameters that tell about the performance of a LF. You will explore them in this chapter.

3) **Model training**

Snorkel's output uses probabilistic labels which can then be used to train any discriminative models. This discriminative model fills in the gap of low recall. See Figure 6-6.

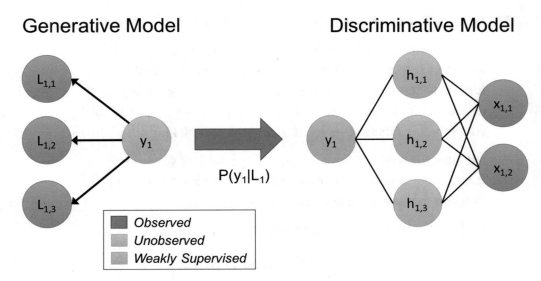

Figure 6-6. *Model training using Snorkel probabilities. Source:* `http://ai.stanford.edu/blog/weak-supervision/`

You will explore labeling functions and how to apply them in depth in this chapter but there are some other ways that Snorkel increases performance of the overall process of labeling (Figure 6-7). The Snorkel team introduced two more concepts:

1) Transformation functions (TFs)

2) Slicing functions (SFs)

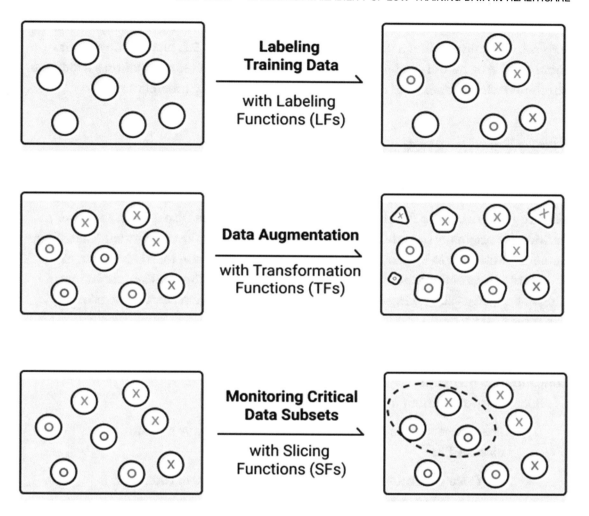

Figure 6-7. *Different programming interfaces. Source: Snorkel.org*

Just like you tend to data augmentation to increase your dataset, similarly in Snorkel you can write TFs to each training data point using a policy (determines how you apply the transformation to each point or some points, etc.) to generate an augmented training set. Some of the common ways can be to replace words with synonyms or replace named entities with other entities. Similar to labeling functions, you use a `transformation_function` decorator, which wraps a function that takes in a single data point and returns a transformed version of the data point.

Often in your training data you will find that certain subsections or slices are more important than others, like patients receiving critical care being used for drug performance testing, hence not only global performance but less failure on such local slices is expected.

Snorkel provides a way to measure performance on such slices. SFs output binary masks indicating whether a data point is in the slice or not. The ones in the slice are monitored. Any model can leverage SFs to learn slice expert representations, which are combined with an attention mechanism to make slice-aware predictions.

Data Exploration

Introduction

You are going to use the data capturing relation between the Disease and Treatment entities. It's originally provided from the research shared in the paper titled "Classifying Semantic Relations in Bioscience Text" by Barbara Rosario and Marti A. Hearst, in the proceedings of the 42nd Annual Meeting of the Association for Computational Linguistics (ACL 2004), Barcelona, July 2004 (`https://biotext.berkeley.edu/dis_treat_data.html`).

The text is taken randomly from Medline 2001, which is a bibliographic database that contains more than 26 million references to journal articles in life sciences, with a concentration on biomedicine.

Some key points about the data:

1) The dataset covers multiple relations between treatment and disease, like

    – **Cure**: Treatment cures the disease irrespective of whether it is clinically proven or not.

    – **Only disease**: No mentions of treatment in the sentence.

    – **Only treatment**: No mentions of disease in the sentence.

    – **Prevent**: Treatment prevents or inhibits a disease from happening.

    – **Side effect**: Disease is a result of treatment.

    – **Vague**: The relationship is semantically unclear.

    – **Does NOT Cure**: Treatment is not effective.

    – **Complex**: Same entities taking part in several interconnected relationships, or there are many-many relationships possible.

2) `<label>` means that the word that follows it is the first of the entity and `</label>` means that the word that proceeds it is the last of the entity.

3) There is unlabeled data shared for testing.

You will download the sentences with roles and relations file from the above mentioned link and place the files as shown below:

```
Data
├── sentences_with_roles_and_relations.txt
├── labeled_titles.txt
├── labeled_abstracts.txt
```

Load the data from the text file. You will not be working with all of the relations; you will just be focusing on the Cure, Prevent, and Side Effect relations. The rest are discarded.

```python
import re
import pandas as pd
import numpy as np
import os

    f = open('./Data/sentences_with_roles_and_relations.txt',
    encoding = "ISO-8859-1")
f_data = []
for line in f.readlines():
        line = line[:-1] # Remove linebreak
        f_data.append(line.split('||'))
f.close()

rows = []
for l in f_data:
        if l[1] not in ['NONE', 'TREATONLY', 'DISONLY', 'TO_SEE', 'VAGUE',
        'TREAT_NO_FOR_DIS']:
            sent = ' '.join(l[0].split())
            dis_re = re.compile('<DIS.*>(.*)</DIS.*>')
            disease = dis_re.search(sent).group(1)
            treat_re = re.compile('<TREAT.*>(.*)</TREAT.*>')
            treat = treat_re.search(sent).group(1)
```

```
        sent = re.sub(r'<.*?> ', '', sent).strip()
    # Handles sentences ending with <*> structure
        sent = re.sub(r'<.*?>', '', sent)

        rows.append([sent, l[1], treat.strip(), disease.strip()])

biotext_df = pd.DataFrame(data=rows, columns=['sentence', 'relation',
'term1', 'term2'])
```

The above code leverages the file that already contains the relation labels but you can also use other files present in the folder, but some preprocessing needs to be done in order to leverage it for your purpose.

```
biotext_df.relation.value_counts()
```

Output

```
TREAT_FOR_DIS     830
PREVENT            63
SIDE_EFF           30
```

You can see that there is a lot of imbalance in relations, with the majority being occupied by TREAT_FOR_DIS or Cure relations. This can be handled during label modeling by passing a class imbalance array that contains a proportion of each class.

Labeling Functions

What you have is tagged data on Treatment, Disease, and their relations from biomedical journals. Effectively, there can be three major types of labeling functions that you can create for an information extraction task like yours.

1) **Syntactic information**: Syntactic information helps you capture grammatical dependencies between words and helps you discover common patterns for a relation class.

2) **Distance supervision**: Use of external ontology like UMLs to capture biomedical entities other than Treatment and Disease.

3) **Regex**: There are certain patterns that can be indicative of a relation type with good precision. For example, words like *prevent, prevention, reduce,* or *reduction* can easily indicate the Prevent relation class.

Regex

A quick way to get started with creating label functions is to scan the bunch of text belonging to the category you want to predict.

You can start with seeing the count plot for different n-grams of the text. You will be using the sklearn module for this, specifically `sklearn.feature_extraction.text.CountVectorizer`.

> `sklearn.feature_extraction.text.CountVectorizer`: "Convert a collection of text documents to a matrix of token counts"

But before directly running the `Countvectorizer` there are some preprocessing steps that you should carry out in order to make the exercise more effective:

1) Normalize words to their lemmas so that words that are semantically the same are not counted differently, such as "providing" and "provide."

2) Remove all numerical mentions.

3) Remove common English stop words.

4) Lower the text.

You are going to use WordNet Lemmatizer from the nltk package to lemmatize individual things. One of the important aspects of using the WordNet Lemmatizer is that you need to provide an appropriate pos tag for the word. If this is not done, it can lead to abrupt or no lemmatization.

Let's understand this with an example.

You start by importing the relevant packages and classes.

```
from nltk import pos_tag
from nltk.stem import WordNetLemmatizer

lemmatizer = WordNetLemmatizer()
```

If you provide a word without any context of a pos tag, the word doesn't get lemmatized.

```
lemmatizer.lemmatize("sitting")
```

Output

sitting

If you provide the context of the pos tag, lemmatization works.

```
lemmatizer.lemmatize("sitting", pos = "v")
```

Output

sit

There are five types of pos tags for WordNet:

- Adjective

- Adjective satellite

- Adverb

- Noun

- Verb

Most of you have heard about adjectives, adverbs, nouns, and verbs, but adjective satellite might be a new term. An adjective satellite is a class of adjectives that are used specifically in certain contexts. For example, there can only be "arid climate;" there can't be "arid skin." However, PennTreeBank, which is used for creating pos tags, doesn't differentiate between satellite and normal adjectives and hence you will consider both of them as adjectives.

Armed with the info above, let's design your preprocessing function. For lemmatization, you will maintain a label map of a pos tag to its label used for the WordNet Lemmatizer.

```
mapping_pos_label = {"JJ":'a',
  "RB":'r',
"NN": 'n',
  "VB":'v'}
```

Next, you define a function that returns WordNet pos label if the pos tag of the word is either an adjective (JJ*), adverb(RB*), noun(NN*), or verb(VB*).

```
def get_pos_label(w, postag, mapping_pos_label):
for k, v in mapping_pos_label.items():
    if postag.startswith(k):
        return v
    return "n"
```

Note in the above function you return a NOUN tag if the regex doesn't find a match as by default the WordNet Lemmatizer uses Noun as the pos tag.

You have everything you need to create a preprocessing function.

```
import re
    def preprocess_text(text):
    text = text.lower()
        text = " ".join([lemmatizer.lemmatize(w,
                                  pos= get_pos_label(w,
                                              pos_w,
                                              mapping_pos_label))\
                    for w, pos_w in pos_tag(text.split()) \
                        if w not in list(set(stopwords.words('english')))])
        text = re.sub(r'\d+', '', text)
    return text
```

You can use this preprocessor function either before using CountVectorizer or pass it in the CountVectorizer function. Since the latter looks neater, let's use it.

```
cv = CountVectorizer(preprocessor = preprocess_text,
                ngram_range = (1,3),
                min_df = 0.01)
```

Besides preprocessor, you also see two other parameters. The values for them are chosen empirically. Please feel free to experiment. See the results in Figure 6-8.

- ngram_range: Tells you about the length of phrases you should consider finding a count for.

- min_df: If it's a float, you can assume at least a percentage of samples should have a mention of vocabulary words. If it's an integer, assume that at least that many rows should have a mention of vocabulary words.

```
count_mat = cv.fit_transform(biotext_df[biotext_df.relation.isin([
"TREAT_FOR_DIS"])].sentence)
count_df = pd.DataFrame(count_mat.todense(), columns=cv.get_feature_names())

count_df = count_df.sum().reset_index()
    count_df.columns = ["word","val"]
    count_df = count_df.sort_values('val', ascending = False)

import plotly.express as px
    fig = px.pie(count_df.head(20), values='val', names='word', title="Top
    Words for 'TREAT_FOR_DIS' Text")
fig.show()
```

Top Words for 'TREAT_FOR_DIS' Text

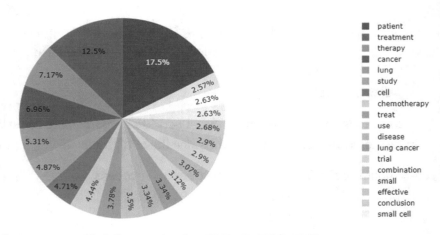

Figure 6-8. *Most frequent words/phrases in the TREAT_FOR_DIS category*

Similarly, repeat the process for the SIDE_EFF and PREVENT classes. See Figures 6-9 and 6-10.

Top Words for 'PREVENT' Text

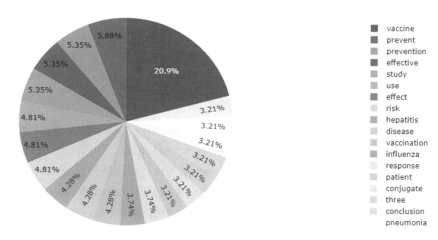

Figure 6-9. *Most frequent words/phrases for the PREVENT category*

Top Words for 'SIDE_EFF' Text

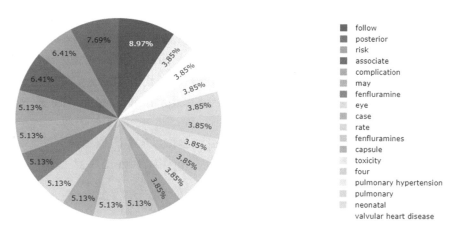

Figure 6-10. *Most frequent words/phrases for the SIDE_EFF category*

The three figures above yield some really useful insights into the key words from the corpus and can help you form some regex-based LFs.

```
treatment_keywords = ['treatment', 'therapy','effective','treat', "reduce"]
```

Note that for treatment keywords you are seeing a lot of oncology-related terms like lung cancer, breast cancer etc. but I would avoid taking them for a label function as they can be just because of the limited corpus you have. You should try to create more robust functions keeping precision in check.

Similarly,

```
prevent_keywords = ["protect", "prevent", "inhibit", "block",
"control", 'effect']
side_effect_keywords = ["risk","follow", "associate", "toxic"]
```

Syntactic

There will be certain words that will not be very frequent but are still useful in tying a disease to the treatment and its various relations.

To find such words, you will leverage the syntactic structure of the text. Specifically, you will work on the dependency parsed tree of the sentence. This is a computational linguist technique used to analyze the grammatical structure of the sentence, establishing "head" words and establishing relations between those words. For more info, refer to `https://nlp.stanford.edu/software/nndep.html`.

You will parse the dependency tree into a graph using the networkx library and look for patterns of the words occurring in between the disease and treatment paths.

Generally there can be multiple paths connecting two paths, but what you are most interested in is the shortest dependency path. This is preferred as it contains only the necessary information to establish a relationship between any two entities.

For example, consider this statement from the PREVENT class:

Modified|bra in the prevention of mastitis in nursing mothers.

Here

Modified|bra is the *treatment* and **mastitis** is the *disease.*

The dependency graph looks something like Figure 6-11.

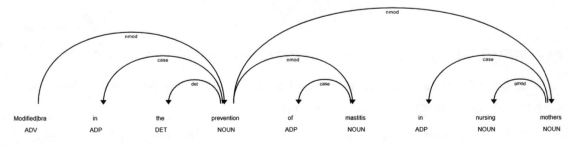

Figure 6-11. *Dependency graph, scispacy*

Note   "|" is introduced instead of a " " for a reason. More on this later.

Now if you want to traverse the dependencies from modified bra to mastitis, there are multiple words and dependency jumps between the two entities. However, the SDP is rather simple.

The SDP is

Modified|bra−−prevention−−mastitis

Some other examples are

1) CONCLUSIONS: These data, the first evidence that chronic stress can inhibit the stability of the IgG antibody response to a **bacterial|vaccine** for **pneumonia**, provide additional evidence of health risks associated with dementia caregiving.

   bacterial|vaccine−−stability−−pneumonia

2) Protective effect of **pralidoxime** on **muscle|fiber|necrosis** induced by organophosphate compounds.

   pralidoxime−−effect−−muscle|fiber|necrosis

You can see how perfectly the SDP captures the relevant information to relate two entities just based on sentence structure and hence you will be using this to identify some new relations or words.

For this you will be using the scispacy package used previously in Chapter 4 to analyze the vocabulary of the BERT model. You will also be loading the networkx library to find the shortest dependency path.

```
import spacy
import scispacy
import networkx as nx

from scispacy.linking import EntityLinker
    nlp = spacy.load('en_core_sci_lg')
```

Before diving into the main code, there are some things you should understand.

1) You are using scispacy for dependency parsing and not the spacy general text parser for the simple reason that scispacy's dependency parsing is trained on the GENIA 1.0 corpus and OntoNotes 5.0, which increases the accuracy and robustness of the parser on biomedical text.

2) Spacy doesn't tokenize on white spaces, while most of your labeling (by a human annotator or otherwise) is based on white spaces. This can lead to some misalignments of the pos tag for a target token as it can get tokenized into smaller constituents based on spacy's logic. To counter this you will

   a) Write a remerge logic to merge entities (disease or treatment) that got split. Generally words with parentheses were showing erratic behavior.

3) You will have noticed in the examples above the use of the "|" character to replace spaces in the disease and treatment phases. This is because you want to use these phrases as one single entity and not separate entities in the dependency tree for SDP calculation.

For more information on scispacy please refer to "ScispaCy: Fast and Robust Models for Biomedical Natural Language Processing" by Neuman et al.

You start by writing the retokenization logic. For this, you use the merge functionality of spacy's Doc class. It merges tokens that are not white spaces in place. Effectively the tokens available from the Doc object become white space-separated.

```python
def remerge_sent(sent):
    i = 0
    while i < len(sent)-1:
    tok = sent[i]
    if not tok.whitespace_:
            ntok = sent[i+1]
        # in-place operation.
        sent.merge(tok.idx, ntok.idx+len(ntok))
        i += 1
return sent
```

Next you initialize an empty list.

```
sdp_list = {'PREVENT': [],
            'SIDE_EFF': [],
            'TREAT_FOR_DIS': []}
```

In the main code, you take these main steps:

1) You start by running two for loops, one for the different relation types of disease and treatment and another for the different sentences of the class.

2) You initialize an empty Graph using the networkx library.

   a) For each token, you add a relation with all its children by maintaining a separate **edges** list and adding them to the Networkx Graph object using the add_edges_from function.

   b) You also add a node with its properties using the add_nodes_from function.

3) You also maintain a Python dictionary (meta_info) containing different info that you can leverage for analysis.

```
for KEY in sdp_list.keys():
    for i,row in biotext_df[biotext_df.relation.isin([KEY])].iterrows():
        # Entities to find SDP between
            entity1 = row["term1"].replace(" ","|").replace("`","")
            entity2 = row["term2"].replace(" ","|").replace("`","")

        # Adjusting for Space
            new_sentence = row["sentence"].replace(row["term1"], entity1)
            new_sentence = new_sentence.replace(row["term2"], entity2)

        # Spacy Pipeline
        doc = nlp(new_sentence)
        doc = remerge_sent(doc)

            entity1_idx = [token.i for token in doc if token.text in
            [entity1]][0]
            entity2_idx = [token.i for token in doc if token.text in
            [entity2]][0]
```

```python
# Load Networkx Graph
G = nx.Graph()

# Load spacy's dependency tree into a networkx graph
edges = []
for token in doc:
    for child in token.children:
        G.add_nodes_from([(token.i, {"pos": token.pos_,
                                     "text": token.text}),
                          (child.i, {"pos": child.pos_,
                                     "text": child.text})])
        edges.append((token.i,
                      child.i))

# Adddding Edges
G.add_edges_from(edges)

meta_info = {}
    meta_info["entity1"] = entity1
    meta_info["entity2"] = entity2
    meta_info["entity1_idx"] = entity1_idx
    meta_info["entity2_idx"] = entity2_idx
    meta_info["graph_object"] = G

shortest_path_list = nx.all_shortest_paths(G, source = entity1_idx,
target = entity2_idx)

    meta_info["word_list"] = [(G.node[n]['text'], G.node[n]['pos']) \
                          for shortest_path in shortest_path_list \
                          for i,n in enumerate(shortest_path) \
                              if i>0 and i<len(shortest_path)-1]

sdp_list[KEY].append(meta_info)
```

Since you have the SDP list for the tree relations, let's analyze what words/phrases you get in the dependency path of the sentence.

Similar to the strategy adopted earlier, you will lemmatize your words using the WordNet Lemmatizer.

```
mapping_pos_label_spacy = {"ADJ":'a',
  "ADV":'r',
  "NOUN": 'n',
  "VERB":'v'}

lemmatized_list = [[lemmatizer.lemmatize(word[0].lower(),
                                    get_pos_label(word[0],
                                              word[1],
                                      mapping_pos_label_
                                      spacy)) \
                  for word in val['word_list']] \
                  for val in sdp_list["TREAT_FOR_DIS"] \
                  if len(val['word_list']) > 0]
```

Next, you create a function named get_top_words, in which you

- Take individual wordlists from the lemmatized tokens.

- Create 1-3 gram tokens.

- Find the frequency and sort.

```
def get_top_words(lemmatized_list, n):
    """

    Show Top 'n' words
    """

    count_df = pd.Series([" ".join(word_phrase) \
                  for word_list in lemmatized_list \
                      for i in range(1,4) \
                  for word_phrase in nltk.ngrams(word_list, i)]).
                  value_counts().reset_index()
    count_df.columns = ["word","counts"]

    count_df = count_df[count_df.counts > 1]
for i,row in count_df.head(n).iterrows():
        print(row["word"] ,"---->", row["counts"])
```

With this, you get the following values for the three classes.

1) TREAT_FOR_DIS

patient ----> 189
treatment ----> 134
treat ----> 59
use ----> 43
effective ----> 36
effect ----> 31
therapy ----> 23
treat patient ----> 20
trial ----> 19
management ----> 16
undergo ----> 16
study ----> 15
perform ----> 13
show ----> 13
rate ----> 13
effectiveness ----> 13
improve ----> 11
efficacy ----> 11
result ----> 11
receive ----> 11

2) PREVENT

prevent ----> 9
prevention ----> 6
effective ----> 4
use ----> 4
reduce ----> 4
vaccine ----> 3
patient ----> 3
effect ----> 3
study ----> 2
incidence ----> 2
effective prevent ----> 2

```
risk ----> 2
stability ----> 2
trial ----> 2
safe ----> 2

 3) SIDE_EFF

associate ----> 5
rate ----> 4
risk ----> 4
case ----> 3
eye ----> 3
administration ----> 2
complication ----> 2
neurotoxicity ----> 2
patient ----> 2
associate risk ----> 2
develop ----> 2
had eye ----> 2
had ----> 2
```

As you can observe, the words highlighted above have now "weakly" added new information to help classify the relations. Moreover, some of them didn't make sense to include in a wild search, but within the SDP context chances of having false positives gets reduced, like "patient" in the TREAT_FOR_DIS sentences.

Distance Supervision

There are many words or phrases that carry semantic meaning along with them and hence they can just be substituted with a statistical frequency-based analysis. For you to identify such phrases, you will be leveraging UMLs ontology, which captures over 110 medical concepts such as therapeutic or preventive procedures, pharmacologic substances, health care activity, pathologic functions, etc.

You learned about UMLs in Chapter 4, so here you'll look at the code and analyze the output.

Firstly, make sure you add the UMLs pipeline to spacy. For this you will just call the EntityLinker class to add the umls database.

```
      linker = EntityLinker(resolve_abbreviations=False, name="umls")
# keeping default thresholds for match percentage.
nlp.add_pipe(linker)

# UMLs provides a class name to each of its TXXX identifier, TXXX is code
for parents for each of the CUI numbers a unique concept
# identifier used by UMLs Kb

# To obtain this file please login to https://www.nlm.nih.gov/research/
umls/index.html
# Shared in Github Repo of the book :)
    type2namemap = pd.read_csv("SRDEF", sep ="|", header = None)
    type2namemap = type2namemap.iloc[:,:3]
    type2namemap.columns = ["ClassType","TypeID","TypeName"]
    typenamemap = {row["TypeID"]:row["TypeName"] for i,row in type2namemap.
    iterrows()}
```

Then for each of the relation classes you create a concept dataframe that contains how often a particular concept occurred. Unlike the previous setup where you were just focused on frequency, here you will also look for uniqueness.

```
    KEY = "TREAT_FOR_DIS"

umls_concept_extracted = [[umls_ent for entity in doc.ents for umls_ent in
entity._.umls_ents] for doc in nlp.pipe(biotext_df[biotext_df.relation.
isin([KEY])].sentence.tolist())]
    umls_concept_cui = [linker.kb.cui_to_entity[concept[0]] for concepts in
    umls_concept_extracted for concept in concepts]
# Capturing all the information shared from the UMLS DB in a dataframe
umls_concept_df = pd.DataFrame(umls_concept_cui)
concept_df = pd.Series([typenamemap[typeid] for types in umls_concept_
df.types for typeid in types]).value_counts().reset_index()
    concept_df.columns = ["concept","count"]

    umls_concept_df["Name"] = pd.Series([[typenamemap[typeid] for typeid in
    types] for types in umls_concept_df.types])
```

Based on the concept_df dataframe from each of the keys, Table 6-1 shows the major UML types that can be used to discriminate between relation types.

Table 6-1. *UML Types for Each Relation*

Relation	UML Types	Reason	Concepts Example
TREAT_FOR_DIS	Therapeutic or preventive procedure	Therapy and treatments	Surgical procedures, chemo/radiation/aspirin therapy, treatment protocols, etc.
TREAT_FOR_DIS	Intellectual product	Methods, objective, and processes	Methods, objectives, and processes
TREAT_FOR_DIS	Qualitative concept	Assesses quality	Effectiveness, typical, simple, complete
TREAT_FOR_DIS	Patient or disabled group	Captures word *patient* and its aliases	Patients, patient, etc.
TREAT_FOR_DIS	Temporal concept	Pertains to time and duration mentions	Year, postoperative period, weekly, transitory, etc.
TREAT_FOR_DIS	Healthcare activity	Evaluation and reporting	Evaluation and reporting
PREVENT	Immunologic factor	Identifies active substance whose activities affect or play a role in the functioning of the immune system	Vaccines and combination therapies
PREVENT	Idea or concept	Conclusions or outcomes	Conclusion
PREVENT	Occupational activity	Analysis and activity of the occupation	Economic analysis
SIDE_EFF	Sign or symptom	Shows effect of a drug	Growing pain
SIDE_EFF	Injury or poisoning	Shows effect of a drug	Wounds/injuries
SIDE_EFF	Body part, organ, or organ component	Shows effect of a drug	Any body part
SIDE_EFF	Pathologic function	Adverse reactions and effect	Brain hemorrhage, adverse reaction to drug, spontaneous abortion

Pipeline

In order to demonstrate Snorkel's capabilities, you need to create an experiment by splitting your data into two datasets:

- An unlabeled training dataset named `train_df` that Snorkel's `LabelModel` will use to learn the labels

- A hand-labeled development dataset named `val_df` you will use to determine if your LFs work

You will maintain the distribution of the target class by sampling in a stratified fashion.

```
from sklearn.model_selection import train_test_split

train_df, val_df, train_labels, val_labels = train_test_split(
    biotext_df,
        biotext_df['relation'],
        test_size=0.4,
        stratify = biotext_df['relation'],
        random_state = 42
)
```

As discussed, Snorkel has three primary interfaces

- Labeling functions

- Transformation functions

- Slicing functions

I will be discussing labeling function in depth in this chapter. A labelling function deterministically determines the class of the data. These functions can work at any level (text/para/metadata) and can leverage multiple sources of information (models/external databases/ontologies)

In order to write labeling functions, you need to define the label schema for your problem.

$$L_i(x) = \begin{cases} -1, ABSTAIN \\ 0, TREAT\_FOR\_DIS \\ 1, PREVENT \\ 2, SIDE\_EFF \end{cases}$$

It is mandatory to define an ABSTAIN label, besides the classes present in the data, because this allows Snorkel to vote for a class only if there is enough evidence. If you get a lot of abstain values as your output from Snorkel, then you will have to increase the coverage for your LFs.

```
# Define our numeric labels as integers
    ABSTAIN = -1
    TREAT_FOR_DIS = 0
    PREVENT = 1
    SIDE_EFF = 2

    def map_labels(x):
        """Map string labels to integers"""
        if x == 'TREAT_FOR_DIS':
        return TREAT_FOR_DIS
        elif x == 'PREVENT':
        return PREVENT
        elif x == 'SIDE_EFF':
        return SIDE_EFF

val_labels  =  val_labels.apply(map_labels, convert_dtype=True)
```

Writing Your LFs

The program interface for labeling functions is snorkel.labeling.LabelingFunction. They are instantiated with a name, a function reference, any resources the function needs, and a list of any preprocessors to run on the data records before the labeling function runs.

There are two ways to define a LF function:

1) Using the base class LabelingFunction.

snorkel.labeling.LabelingFunction(name, f, resources=None, pre=None)

- "name" = Name of the LF.
- "f" = Function that implements the LF logic.
- "resources" = Labeling resources passed into f
- "pre" = Preprocessors to run on the data

2)   Using the decorator `labeling_function`.

snorkel.labeling.labeling_function(name=None, resources=None, pre=None)

- **"name" = Name of the LF.**
- **"resources" = Labeling resources passed into f**
- **"pre" = Preprocessors to run on the data**

You will be using the decorator method as it is much easier.

For those who don't understand decorators, decorators basically take a function, add some functionality (a.k.a. decorate it), and return it by calling it.

Working with Decorators

Based on your analysis, you have shortlisted the following words for each of the relation classes. Hence, you will just write a labeling function that returns the relation class if any of their respective words are found and otherwise abstains from the label.

```
treatment_keywords = ['treatment', 'therapy','effective','treat',
"reduce"]
prevent_keywords = ["protect", "prevent", "inhibit", "block",
"control", 'effect']
side_effect_keywords = ["risk","follow", "associate", "toxic"]
```

```
@labeling_function()
    def sent_contains_TREAT_FOR_DIS(x):
    text = x.sentence.lower()
    lemmatized_word = [lemmatizer.lemmatize(w,
                              pos= get_pos_label(w,
                                          pos_w,
                                          mapping_pos_label))\
                for w, pos_w in pos_tag(text.split()) \
                    if w not in list(set(stopwords.words('english')))]
    return TREAT_FOR_DIS if any([ True if key in lemmatized_word else False
    for key in treatment_keywords]) else ABSTAIN
```

```python
@labeling_function()
    def sent_contains_SIDE_EFF(x):
    text = x.sentence.lower()
    lemmatized_word = [lemmatizer.lemmatize(w,
                               pos= get_pos_label(w,
                                            pos_w,
                                            mapping_pos_label))\
                    for w, pos_w in pos_tag(text.split()) \
                        if w not in list(set(stopwords.words('english')))]
    return SIDE_EFF if any([ True if key in lemmatized_word else False for
    key in side_effect_keywords]) else ABSTAIN

@labeling_function()
    def sent_contains_PREVENT(x):
    text = x.sentence.lower()
    lemmatized_word = [lemmatizer.lemmatize(w,
                               pos= get_pos_label(w,
                                            pos_w,
                                            mapping_pos_label))\
                    for w, pos_w in pos_tag(text.split()) \
                        if w not in list(set(stopwords.words('english')))]
    return PREVENT if any([ True if key in lemmatized_word else False for
    key in prevent_keywords]) else ABSTAIN
```

Yes, it is that simple.

Preprocessor in Snorkel

But there is one problem with the above code. You must repeat the lemmatization and text lower logic every time for each function. Can't you preprocess your data beforehand and then use it without repeating logic in each function?

Well, Snorkel has a preprocessor that maps a data point to a new data point.

LabelingFunctions can use preprocessors, which lets you write LFs over transformed or enhanced data points.

You add the @preprocessor(...) decorator to preprocessing functions to create preprocessors. Preprocessors also have extra functionality, such as memoization (i.e. input/output caching, so it doesn't re-execute for each LF that uses it).

```python
from snorkel.preprocess import preprocessor

@preprocessor(memoize = True)
    def get_syntactic_info(x):

    # Entities to find SDP between
        entity1 = x.term1.replace(" ","|").replace("`","")
        entity2 = x.term2.replace(" ","|").replace("`","")

    # Adjusting for Space
    new_sentence = x.sentence.replace(x.term1, entity1)
    new_sentence = new_sentence.replace(x.term2, entity2)

    # Spacy Pipeline
    doc = nlp(new_sentence)
    doc = remerge_sent(doc)

        entity1_idx = [token.i for token in doc if token.text in [entity1]][0]
        entity2_idx = [token.i for token in doc if token.text in [entity2]][0]

    # Load Networkx Graph
    G = nx.Graph()

    # Load spacy's dependency tree into a networkx graph
    edges = []
    for token in doc:
        for child in token.children:
                G.add_nodes_from([(token.i, {"pos": token.pos_,
                                             "text": token.text}),
                                  (child.i, {"pos": child.pos_,
                                             "text": child.text})])
            edges.append((token.i,
                        child.i))

    # Addding Edges
    G.add_edges_from(edges)

    shortest_path_list = nx.all_shortest_paths(G, source = entity1_idx,
    target = entity2_idx)
```

```
word_list = [(G.node[n]['text'], G.node[n]['pos']) \
                    for shortest_path in shortest_path_list \
                    for i,n in enumerate(shortest_path) \
                        if i>0 and i<len(shortest_path)-1]

lemmatized_list = [lemmatizer.lemmatize(word[0].lower(),
                                    get_pos_label(word[0],
                                                word[1],
                                            mapping_pos_label_
                                            spacy)) \
                for word in word_list]

x.sdp_word = lemmatized_list
return x
```

Similarly, you know the important words from the SDP path for each of the relation classes. Hence you start by initializing them.

```
treatment_sdp_keywords = ['patient', 'use','trial','management',
"study", "show", "improve"]
prevent_sdp_keywords = ["reduce", "vaccine", "incidence", "stability"]
side_effect_sdp_keywords = ["rate","case", "administration",
"complication", "develop"]
```

```
@labeling_function(pre=[get_syntactic_info])
    def sent_sdp_TREAT_FOR_DIS(x):
    return TREAT_FOR_DIS if any([True if key in x.sdp_word else False for
    key in treatment_sdp_keywords]) else ABSTAIN
```

```
@labeling_function(pre=[get_syntactic_info])
    def sent_sdp_SIDE_EFF(x):
    return SIDE_EFF if any([True if key in x.sdp_word else False for key in
    side_effect_sdp_keywords]) else ABSTAIN
```

```
@labeling_function(pre=[get_syntactic_info])
    def sent_sdp_PREVENT(x):
    return PREVENT if any([True if key in x.sdp_word else False for key in
    prevent_sdp_keywords]) else ABSTAIN
```

See how easy and clean the code becomes now.

Lastly, you get your distance-based weak learners as well. Similar to the preprocessing done above, you use the preprocessing decorator to do another preprocessing.

```python
@preprocessor(memoize = True)
    def get_umls_concepts(x):

    umls_concept_extracted = [[umls_ent for entity in doc.ents for umls_ent
    in entity._.umls_ents] for doc in nlp.pipe([x.sentence])]

    try:
            umls_concept_cui = [linker.kb.cui_to_entity[concept[0]] for
            concepts in umls_concept_extracted for concept in concepts]
        # Capturing all the information shared from the UMLS DB in a
        dataframe
        umls_concept_df = pd.DataFrame(umls_concept_cui)
        concept_df = pd.Series([typenamemap[typeid] for types in umls_
        concept_df.types for typeid in types]).value_counts().reset_index()
            concept_df.columns = ["concept","count"]

            x["umls_concepts"] = concept_df.concept.tolist()
    except Exception as e:
            x["umls_concepts"] = []

    return x
```

Based on Table 6-1, you also know the dominant and significant UML concepts from the sentences.

```python
treatment_umls_concepts = ['Therapeutic or Preventive Procedure',
                           'Intellectual Product',
                           'Qualitative Concept',
                           'Patient or Disabled Group',
                           "Temporal Concept",
                           "Health Care Activity"]
```

```
prevent_umls_concepts = ["Immunologic Factor",
                         "Idea or Concept",
                         "Finding",
                         "Occupational Activity"]

side_effect_umls_concepts = ["Sign or Symptom",
                             "Injury or Poisoning",
                             "Body Part, Organ, or Organ Component",
                             "Pathologic Function"]
```

Finally, you write the labeling functions for this distance supervision setup.

```
@labeling_function(pre=[get_umls_concepts])
    def sent_umls_TREAT_FOR_DIS(x):
    return TREAT_FOR_DIS if any([True if key in x.umls_concepts else False
    for key in treatment_umls_concepts]) else ABSTAIN


@labeling_function(pre=[get_umls_concepts])
    def sent_umls_SIDE_EFF(x):
    return SIDE_EFF if any([True if key in x.umls_concepts else False for
    key in prevent_umls_concepts]) else ABSTAIN


@labeling_function(pre=[get_umls_concepts])
    def sent_umls_PREVENT(x):
    return PREVENT if any([True if key in x.umls_concepts else False for
    key in side_effect_umls_concepts]) else ABSTAIN
```

Training

For training, you must apply your weak labels to each sentence. Since your data is stored in a pandas dataframe, you will leverage a built-in function called PandasLFApplier.

It is a LFApplier class that gives a label matrix. It's a NumPy array L with one column for each LF and one row for each data point, where L[i, j] is the label that the jth labeling function output for the ith data point. You'll create a label matrix for the train set.

```
lfs = [sent_contains_TREAT_FOR_DIS, sent_contains_SIDE_EFF, sent_contains_
PREVENT,
       sent_sdp_TREAT_FOR_DIS, sent_sdp_SIDE_EFF, sent_sdp_PREVENT,
       sent_umls_TREAT_FOR_DIS, sent_umls_SIDE_EFF, sent_umls_PREVENT]

# Instantiate our LF applier with our list of LabelFunctions (just one for now)
applier = PandasLFApplier(lfs=lfs)

# Apply the LFs to the data to generate a list of labels
L_train = applier.apply(df=train_df)
L_dev   = applier.apply(df=val_df)
```

Evaluation

Snorkel nicely packs lots of analysis for us in a simple function named LFAnalysis. There are many summary statistics that are reported (see Figure 6-12):

- **Polarity**: The set of unique labels this LF outputs (excluding abstains)

- **Coverage**: The fraction of the dataset the LF labels

- **Overlaps**: The fraction of data points with at least two (non-abstain) labels.

- **Conflicts**: The fraction of the dataset where this LF and at least one other LF label disagree (non-abstain labels)

- **Correct**: The number of data points this LF labels correctly (if gold labels are provided)

- **Incorrect**: The number of data points this LF labels incorrectly (if gold labels are provided)

- **Empirical Accuracy**: The empirical accuracy of this LF (if gold labels are provided)

```
# Run a label function analysis on the results, to describe their output
against the labeled development data
LFAnalysis(L=L_dev, lfs=lfs).lf_summary(val_labels.values)
```

	j	Polarity	Coverage	Overlaps	Conflicts	Correct	Incorrect	Emp. Acc.
sent_contains_TREAT_FOR_DIS	0	[0]	0.505405	0.502703	0.305405	177	10	0.946524
sent_contains_SIDE_EFF	1	[2]	0.051351	0.051351	0.051351	4	15	0.210526
sent_contains_PREVENT	2	[1]	0.113514	0.113514	0.113514	11	31	0.261905
sent_sdp_TREAT_FOR_DIS	3	[0]	0.329730	0.324324	0.229730	113	9	0.926230
sent_sdp_SIDE_EFF	4	[2]	0.040541	0.040541	0.040541	5	10	0.333333
sent_sdp_PREVENT	5	[1]	0.024324	0.024324	0.024324	5	4	0.555556
sent_umls_TREAT_FOR_DIS	6	[0]	0.943243	0.875676	0.627027	316	33	0.905444
sent_umls_SIDE_EFF	7	[2]	0.294595	0.291892	0.291892	7	102	0.064220
sent_umls_PREVENT	8	[1]	0.454054	0.443243	0.443243	21	147	0.125000

Figure 6-12. *LFAnalysis output with various metrics*

Some observations:

- You see that TREAT_FOR_DIS performs very well on the coverage and accuracy metrics.

- PREVENT's SDP label sees a much better empirical accuracy as compared to other label functions.

- SIDE_EFF doesn't seem to perform that well on UMLs LF. You can check for combinations of UMLs tags either in the whole sentence or just in the SDP. You will have to iteratively make these LFs better.

Generating the Final Labels

So far you have covered a lot of ground. You have

- Loaded and prepared the data

- Split it into train and test sets

- Scanned the data for LF ideas

- Created the LF

- Looked at preprocessing steps and how you can memoize them

- Evaluated the performance of these LFs against a validation data

You are finally ready to generate labels. Snorkel provides two main ways to generate final labels. One is the `MajorityLabelVoter`, which basically assigns the sample the label that is given by most LFs.

This generally yields subpar or in some cases equal performance to Snorkel's more noise-aware generative model and hence acts as a baseline. A very intuitive way of understanding this subperformance is due to the fact in `MajorityLabel` all LFs are treated equal. However, as you can see for SIDE_EFF, "regex" makes more sense than "umls" based LFs.

```
from snorkel.labeling.model import MajorityLabelVoter

    majority_model = MajorityLabelVoter(cardinality = 3)
preds_train = majority_model.predict(L=L_train)
```

As you can see, you need to provide a cardinality value to the `MajorityLabelVoter`, which basically is nothing but the number of non-abstain classes.

This helps establish a baseline. You can now comfortably move to using a more noise-aware and weighted voting strategy. Details of the strategy are out of scope for this chapter but for the interested souls, please read the paper titled "Data Programming: Creating Large Training Sets, Quickly" by Ratner et al.

```
from snorkel.labeling.model import LabelModel

label_model = LabelModel(cardinality=3, verbose=True)
```

Before you fit the model, you should understand the different options available for you to play with.

`LabelModel.fit()` allows you to play with the following hyperparameters:

- n_epochs: The number of epochs to train (where each epoch is a single optimization step)

- lr: Base learning rate (will also be affected by lr_scheduler choice and settings)

- l2: Centered L2 regularization strength

- optimizer: Which optimizer to use (one of ["sgd", "adam", "adamax"])

- optimizer_config: Settings for the optimizer

- lr_scheduler: Which lr_scheduler to use (one of ["constant", "linear", "exponential", "step"])

- lr_scheduler_config: Settings for the LRScheduler

- prec_init: LF precision initializations/priors

- seed: A random seed to initialize the random number generator with

- log_freq: Report loss every this many epochs (steps)

- mu_eps: Restrict the learned conditional probabilities to [mu_eps, 1-mu_eps]

You will train the model with defaults for now, but I urge you to experiment and learn more about the effects of these hyperparameters on tuning.

```
label_model.fit(L_train=L_train, n_epochs=100, seed=42)
```

Let's see how the generative model compares to the majority vote baseline.

```
majority_acc = majority_model.score(L=L_dev, Y=val_labels, tie_break_
policy="random")[
    "accuracy"
]
print(f"{'Majority Vote Accuracy:':<25} {majority_acc * 100:.1f}%")

label_model_acc = label_model.score(L=L_dev, Y=val_labels, tie_break_
policy="random")["accuracy"
]
print(f"{'Label Model Accuracy:':<25} {label_model_acc * 100:.1f}%")
```

Majority Vote Accuracy: 80.8%

Label Model Accuracy: 87.6%

As you can see, the Label model outperforms the Majority Vote by over 7.5%. This is a major lift. Although nothing conclusive can be said, you should always experiment to see the sensitivity of the performance by changing the hyperparameters.

One thing you will notice while scoring the performance on validation set is the use of policy,

Policies to break ties include

- `abstain`: Return an abstain vote (-1).

- `true-random`: Randomly choose among the tied options.

- `random`: Randomly choose among tied option using a deterministic hash (the values remain consistent over different runs).

Conclusion

There is no perfect way of weakly learning from your data. You just have to be better than random. Your LFs can differently predict the output for a data point. You just need to keep generating ideas by analyzing the data, writing the LF, and then refining and debugging. As data increases at a much faster veracity and velocity, it is imperative for organizations to adopt such innovative methods to get started with labeled data and training powerful models. I hope this chapter has sparked your curiosity to learn more about these methods. If yes, then it is a win for us.

CHAPTER 7

Federated Learning and Healthcare

With better and more computer and hardware technology so easily accessible, there is a huge influx of analytical data available from different healthcare stakeholders, from clinical institutions to insurance companies and from patients to pharmaceutical industries. This huge amount of data is a gold mine for uncovering insights that can help design an AI-integrated healthcare system aimed at providing better outcomes and quality at a reasonable cost.

Healthcare data, however generated in volumes, is still fragmented, with legal, ethical, and privacy concerns inhibiting large scale data analysis for robust research. For example, as you saw in Chapters 3 and 4, the EHR data collected by Beth Israel Deaconess Medical Center, although still a large data set, lacked aspects like distribution of white and non-white population, difference in age distribution, etc. whereas it could be possible that data that contains more of such unrepresented groups might be present elsewhere. Hence a more ingenious way of thinking is required.

Federated learning helps us address such issues of privacy and legal limitations by bringing models to the data rather than the other way around. In this chapter, you are going to deep dive into federated machine learning. What is TensorFlow Federated? What are the different privacy mechanisms? The objective of the chapter is not to introduce you to a novel case study but rather to learn more about the TensorFlow Federated ecosystem (Federated, Privacy, and Encryption) and its capabilities.

© Anshik 2021
Anshik, *AI for Healthcare with Keras and Tensorflow 2.0*, https://doi.org/10.1007/978-1-4842-7086-8_7

Introduction

Federated learning (FL) is a distributed machine learning concept that allows model training on decentralized data while addressing the issues of data transfer, privacy, and security for every stakeholder. There are four main components to a FL system and they work in sync to do federated learning:

- **Central server/node**: Orchestrates training and deployment of local models and serves as the playground to create a global model. Local models are those that are trained on local nodes/edge devices, and global models are those whose weights are updated using weights from local nodes.

- **Local server/devices/node**: This is where the real-world data lies. They are generally edge devices of installed machines collecting customer data.

- **Local model**: This is any type of machine learning model that trains on the data present in the local server. These models learn specific to the data of local devices.

- **Global model**: The final model obtained by assembling information from different local models.

How Does Federation Learning Work?

There are four key steps in federated learning training.

Step 1: Transferring the initial model from the central node (see Figure 7-1)

- The initial model obtained from the central server is trained on data available with the model's owner (i.e. this model is trained with the available data on a central server).

- This global model is then transferred over a network to all of the local nodes.

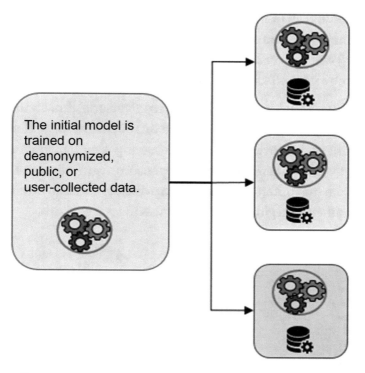

Figure 7-1. *Step 1*

Step 2: Model training

- Any type of machine learning model, from basic models like Naive Bayes and SVM to DeepNets, can be trained.

- A fraction of clients are selected for local model training because selecting lots of clients has diminishing returns over performance and costs.

- The local node's compute resources are used for training, which saves the central server compute time and resources.

- Sometimes the data is insufficient at a local node, which can make that node's contribution futile to the global model, hence techniques like secure aggregation which allows data sharing between nodes using public-private keys. Also such a technique helps prevent individual data leakage issues.

Step 3: Local models transferred to the central node (see Figure 7-2)

- After training, all models can be passed back to the central server. For edge devices, this can cause huge network overheads (cross-device training) while in cross-silos federal training (groups/institutes as local nodes) this effect is less pronounced.

- Sometimes models can be subjected to adversarial attacks that can help identify user-sensitive data used to train the models. Hence, to prevent such attacks, a privacy-preserving layer that implements techniques like differential privacy or secure aggregation can be used. Note that differential privacy in principle can also be applied locally rather than globally. More on this in later sections.

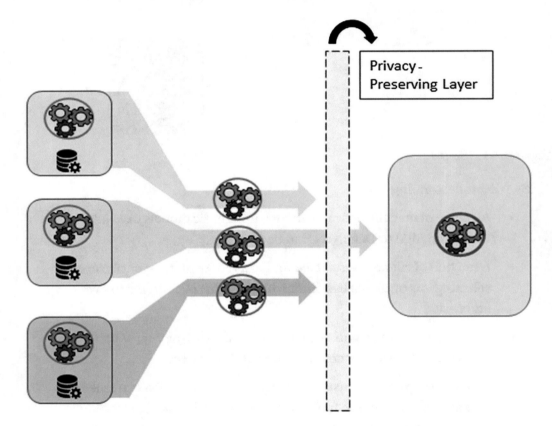

Figure 7-2. *Step 3*

Step 4: The central node aggregates the result from all the local models.

- Federated averaging is more than simple averaging of output probabilities or majority voting.

- Whatever parameter needs to be learned, like for example a deep learning model works on weight updates. Hence a global weight vector is decided by weighing on the loss metric and normalizing with the number of samples observed. This way you get more representation of weights, which statistically (number of samples) lead to better performance.

- There can be many other averaging techniques depending on how results are transferred from local nodes.

Types of Federated Learning

Depending upon how the data is distributed across multiple local nodes in the FL training process, you can classify FL into three major categories.

Horizontal Federated Learning

In horizontal federated learning, datasets of different local nodes have the same set of feature space but the amount of overlap of samples is minimal.

This is a natural partitioning for a cross-device setting, where different nodes/users are trying to improve on a common task, say keyboard suggestions while typing using GBoard on a mobile app or risk prediction of a disease using wearable device data. See Figure 7-3.

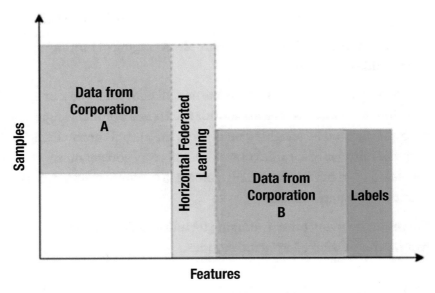

Figure 7-3. *Horizontal federated learning. Source: "Survey On Federated Learning Towards Privacy Preserving AI" by Kurupathi et al*

Vertical Federated Learning

Here datasets of different local nodes have the same set of samples/persons but the amount of overlap of feature space can be different depending on organization data.

When multiple organizations are coordinating, they can look forward to implementing vertical FL. A feature alignment approach is used to align features of different individuals and then a single model is trained. The alignment is privacy preserved, meaning it is not easy to identify protected information. This can be achieved using encryption. You'll learn more about this in the secure aggregation discussion.

Some examples are joint collaboration between insurance and banking companies on common data of shared customers. Labels can be a default rate or any fraudulent transactions. In healthcare, different hospitals can share info on different tests which they have expertise in to chart out a comprehensive medical history of the patient. See Figure 7-4.

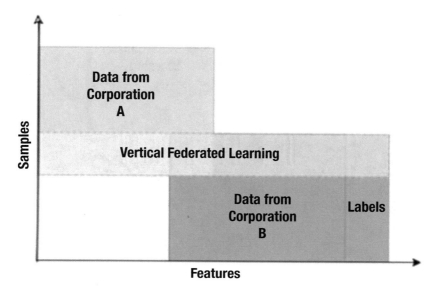

Figure 7-4. *Vertical federated learning. Source: "Survey On Federated Learning Towards Privacy Preserving AI" by Kurupathi et al*

Federated Transfer Learning

This is implemented in scenarios where both feature space and samples differ. Say a group of hospitals wants to do breast cancer research. Each hospital has a distinct set of patients (samples) and they may be capturing different metrics (feature space) with some minimal capture in both dimensions.

Generally, a common representation is learned between the two feature spaces using limited common sample sets and then later applied to obtain predictions for only one-side feature samples. See Figure 7-5.

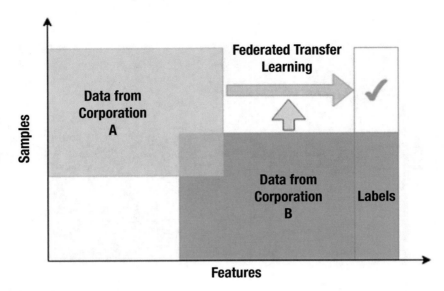

Figure 7-5. *Federated transfer learning. Source: "Survey On Federated Learning Towards Privacy Preserving AI" by Kurupathi et al*

Privacy Mechanism

The larger acceptance of FL in the real word came only when multiple privacy mechanisms were implemented in addition to the flow discussed in the introduction. Although the dataset resides on local nodes, there can be re-engineering of model parameters to obtain information about data. Also, multiple privacy mechanism techniques can be applied together to ensure more robust security of an individual's identity/data.

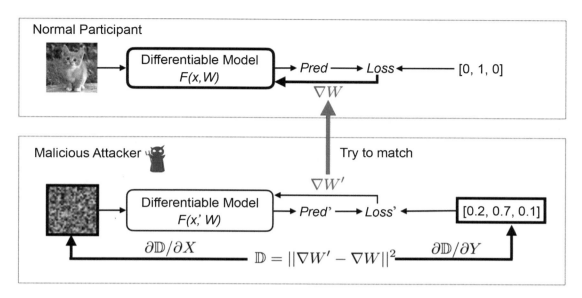

Figure 7-6. *Gradient matching attack*

As shown in Figure 7-6, a malicious attacker can try to match gradients to the local gradient updates and reconstruct the data.

There are many privacy mechanism techniques, but in this chapter we are going to discuss the two most common ones that are used in current FL systems.

For a more thorough deep-dive of privacy mechanisms and ways to measure their effectiveness, refer to the paper "Technical Privacy Metrics: A Systematic Survey" by Wagner et al, released in 2018.

Secure Aggregation

Secure aggregation is a privacy-preserving machine learning technique that relies on multi-party computation to compute sums of model parameters when updated from individual user devices in a secure manner.

In 2017, Google originally proposed a secure aggregation technique in the paper titled "Practical Secure Aggregation for Privacy-Preserving Machine Learning." For mathematical details you can have a look at the paper, but for now let's understand it intuitively.

1)   Public and private keys are generated using a schema.

2)   The public keys are shared with each local node.

3) These keys are used to encrypt the model parameters changes.

4) All the local nodes accumulate model weights using mathematical operations like addition or multiplication.

5) The accumulated changes are sent to the central server, which uses the private key to decrypt the data.

Two things to note in the above process are

- We can do ALU (arithmetic and logical) operations on the encrypted data itself as the encryptions are homomorphic in nature. We can perform ALU operations on data without decrypting it.

- The central server sees the accumulated results, which can be decrypted using the private key.

Also, certain users can drop out abruptly due to network issues. Any change that happens on the central server only happens when the sum comes from at least n number of local nodes.

Internally TFF (TensorFlow Federated) uses TensorFlow Encrypted to carry out this exercise, but for simplicity let's use the pallier package to see how this can work.

You will be using python-pallier, which uses the Paillier Crypto system (a homomorphic encryption scheme, see `https://blog.openmined.org/the-paillier-cryptosystem/` for how homomorphic encryption works).

```python
import phe
import numpy as np
# Generate Public and Private Key
    public_key, private_key = phe.generate_paillier_keypair(n_length=1024)
    weight1 = np.random.rand(10)
    weight2 = np.random.rand(10)
# Note : This is a simple addition but it can be more complex as well
sum_of_local_weights = np.add(weight1, weight2)
    print("Addition Of w1 and w2: " + str(sum_of_local_weights))
encrypted_w1 = [public_key.encrypt(i) for i in weight1]
encrypted_w2 = [public_key.encrypt(j) for j in weight2]
encrypted_sum_of_w1_and_w2 = [i+j for i,j in zip(encrypted_w1, encrypted_w2)]
```

```
decryped_sum_of_w1_and_w2 = [private_key.decrypt(k) for k in encrypted_sum_
of_w1_and_w2]
    print("Addition Of Encrypted Number: " + str(decryped_sum_of_w1_and_w2))
```

Output

```
Addition Of w1 and w2: [0.01965569 1.38181926 0.95724207 1.40539024
0.56162914 1.26444545
 0.84660776 0.55585975 1.60470971 0.74662359]
Addition Of Encrypted Number: [0.01965569240712506, 1.381819260975988,
0.957242068080129, 1.4053902417875905, 0.5616291366817605,
1.2644454455590868, 0.8466077626079891, 0.5558597475342251,
1.604709707486859, 0.7466235859816883]
```

You can see how easily homomorphic encryption along with multiple parties (to ensure robustness and better up-time) can secure data of an individual by sharing the aggregated result itself.

As you may have thought by now, this technique contains a lot of overhead in terms of computation, which can scale with the number of local nodes and parameter vector size.

Differential Privacy

Differential privacy is a privacy mechanism that tries to quantify the amount of privacy ensued as a result of adding noise to the data either at the local node (Local DP) or at an aggregate level (Global DP) such that the end analysis stays the same. Let's understand it through an example.

Suppose you take a survey in your class to see how many students have color blindness to the color green. You plan to include a lot of visuals that might use green color while explaining some of the concepts.

Objective: Are the majority of people not color blind to green?

Say you administer the survey and the results are as shown in Figure 7-7.

Note   For simplicity, we are using a very small sample size.

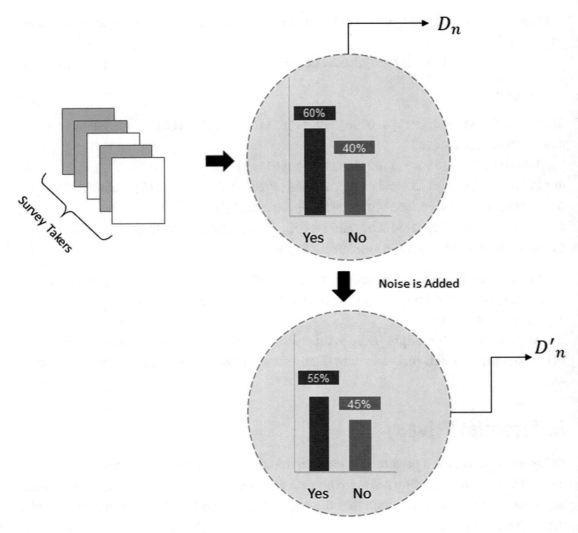

Figure 7-7. *Differential privacy*

Let's also imagine your secondary research tells you that people from a certain ethnicity tend to show color blindness to the color green. So if you are presented with data D_n, you can in some way identify those particular individuals in the classroom. But what if you add some noise so that the number becomes non-intuitive and can't be pinpointed to a certain section of the classroom.

That's exactly what differential privacy guarantees. It safeguards individuals participating in the analysis and yet doesn't affect the result, as in the above case of finding that the majority of the class is not sensitive to the green color.

Differential privacy introduces a metric called an epsilon, which quantifies how close the distributions of data is:

$$\frac{P(f(D_n))}{P(f(D'_n))} = e^{\varepsilon}$$

If $\varepsilon = 0$, then you have an exact distribution and you have achieved peak privacy. $f(D_n)$ represents the data function and $f(D'_n)$ represents the data function after adding the noise.

In practice, Laplace and normal distributions are used to generate answer to queries because these functions are more likely to predict numbers closer to the mean (<=1 standard deviations from means; for standard normal it is 68% while for Laplace it is 74% (b=1)) and yet not giving the correct answer. The mean here will be your true value.

As you know, you can estimate the mean of any distribution if enough random samples are taken from it by the Central Limit Theorem. In the same way, if multiple queries are fired to the database containing data from local nodes, an estimate of the mean can be formed.

For example,

1) What is the number of non-color blind students in the survey?

2) What is the number of students belonging to "this" ethnicity?

3) What is the total number of people?

So each time you throw a number, you are giving an adversary a better chance to guess the right number/data coming from a local node or any of its characteristics.

While implementing differential privacy, you must make sure that the two probability distributions are as close as possible. In small sample cases, noise can completely change the data; with large numbers of samples, noise has a limiting effect (because more variations are introduced so a single noise can't mask all samples well). Hence, designing a noise function is an extremely difficult task sometimes.

Since noise can sometimes overwhelm small samples, you can introduce another parameter called δ, a threshold that helps you drop rare categories. So a unique differential privacy mechanism is actually a function of two things:

- Threshold (δ)

- Amount of noise (ε)

TensorFlow Privacy is a library in the TensorFlow ecosystem for training machine learning models with privacy for training data. There are three distinct features that this library provides:

1) A training algorithm, specifically gradient descent

   a) It limits the influence of a single datapoint in the resulting gradient computation by clipping the gradients.

   b) It make the gradient value agnostic of any particular point in the training batch by adding random noise to the clipped gradients.

2) Selection and configuration (hyperparameter tuning) of the privacy mechanisms to apply to each of the aggregates collected (model gradients, batch normalization weight updates, metrics)

3) Performance measures

   a) Privacy budget

   b) Epsilon

Note   Differential privacy is an independent privacy-maintaining technique that can be used with FL architecture, in which case the updates come from multi-parties.

TensorFlow Federated

TensorFlow Federated (TFF) is an open-source framework for applying federated learning locally through simulated experiments. TFF enables developers to simulate the included federated learning algorithms on their models and data, as well as to experiment with novel algorithms.

TFF's interfaces are organized in two layers:

- **Federated Learning (FL) API**: This layer offers a set of high-level interfaces that allow developers to apply the included implementations of federated training and evaluation to their existing TensorFlow models.

- **Federated Core (FC) API**: At the core of the system is a set of lower-level interfaces for expressing novel federated algorithms by combining TensorFlow with distributed communication operators.

Input Data

You are going to use the malaria dataset, which contains a total of 27,558 cell images with equal instances of parasitized and uninfected cells from the thin blood smear slide images of segmented cells. The data set can be obtained from `https://ceb.nlm.nih.gov/proj/malaria/cell_images.zip`.

There are simulated datasets present in the TensorFlow Federated library ecosystem but the malaria dataset is close to the healthcare domain. In the next chapter, you are going to see how medical image analysis works on 2D and 3D image data and hence it's a good start.

The malaria dataset contains two classes, shown in Figure 7-8:

- Parasitized (a.k.a. infected cells)

- Non-parasitized (a.k.a. uninfected cells)

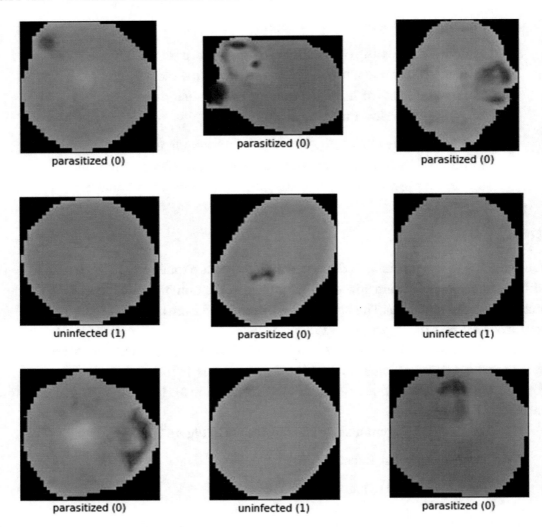

Figure 7-8. *Examples of parasitized and uninfected cells*

You start by loading the data from the local directory and see the distribution of infected and non-infected image samples.

```
import os
import glob

    BASE_DIR = os.path.join('./Data')
    parasitized_dir = os.path.join(BASE_DIR,'Parasitized')
    uninfected_dir = os.path.join(BASE_DIR,'Uninfected')
```

```
    parasitized_files = glob.glob(parasitized_dir+'/*.png')
    uninfected_files = glob.glob(uninfected_dir+'/*.png')
len(parasitized_files), len(uninfected_files)
```

Output

```
(13779, 13779)
```

It looks like you have a balanced representation for both the classes.

Federated learning requires a federated data set (a collection of data from multiple users, also known as local nodes). Any federated data is expected to be non-iid which means different clients should have at least some reasonably similar distributions (local node-specific characteristics affect the distribution of data on each system).

In your case, you won't have distinct distributions of the datasets but it would be good to explore them through visualizations.

Custom Data Load Pipeline

If you were using a simulated dataset already present in the tff library, you could simply call the function load_data().

```
_train, _test = tff.simulation.datasets.<dbname>.load_data()
```

The data sets returned by load_data() are instances of tff.simulation. ClientData, which enumerates the set of local nodes to construct a tf.data.Dataset that represents the data of a particular node and to query the structure of individual data elements.

Since you are not using a presimulated dataset, you need to construct one yourself. Since your directory structure is organized in the following fashion

```
Data/
...Parasitized/
......image_1.png
......image_2.png
...Uninfected/
......image_1.png
......image_2.png
```

231

you can leverage the tf.keras preprocessing function image_dataset_from_
directory.

Calling image_dataset_from_directory(data_directory, labels='inferred')
will return a tf.data.Dataset that yields batches of images from the subdirectories
Parasitized and Uninfected, together with labels 0 and 1 (0 corresponding to
Parasitized and 1 corresponding to Uninfected).

```
tf.keras.preprocessing.image_dataset_from_directory(
        BASE_DIR, labels='inferred', label_mode='int',
        class_names=None, color_mode='rgb', batch_size=32, image_size=(256,
        256), shuffle=True, seed=None, validation_split=None, subset=None,
        interpolation='bilinear', follow_links=False
)
```

In the above function, there is also an option to resize the images, but for you to
resize the image you need to know the correct resized shape. Since these are cell images,
they might have different shapes. Let's quickly check that and then use the preprocessing
function to load the data.

Since you have roughly 30k images, loading each one of them sequentially can take
some time, so you should try to parallelize the operation on different CPU cores and use
the OpenCV library to return the shape of each image.

You start by loading the libraries and using the built-in os library to calculate the
CPU count.

```
from joblib import Parallel, delayed
import os
nprocs = os.cpu_count()
```

You use one less CPU than the total number to not disrupt other applications'
compute resources. It's just a good practice to follow.

You are going to use OpenCV 3 to read in the images. It can be downloaded by
running the following command:

```
pip install opencv-python==3.4.6.27
```

```
    def load_image_shape(img):
    return cv2.imread(img).shape
```

```
results = Parallel(n_jobs=nprocs-1)(delayed(load_image_shape)
(img_file) for img_file in parasitized_files + uninfected_files)

print('Min Dimensions:', np.min(results, axis=0))
print('Avg Dimensions:', np.mean(results, axis=0))
print('Median Dimensions:', np.median(results, axis=0))
print('Max Dimensions:', np.max(results, axis=0))

Min Dimensions: [40 46  3]
Avg Dimensions: [132.98345308 132.48715437    3.         ]
Median Dimensions: [130. 130.   3.]
Max Dimensions: [385 394   3]
```

Note this process just makes the load time faster, but you are still loading the full data in memory, which is generally not recommended for large datasets. You use generators for such cases, which loads data as and when required.

So, the median dimensions for the image shape comes at 130 and hence you can safely rescale all of the images to a standard shape of (128,128,3).

Also, to reshape, the Keras preprocessing library will use bilinear interpolation, which is the default option so you will just use it (*bi* here means two dimensions (x,y) of the image).

```
import numpy as np
import pandas as pd
import tensorflow as tf
import matplotlib.pyplot as plt
from sklearn.model_selection import train_test_split

import tensorflow_federated as tff

    IMG_HEIGHT = 128
    IMG_WIDTH = 128
    BATCH_SIZE = 32

    train_ds = tf.keras.preprocessing.image_dataset_from_directory(BASE_DIR,
    seed=123,
    labels='inferred',
    label_mode='int',
image_size=(IMG_HEIGHT, IMG_WIDTH),
    color_mode='rgb',
```

```
    subset="training",
shuffle=True,
    validation_split = 0.2,
batch_size= BATCH_SIZE)
```

```
    Found 27558 files belonging to 2 classes.
    Using 22047 files for training.
```

```
    val_ds = tf.keras.preprocessing.image_dataset_from_directory(BASE_DIR,
    seed=123,
    labels='inferred',
    label_mode='int',
image_size=(IMG_HEIGHT, IMG_WIDTH),
    color_mode='rgb',
    subset="validation",
shuffle=True,
    validation_split = 0.2,
batch_size= BATCH_SIZE)
```

```
    Found 27558 files belonging to 2 classes.
    Using 5511 files for validation.
```

Note   TF 2.2.0, which has been the version thus far in our journey, doesn't support the `image_dataset_from_directory` function so it is recommended to use the latest TensorFlow Federated library, which by default installs TF 2.3.0. In TF 2.3 and onwards `image_dataset_from_directory` is supported.

You can also see the class names that the labels are mapped to.

```
class_names = train_ds.class_names
print(class_names)
```

Output:

```
    ['Parasitized', 'Uninfected']
```

This means integer 0 is the class `Parasitized` and 1 is the class `Uninfected`.

The malaria dataset is a large dataset. Depending on your machine setting, you can either load the full data into memory or not. To avoid any issues during runtime, you will enclose your federated data creation in a `try-catch` block.

```
NUM_CLIENTS = 10 # Local Nodes
CLIENT_LR = 1e-2
SERVER_LR = 1e-2 # Central Node
```

```
NUM_BATCH_CLIENT = int(len(train_ds)/NUM_CLIENTS)
```

```
import collections
    client_train_dataset = collections.OrderedDict()
    skip = 0
try :
        for i in range(1, NUM_CLIENTS+1):
            client_name = "Client_" + str(i)
        take = NUM_BATCH_CLIENT
        client_data = train_ds.skip(skip).take(take)
        x_train, y_train = zip(*client_data)

            print(f"Adding data from Batch No {skip} to {take*i} for client :
            {client_name}")

        # We are going to unbatch and load the data to prevent data
        dropping in creating client data later on
            data = collections.OrderedDict((('label', [y for x in y_train
                                            for y in x]),
                                            ('pixels', [y for x in x_train
                                            for y in x])))
        client_train_dataset[client_name] = client_data
        skip = take*i
except Exception as e:
        print("Memory Error - Client Data creation stopped")
        print(f"Total number of clients created are {len(client_train_
        dataset)}")
    NUM_CLIENTS = len(client_train_dataset)
```

Output

```
Adding data from Batch No 0 to 68 for client : Client_1
Adding data from Batch No 68 to 136 for client : Client_2
Adding data from Batch No 136 to 204 for client : Client_3
Adding data from Batch No 204 to 272 for client : Client_4
Adding data from Batch No 272 to 340 for client : Client_5
```
```
Memory Error - Client Data creation stopped
    Total number of clients created are 4
```

In the above code you are trying to create an ordered dictionary so that the order of clients is maintained while creating client data from tensor slices.

As I said, you can start with an expected number of clients but depending on the compute resources available in your local you can expect a lower number of clients as well. Here you are finally left with four clients and hence reduced data for training. For now you shouldn't worry about this as with a larger machine such issues can be easily mitigated.

Also, as per the TFF team, "our near-term future roadmap includes a high-performance runtime for experiments with very large data sets and large numbers of clients."

Next, you create client data in a simulation environment by passing a key-value pair of client data (see Figure 7-9).

```
train_dataset = tff.simulation.FromTensorSlicesClientData(client_train_
dataset)
    sample_dataset = train_dataset.create_tf_dataset_for_client(train_
    dataset.client_ids[0])
sample_element = next(iter(sample_dataset))
```

The total number of training examples at a local node is

```
len(sample_dataset)
```

Output

```
2176
```

```
    plt.imshow(sample_element['pixels'].numpy().astype('uint8'))
plt.grid(False)
plt.show()
```

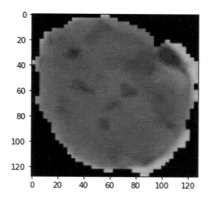

Figure 7-9. *Image from the federated data*

At this point, once you have the federated data available, since this is a simulation environment you can do several tests to check the intensity of non-iid behavior of the client's data. I will leave this exercise for you to explore and experiment with, but keep in mind that in a real-world setting this type of analysis is not possible as the data is not available centrally.

Preprocessing Input Data

For preprocessing, you must make sure of the following:

- Data quality

    - You have normalized the pixel values by rescaling all of the channels by multiplying pixel intensities by 1/255.

    - Proper scale: Already ensured when loaded

    - Augmentation to create more data and avoid overfitting the OOB/Validation dataset. Since the case study is meant to discover federated principles, you will skip this for now and return to it in Chapter 8.

- Training improvements:

    - Create batches for training using gradient descent

    - Shuffle to induce randomness and make the loss independent of sample selection

- Prefetch certain samples to reduce possibility of lag in training since you have to run preprocessing because the samples are used for training

```
SHUFFLE_BUFFER = len(sample_dataset) # How much data to shuffle
    EPOCHS = 5 # Number of epochs to run for training @ individual node
    PREFETCH_BUFFER = 100 # Preloading some number of samples to aid faster
    training.

# Normalizing the pixel values
    normalization_layer = tf.keras.layers.experimental.preprocessing.
    Rescaling(1.0/255)

    def preprocess(dataset):

        def batch(sample):
            _x = normalization_layer(sample['pixels'])
        return collections.OrderedDict(
            x = _x
                y = tf.reshape(sample['label'], [-1, 1]))

    return dataset.repeat(EPOCHS).shuffle(SHUFFLE_BUFFER).batch(
            BATCH_SIZE).map(batch).prefetch(PREFETCH_BUFFER)
```

Creating Federated Data

Since you have the preprocess function ready, you can finally create the final federated data by creating an iterator of the client dataset.

Also, in a real-world setting you generally select a sample of clients from a large population of clients, as only a fraction of them are available (cross-device setting).

```
selected_clients = np.random.choice(train_dataset.client_ids,NUM_CLIENTS,
replace = False)
federated_train_data = (preprocess(train_dataset.create_tf_dataset_for_
client(i)) for i in selected_clients)
```

You also use the sample batch created earlier to create a sample preprocessed federated dataset as it can be later used for input specification.

```
sample_federated_dataset = preprocess(sample_dataset)
```

Federated Communications

Within the TFF framework, any model that is trained locally needs to be wrapped in the `tff.learning.Model` interface. This allows two things:

- Helps in computing federated metrics and performance at individual nodes

- A set of variables are impacted in silos on each local node.

You start by creating a train model function that builds the NNet architecture you are using.

- The Conv2D layer is to do a convolution operation over the input images to capture locality effects for each pixel.

- The Pooling layer is to reduce the dimensions and concentrate information.

- You drop out random neurons during training to prevent overfitting.

- Finally, you add a dense layer after flattening the 2-D output from the dropout layer for prediction.

```
def train_model():
model = Sequential([
        tf.keras.layers.InputLayer(input_shape=(IMG_HEIGHT,IMG_WIDTH, 3)),
    # Ingesting a 2-d Image with 3 channels
        tf.keras.layers.Conv2D(16, 3, padding='same', activation='relu'),
    # Max pooling to reduce dimensions
    tf.keras.layers.MaxPooling2D(),
        tf.keras.layers.Conv2D(32, 3, padding='same', activation='relu'),
    tf.keras.layers.MaxPooling2D(),
        tf.keras.layers.Conv2D(64, 3, padding='same', activation='relu'),
    tf.keras.layers.MaxPooling2D(),
    # Dropout to prevent over-fitting
```

```
        tf.keras.layers.Dropout(0.2),
    # Flattening to feed data for sigmoid activation
    tf.keras.layers.Flatten(),
        tf.keras.layers.Dense(128, activation='relu'),
        tf.keras.layers.Dense(len(class_names)-1, activation = 'sigmoid')
])
```

```
return model
```

```
def federated_train_model():
local_train_model = train_model()
return tff.learning.from_keras_model(
    local_train_model,
    input_spec=sample_federated_dataset.element_spec,
    loss=tf.keras.losses.BinaryCrossentropy(),
    metrics=[tf.keras.metrics.AUC()])
```

Next, you create the process for the central server to make updates for the central model using parameter updates from all of the local nodes.

```
parameter_iteration_process = tff.learning.build_federated_averaging_process(
    federated_train_model,
    client_optimizer_fn = lambda: tf.keras.optimizers.SGD(learning_rate=
    CLIENT_LR),
    server_optimizer_fn = lambda: tf.keras.optimizers.SGD(learning_rate=
    SERVER_LR))
```

TFF has constructed a pair of federated computations and packaged them into a tff.templates.IterativeProcess in which these computations are available as a pair of properties called initialize and next.

- initialize represents the state of the Federated Averaging process on the server. It consists of

  - **Model**: The initial parameters distributed to all devices

  - **Optimizer state**: Maintained for federated metrics calculation and averaging. It keeps track of gradient updates.

  - Delta aggregates

- The next_fn will make use of the client_update and server_update and represents one cycle of federated averaging.

```
state = parameter_iteration_process.initialize()

state, metrics = parameter_iteration_process.next(state, federated_train_data)
    print('round 1, metrics={}'.format(metrics))
```

Output

```
round 1, metrics=OrderedDict([('broadcast', ()), ('aggregation',
OrderedDict([('value_sum_process', ()), ('weight_sum_process', ())])),
('train', OrderedDict([('auc', 0.5897039), ('loss', 0.6823319)]))])
```

Similarly, you can have multiple rounds.

```
NUM_ROUNDS = 6 # Total 5 rounds of training
for round_num in range(2, NUM_ROUNDS):
state, metrics = parameter_iteration_process.next(state, federated_
train_data)
    print('round {:2d}, metrics={}'.format(round_num, metrics))
```

Output

```
round 2, metrics=OrderedDict([('broadcast', ()), ('aggregation',
OrderedDict([('value_sum_process', ()), ('weight_sum_process', ())])),
('train', OrderedDict([('auc', 0.60388386), ('loss', 0.67804503)]))])
round 3, metrics=OrderedDict([('broadcast', ()), ('aggregation',
OrderedDict([('value_sum_process', ()), ('weight_sum_process', ())])),
('train', OrderedDict([('auc', 0.61434853), ('loss', 0.6752475)]))])
round 4, metrics=OrderedDict([('broadcast', ()), ('aggregation',
OrderedDict([('value_sum_process', ()), ('weight_sum_process', ())])),
('train', OrderedDict([('auc', 0.62443274), ('loss', 0.67076266)]))])
round 5, metrics=OrderedDict([('broadcast', ()), ('aggregation',
OrderedDict([('value_sum_process', ()), ('weight_sum_process', ())])),
('train', OrderedDict([('auc', 0.6333971), ('loss', 0.6674127)]))])
```

Some of you might find the training process (convergence) to be a little slow. Actually this is due to a lower server learning rate. I kept it at 0.1. If you keep it at 1, that means each iteration contributes in full strength to the central model's parameters. In other words the updates are completely learned.

Note   If you are running the same code in a Jupyter notebook, you must allow async operations. In Python, you can do it by calling

---

```
import nest_asyncio
nest_asyncio.apply()
```

Evaluation

The TensorFlow library provides build_federated_evaluation, which allows aggregation of metrics via federated communication (across local nodes).

```
    def evaluate(train_fn, state, train_data, test_data):

    # Print training metrics
    evaluation = tff.learning.build_federated_evaluation(train_fn)
    train_metrics = evaluation(state.model, train_data)
        print("Training Metrics: AUC : {}, Binary Cross Entropy Loss: {}".
        format(
            train_metrics['auc'],
            train_metrics['loss']))

    # Print testing metrics
    test_metrics = evaluation(state.model, test_data)
        print("Validation Metrics:  AUC: {}, Binary Cross Entropy
        Loss: {}".format(
            test_metrics['auc'],
            test_metrics['loss']))
```

You have to pass the validation set in the same format as the train data. In order to do so, you create a client_test_dataset which is a dictionary that contains validation data for each local node or server node.

All of the validation is then processed for evaluation using the `preprocess()` function defined above.

```
val_dataset = tff.simulation.FromTensorSlicesClientData(client_test_dataset)
federated_val_data = [preprocess(val_dataset.create_tf_dataset_for_
client(i)) for i in selected_clients]
```

```
evaluate(federated_train_model, state, federated_train_data,
federated_val_data)
```

Output

```
Training Metrics: AUC : 0.6697379946708679, Binary Cross Entropy Loss:
0.6773737072944641
Validation Metrics: AUC: 0.6535744071006775, Binary Cross Entropy Loss:
0.6790395379066467
```

In this section, I discussed the TF learning API. TFF also offers the core API where you can modify several different components of what TFF has to offer like Federated Averaging techniques and Federated Communications (across device network loads and local processing).

Conclusion

Federated learning is an evolving field and is bound to grow as the need for protecting private and expensive data becomes common. In this chapter, you covered privacy mechanisms of differential privacy and multi-party communication in detail, but new research is constantly happening. "A Survey on Federated Learning Systems: Vision, Hype and Reality for Data Privacy and Protection" by Qinbin et al is an excellent paper that unwraps different layers about federated learning.

Having said that, federated learning is not the only way to do protected learning. People are also researching peer-to-peer systems in which there are no central servers orchestrating the work; instead it is self-governed. The reliability of such systems in real-world setting is yet to be established.

Lastly, several companies like Owkin, Google, and Apple are actively investing in federated technologies especially around drug discoveries for patients, typing recommendations, and improving chatbots, respectively. In my opinion, the pace at which ML products are hitting the markets to solve vernacular problems across nations' federated learning means it's an important technology to use.

CHAPTER 8

Medical Imaging

Medical image analysis has evolved dramatically over the last three decades. Initially the analysis in this area was seen as applying pattern recognition and actuarial computer vision methodologies, but with the wide-scale use of advanced image processing and deep learning-based methodologies, the field has evolved quickly not just in terms of algorithmic advancements but also in terms of handling a wide variety of data as different modalities have emerged during this time-frame.

In this case study, you will be touching upon many different aspects of medical imaging. You will be especially focused on seeing the different types of medical data and how is this medical image data captured, digitally stored, and distributed. You will not be touching upon the physics of how these images are formed based on tissue-energy interaction and related statistics.

You will deep-dive into two end applications of image segmentation and classification using both 2-D and 3-D images. Lastly, you will explore various challenges that currently exist such as image quality, explainability, and adversarial attacks.

What Is Medical Imaging?

Medical imaging involves scientific analysis of biomedical images on different image modalities such as X-ray, CT, MRI, etc. to monitor health (via screening), diagnosis, and treatment of diseases and injuries.

These biomedical images are measurements of the human body, organs, or tissues on different scales like macroscopic, mesoscopic, and microscopic. These scales differ on penetration depth and image resolution, as shown in Figures 8-1 and 8-2.

© Anshik 2021
Anshik, *AI for Healthcare with Keras and Tensorflow 2.0*, https://doi.org/10.1007/978-1-4842-7086-8_8

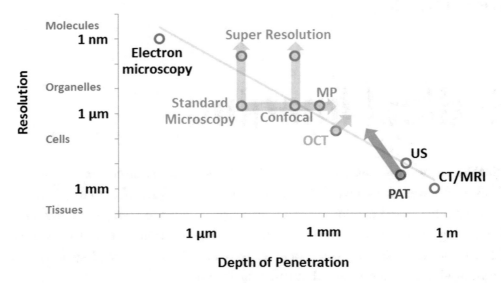

Figure 8-1. *Overview of the optical resolution technique. Source: The Optical Society (OSA)*

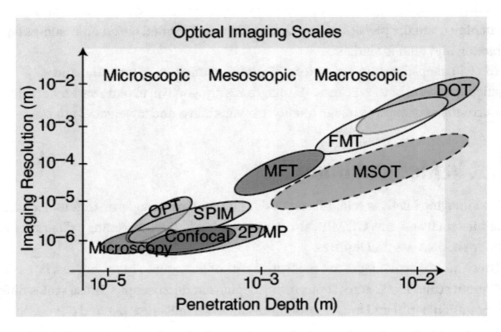

Figure 8-2. *Comparison of optical imaging techniques based on their scales. Source: Subhamoy Mandal et al, "Extending Biological Imaging to the Fifth Dimension"*

Biomedical images are sourced using different imaging modalities which measure different physical properties of the human body.

Image Modalities

Image modalities are various ways to capture organ/tissue characteristics in the form of n-dimensional images by leveraging interaction with the energy type used in the technique/device. For example,

- Radiation absorption in X-ray imaging

- Acoustic pressure in ultrasounds

- Radio frequency (RF) signal amplitude in MRIs

MRI, ultrasound, X-ray, and CT are some of the major image modalities but there are many more, as shown in Figure 2. So many modalities exist because of the simple reason that a single technique is not enough to capture human anatomy and physiology.

In order to provide a brief overview of these techniques, Table 8-1 compares and contrasts the major modalities.

Table 8-1. *Comparing Different Image Modalities*

S. No.	Modalities	Application	Main Characteristic	Shortcomings	Radiation
1	X-rays	Non-uniformly composed materials like bones. These images help in the assessment of the presence or absence of disease, damage, or a foreign object.	Image obtained through the use of X-rays. Non-invasive and painless.	Sometimes structures overlap and can create problems in interpretation.	Ionizing

(*continued*)

Table 8-1. (*continued*)

S. No.	Modalities	Application	Main Characteristic	Shortcomings	Radiation
2	CT	Non-uniformly composed materials like bones. These images help in assessment of the presence or absence of disease, damage, or a foreign object.	Scanning is done using X-rays and later A computer is used to construct a series of cross-sectional images. This eliminates superposition.	High dose of ionizing radiation, and hence can cause carcinogenic diseases in future.	Ionizing
3	MRI	Generally used to analyze torn ligaments and tumors. Also helps examine the brain and spinal cord.	Uses magnetic signals and radio waves.	Strong signals can cause claustrophobic tendencies.	Non-Ionizing
4	Ultrasound	Primarily fetus imaging. Also used for imaging of abdominal organs, heart, breast, muscles, tendons, arteries, and veins.	Uses high frequency sound signals to image internal structures such as organs, soft tissues, and unborn babies.	Prone to noise, and the process is driven by a radiologist and hence is prone to human error.	Non-Ionizing

So why are we even interested in understanding these modalities?

Firstly, to understand that depending upon the use case on hand we must carefully select the modality to use.

- Increased sensitivity towards finding the problem (foreign object/ vascular problems, etc.)

- 3-D image modalities allow better localization as compared to 2-D image modalities like X-ray.

- Better delineation between tissue types. For example, as shown in Figure 8-3, if the objective is to find injured brain tissue from a stroke, you can see that a MRI image shows clearly the damaged area as compared to a CT, where most of the area is dark.

CT Scan of a Brain (Axial)

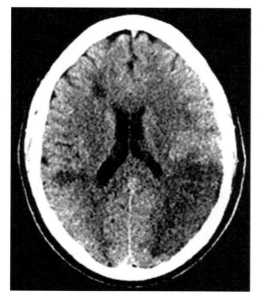

MRI Scan of a Brain (Axial)

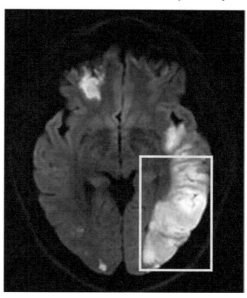

Figure 8-3. *An MRI scan shows the injured brain tissue much more clearly than a CT*

Secondly, these modalities can differ in how they capture the value. Because there are pixel intensities for digital images, there are different metrics for measuring information values in digital medical images.

CT scans and X-ray Hounsfield units (HU) are used to measure intensities of ionizing radiation. A higher HU means that it is more difficult for radiation to pass through, hence there is higher attenuation. See Figure 8-4.

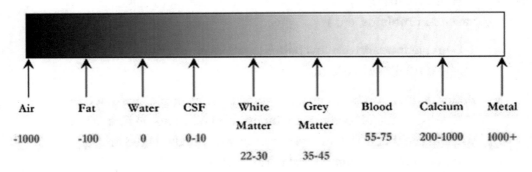

Figure 8-4. *Hounsfield scale ranging from -1000 to + 1000. Source: Osborne et al,* www.southsudanmedicaljournal.com/

Note the many shades of gray. It is impossible for human eyes or even computers in some cases to work on such a small gradient, hence a technique called windowing is used to look at areas of interest such as soft tissue, lungs, and bone. A window level of L and a width of W are decided. Then the gradients are maintained only for the range $L - w/2$ to $L + w/2$ and the rest is made black (less than L - W/2) and white (greater than L + W/2) completely. All of these important decisions are made and known before we model such images.

Lastly, different modalities can use different contrasting agents to highlight certain tissue areas. Since tissues differ in their rate of agent absorption, certain tissues stand out. CT imaging uses an iodine base while MRIs uses a gadolinium base, which is generally given orally (like tablets) or intravenously (pumped into bloodstream directly). As shown in Figure 8-5, due to the use of a contrasting agent, after some time (20-30 second delay) you can see that carcinogenic nodules are highlighted in the liver.

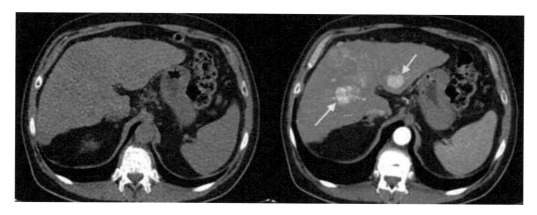

Figure 8-5. *A contrast agent highlights certain tissue areas*

Data Storage

Before we dive deeper into how to handle multiple dimensional image formats and make a machine learning model on them, let's quickly learn about the standard file formats you will find medical image data to be in and the different components.

A typical medical image is made up of four basic components:

- Pixel depth

- Pixel data

- Metadata

- Photometric interpretation

Let's understand this with a very simple example. Suppose you have a black and white image in which you have various intensities of grayscale and you know various other information like the who, what, and when of this image.

From this description, various elements correspond to the basic components you just learned about.

- **The black and white image** tells us about the channels used and hence the photometric interpretation of the image. An image can be monochromatic or colored.

- **Various intensity levels** hint towards two things. Firstly, it tells us about the pixel depth, which is the number of bits used to encode information. For example, an 8-bit pixel can include 28 intensity levels (unsigned being 0 to 255). Secondly, it tells us about the pixel intensity values as well as the range of pixel values.

- **Other information** is the metadata like study date, modality of the image, patient sex, shape, etc.

Special data requires special formats. There are predominantly six different formats for images collected from radiography modalities.

- DICOM (Digital Imaging and Communications in Medicine)

- NIFTI (Neuroimaging Informatics Technology Initiative)

- PAR/REC (Philips MRI scanner formats)

- ANALYZE (Mayo Medical Imaging)

- NRRD (Nearly Raw Raster Data)

- MINC (`www.bic.mni.mcgill.ca/ServicesSoftware/MINC`).

Of these six different formats, DICOM and NIFTI are the most widely used. The main difference between DICOM and NIFTI is that the raw image data in DICOM is stored as a collection of 2-D slice files, making the structure a little cumbersome for 3-D data analysis, whereas in NIFTI we have the entire 3-D image.

All of these different formats, besides just handling, storing, printing, and transmitting information, also help you to get all the features you need for your machine learning model, and as a data scientist this where you should concentrate: on which format can give what kind of information.

In sections ahead, you'll use one example from DICOM and another from NIFTI in order to make you familiar with these formats.

Dealing with 2-D and 3-D Images

Of the modalities we have discussed only X-ray imaging creates a 2-D image. CTs and MRIs create 3-D images because they capture information from various angles. There are two other type of modalities that help us capture 2-D data:

- **Fundal imaging**: Used to scan the health of tiny vessels in the eye. Generally used to identify diabetic retinopathy (DR).

- **Pathology imaging**: Cell-level imaging (remember the last chapter) obtained by staining the cell so that different cell structures appear in different colors and are then digitized.

In this chapter, however, we will be covering 2-D image analysis via the X-ray modality.

Similarly, 3-D images are not limited to CTs and MRIs. Other modalities like ultrasound and PET/SPECT scans also produce 3-D images meant for understanding different parts of the human body. We can consider 3-D images as a stack of 2-D images, such that these images are taken from different angles and then stitched together to create a comprehensive 3-D view.

In this chapter, we will be covering 3-D image analysis via the MRI modality.

You might sometimes hear the term *4-D image*. Well, don't be surprised. It is just several 3-D images captured across time or in different submodalities, like in the case of MRI T1, T2, etc. I won't be covering it, but if you're interested, I urge you to have a look at the paper by Li et al titled "Advances in 4D Medical Imaging and 4D Radiation Therapy."

Handling 2-D Images

You will take the RSNA Pneumonia detection challenge by the Radiological Society of North America. Organized on Kaggle, it has data in the DICOM format. Although the challenge was organized to locate lung capacities on chest radiographs, the DICOM metadata file also contains the following labels for the image:

- Normal

- No Lung Opacity/Not Normal

- Lung Opacity

Hence, you will be using the same labels for your image classification as well.

RSNA organizes competitions on medical imaging each year. Check out their space for different datasets and competitions: `www.rsna.org/education/ai-resources-and-training/ai-image-challenge`.

DICOM in Python

Your directory should look something like this:

```
Data/
    ...2d_lung_opacity_challenge/
......Train/
        .........000db696-cf54-4385-b10b-6b16fbb3f985.dcm
        .........000fe35a-2649-43d4-b027-e67796d412e0.dcm
......Test/
        .........00b4e593-fcf8-488c-ae55-751034e26f16.dcm
        .........00f376d8-24a0-45b4-a2fa-fef47e2f9f9e.dcm
......stage_2_detailed_class_info.csv
```

- Downloaded separate ZIP files from the data section of the Kaggle notebook and create the directory in the format shown above.

- `stage_2_detailed_class_info.csv` contains the label for each patient-id, while each DICOM file in the `train` and `test` folders is named `patient-id`.

- `stage_2_train_labels.csv` contains the target label Pneumonia or No-Pneumonia for each patient-id from both the `train` and `test` folders.

The DICOM file contains a combination of header metadata and the raw image pixel array. In Python, you can use a library called `pydicom` to deal with the DICOM files.

Remember that we discussed how different image modalities can introduce new preprocessing steps other than a typical image analysis pipeline? Happily, in your case you already have preprocessed data. The data shared by RSNA is preprocessed on two aspects:

- Converting a high dynamic range to 8-bit encoding with values ranging from 0 to 255 grayscale.

- Images are usually captured at a higher resolution, but for practical purposes the images are resized to 1024 x 1024 matrices.

For those who are still thinking how to do windowing and resizing if such preprocessing is not already done, here is some code:

```python
def windowed_image(img, center, width):
    img_min = center - width // 2
    img_max = center + width // 2
    windowed_image = img.copy()
    windowed_image[windowed_image < img_min] = img_min
    windowed_image[windowed_image > img_max] = img_max

    return windowed_image
```

You merge the target and the class data to understand the distribution better.

```python
import pandas as pd
import numpy as np
import matplotlib.pyplot as plt

import tensorflow as tf
import pydicom

import glob
import os

    BASE_DIR = "./Data"
    DATA_DIR = os.path.join(BASE_DIR,"2d_lung_opacity_challenge/")
    classes = pd.read_csv(glob.glob(os.path.join(DATA_DIR,"*.csv"))[0])
    target = pd.read_csv(glob.glob(os.path.join(DATA_DIR,"*.csv"))[1])

    train_labels = pd.merge(classes, target[["patientId","Target"]], on =
    "patientId", how="left")
```

Since there are multiple patientIds, there can be multiple bounding boxes for a single image. Just drop the duplicates.

```python
    assert train_labels.drop_duplicates().shape == train_labels.drop_
    duplicates('patientId').shape:

train_labels = train_labels.drop_duplicates().reset_index(drop = True)
```

```
print(train_labels.groupby(['class', 'Target']).size().reset_
index(name='Patient Count').to_markdown())
```

	class	Target	Patient Count
0	Lung Opacity	1	6012
1	No Lung Opacity / Not Normal	0	11821
2	Normal	0	8851

Wherever there is lung opacity, there is pneumonia. However, medically lung opacities can't wholly and solely determine pneumonia because the diagnosis requires other clinical information like laboratory data, symptoms, etc. But for simplicity, all lung opacities are termed as pneumonia. In a real world-setting, though, you can't make the same assumptions; you must consult proper medical researchers and radiologists to make such assumptions.

Next, Non-Pneumonia can be classified into No Lung Opacity/Not Normal and Normal. Well, normal images are those of a healthy chest. You can't say the same for No Lung Opacity/Not Normal. Let's look at a few of them.

```
def draw(input_ids):
# A maximum of 3 images in a row
    ncols, nrows = min(3,len(input_ids)), len(input_ids)//min(3,
    len(input_ids)) +1 if len(input_ids)%min(3,len(input_ids)) !=0 else
    len(input_ids)//min(3,len(input_ids))
# figure size, inches
    figsize = [10, 8]

# create figure (fig), and array of axes (ax)
fig, ax = plt.subplots(nrows=nrows, ncols=ncols, figsize=figsize)

# plot image for single sub-plot
for i, axi in enumerate(ax.flat):
    try:
        dicom_path = input_ids[i]
        data = pydicom.read_file(dicom_path)
        # one can also use plt.cm.bone
            axi.imshow(data.pixel_array, cmap="gray")
        # get indices of row/column
```

```
        rowid = i // ncols
        colid = i % ncols
    except IndexError as e:
        continue

# For some of you who want to add bounding box info to plots as
# well can access by row-id and col-id on the array of axes
# ax[row-id][col-id].plot()

plt.tight_layout(True)
plt.show()

np.random.seed(123)
examples_non_normal = np.random.choice(train_labels[train_labels["class"].\
                                            isin(["No Lung Opacity
/ Not Normal"])].patientId,
                                    size = 3,
                              replace = False)

examples_non_normal = [os.path.join(DATA_DIR,"Train",x+".dcm") for x in
examples_non_normal]

draw(examples_non_normal)
```

Some observations from Figure 8-6.

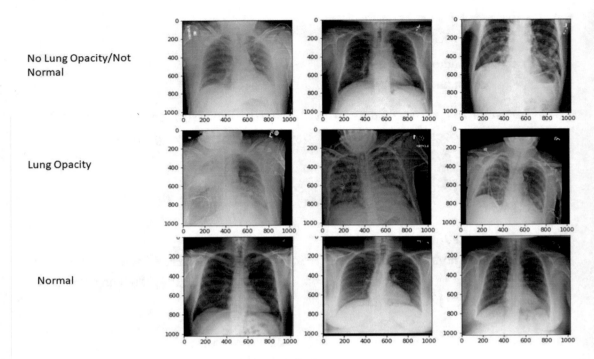

Figure 8-6. *Samples of three different labels*

- Lung Opacity images and No Lung Opacity/Not Normal images share some similar characteristics.

  - The presence of wires and tubes, which shows that there may be some other observed illness than pneumonia where Target is 0.

  - In most cases, the nature of gaps/opacity (gaps filled with fluid/pathogens, etc.) is different for both types although it can overlap due to a diffusion of foreign material in the lungs similar to COPD or asthma.

- Due to pleural effusion, accumulation of fluids or foreign materials can

  - Ooze out to make the lung look smaller. See sample 3 in the No Lung Opacity/Not Normal row.

  - The above can easily be confused with a Lung Opacity case and hence several radiologists may be consulted in such a case to reach a conclusion.

The objective of doing this analysis of a class label and not just following the target label blindly was to make you aware that medical image analysis requires some amount of domain knowledge to understand and implement a robust image analysis system. Especially if you plan to take the model live, the FDA will probe the risk associated with your model and in that case such subtle understanding comes in handy.

EDA on DICOM Metadata

You define a function to select important metadata from the DICOM files.

```
def get_metadata(patient_id):
    """

    Returns metadata from each dicom file
    """

    data = pydicom.read_file(os.path.join(DATA_DIR,"Train",
    patient_id+".dcm"),
                            stop_before_pixels=False)
_id = data.PatientID
_age = data.PatientAge
_sex = data.PatientSex
# col_spacing (horizontal)
    _pixelspacing_x = data.PixelSpacing[1]
# row_spacing (vertical)
    _pixelspacing_y = data.PixelSpacing[0]
_viewpos = data.ViewPosition
_mean = np.mean(data.pixel_array)
_min = np.min(data.pixel_array)
_max = np.max(data.pixel_array)
return pd.DataFrame([[_id, _age, _sex, _pixelspacing_x,
_pixelspacing_y, _viewpos ,_min, _max, _mean]],
                        columns = ["patientId","age","sex","pixel_
                        spacing_x","pixel_spacing_y","view_pos",
                                "min_pixint","max_pixint","mean_pixint"])
```

- Patient age

- Patient sex: There are just two categories, male and female

- Pixel spacing: A higher pixel spacing means less quality in the image

- View position: AP (ray goes from chest to back, laying down position; generally for ill or old-aged people) and PA (ray goes from back to chest, standing position)

Using parallel processing you capture all metadata to see its correlation and impact on the target variable.

```
from joblib import Parallel, delayed, parallel_backend
from tqdm import tqdm
    train_dicom = Parallel(n_jobs=os.cpu_count()-1, backend="threading")
    (delayed(get_metadata)(pt_id) for pt_id in tqdm(train_labels.
    patientId))
```

You then concatenate individual data frames returned from each DICOM.

```
    train_dicom_df = pd.concat(train_dicom, axis = 0)
```

Finally, you merge the target/label dataset with the metadata dataframe and create the data for analysis. See Figure 8-7.

```
# Train Labels with Metadata
    train_labels_w_md = pd.merge(train_labels, train_dicom_df, on =
    "patientId", how="left")
```

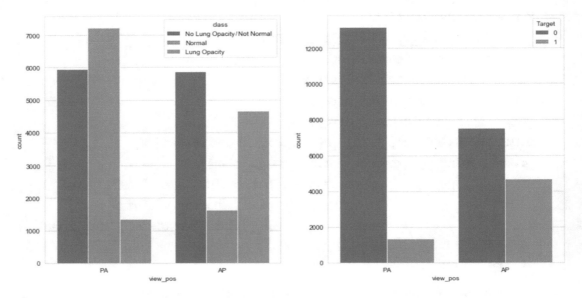

Figure 8-7. *Distribution of patients across view positions*

View Position

```
fig, axes = plt.subplots(1, 2, figsize=(14, 7))
sns.countplot(x='view_pos', hue='class', data=train_labels_w_md, ax=axes[0])
sns.countplot(x='view_pos', hue='Target', data=train_labels_w_md, ax=axes[1])
```

The view position look like an important variable, based on the following reasons:

- Although the number of patients with PA or AP positions are similar, the AP position has more pneumonia patients (Target = 1).

- Also, the lung opacity labels are pronounced for the AP view and the normal labels are more pronounced for the PA view.

Age

You plot the distribution of age against both the target and the class labels to check the distribution.

```
fig, axes = plt.subplots(1, 2, figsize=(14, 7))

p = sns.distplot(train_labels_w_md[train_labels_w_md['class']=='No Lung
Opacity / Not Normal']['age'],
            hist=True,
            kde=False,
                color='red',
                label='No Lung Opacity / Not Normal', ax=axes[0])
p = sns.distplot(train_labels_w_md[train_labels_w_
md['class']=='Normal']['age'],
            hist=True,
            kde=False,
                color='cornflowerblue',
                label='Normal', ax=axes[0])
p = sns.distplot(train_labels_w_md[train_labels_w_md['class']=='Lung
Opacity']['age'],
            hist=True,
            kde=False,
                color='lime',
                label='Lung Opacity', ax=axes[0])
```

```
_ = p.legend()

    p = sns.distplot(train_labels_w_md[train_labels_w_md['Target']==0]['age'],
                hist=True,
                kde=False,
                    color='gray',
                    label='0', ax=axes[1])
    p = sns.distplot(train_labels_w_md[train_labels_w_md['Target']==1]['age'],
                hist=True,
                kde=False,
                    color='lime',
                    label='1', ax=axes[1])
_ = p.legend()
```

As you can see in Figure 8-8, the Age category doesn't show any distinctive characteristics for any target, 0 or 1, likewise for the Class labels. However, certain groups with a spacing of 20 can be formed.

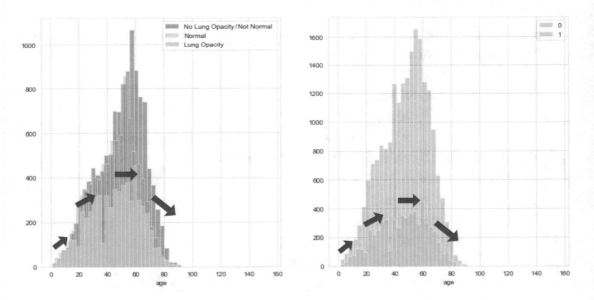

Figure 8-8. *Distribution of patients across age*

Sex

You do two analyses on the Sex column.

- Check the distribution of patients across different targets and labels for different sexes.

  - Although the distribution is not structurally different, women generally have a higher pneumonia percentage (see Figure 8-9).

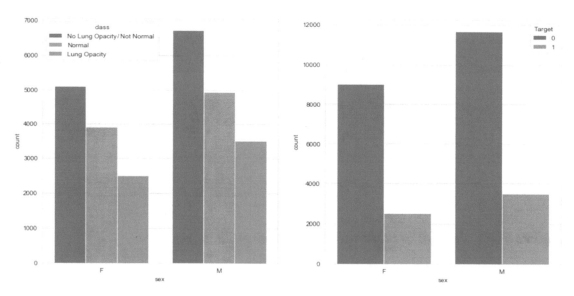

Figure 8-9. *Distribution of patients across the Sex column*

- Age and sex correlation

  - Both sexes show the same distribution pattern, with normal patients generally having lower age mean as compared to No Lung Opacity/Not Normal patients (see Figure 8-10).

```
fig, axes = plt.subplots(1, 2, figsize=(14, 7))
sns.countplot(x='sex', hue='class', data=train_labels_w_md, ax=axes[0])
sns.countplot(x='sex', hue='Target', data=train_labels_w_md, ax=axes[1])

train_labels_w_md["age"] = train_labels_w_md.age.apply(lambda x:int(x))

fig, axes = plt.subplots(1, 2, figsize=(14, 7))
```

```
sns.boxplot(x='sex', y = 'age', hue='class', data=train_labels_w_md,
ax=axes[0])
sns.boxplot(x='sex', y = 'age', hue='Target', data=train_labels_w_md,
ax=axes[1])
```

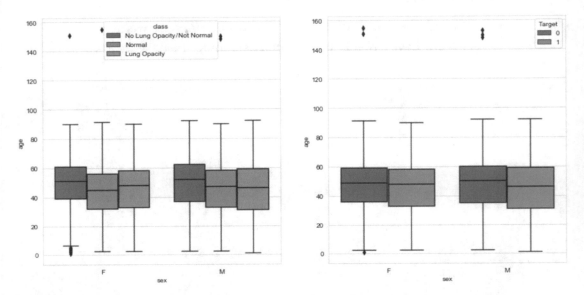

Figure 8-10. *Boxplot to see how age varies for different sexes*

Pixel Spacing

Pixel spacing represents the size of each pixel. Each pixel represents a certain patch of area on the image. Differing pixel spacing can lead to non-uniform distribution of spatial information. Let's see how pronounced this difference is.

Firstly, you round off the pixel spacing by two points.

```
train_labels_w_md["pixel_spacing_x_norm"] = train_labels_w_md.pixel_
spacing_x.apply(lambda x: round(float(x),2))
train_labels_w_md["pixel_spacing_y_norm"] = train_labels_w_md.pixel_
spacing_y.apply(lambda x: round(float(x),2))
```

Next, you plot the patient counts.

```
fig, axes = plt.subplots(2, 2, figsize=(15, 10))
plot = sns.countplot(x='pixel_spacing_x_norm', hue='class', data=train_
labels_w_md, ax=axes[0][0])
plot.set_xticklabels([x for x in plot.get_xticklabels()],rotation=90)
plot.legend(loc='upper right')
plot = sns.countplot(x='pixel_spacing_x_norm', hue='Target',
data=train_labels_w_md, ax=axes[0][1])
plot.set_xticklabels([x for x in plot.get_xticklabels()],rotation=90)
plot.legend(loc='upper right')

sns.countplot(x='pixel_spacing_y_norm', hue='class', data=train_
labels_w_md, ax=axes[1][0])
plot.set_xticklabels([x for x in plot.get_xticklabels()],rotation=90)
plot.legend(loc='upper right')
sns.countplot(x='pixel_spacing_y_norm', hue='Target', data=train_
labels_w_md, ax=axes[1][1])
plot.set_xticklabels([x for x in plot.get_xticklabels()],rotation=90)
plot.legend(loc='upper right')
```

There are two main observations from Figure 8-11:

- Pixel spacing has good amount of variation, ranging from 0.13 to 0.2.

- Lung opacity is more observed for spacing between 0.15 to 0.17.

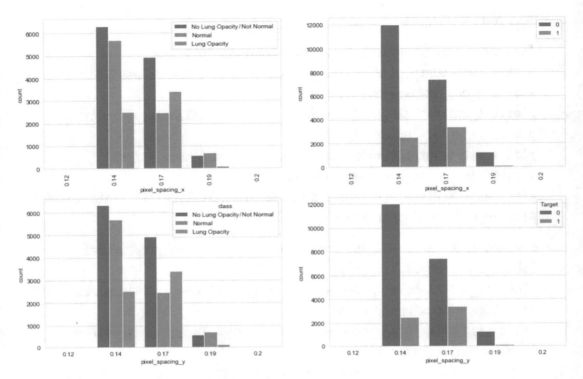

Figure 8-11. *Distribution of patients by pixel spacing*

Although you will not directly use pixel spacing, you will make the spatial information uniform, for which you will resample the images to 1mm X 1mm.

Mean Intensity

Lastly, you will see how the mean intensity varies for labels and targets. If you find different modes for the target or label, you will definitely try to include the metadata

In Figure 8-12, both Pneumonia and Non-Pneumonia patients follow a similar distribution and hence they don't give any special info about any of the classes.

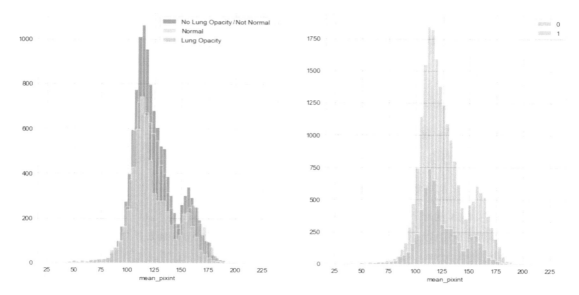

Figure 8-12. *Distribution of patients across mean intensity*

Note   In a similar way you can do many more analyses using DICOM metadata. I hope you got a fairly detailed understanding of dealing with DICOM files and also the metadata.

Handling 3-D Images

Handling a 3-D image is not very different from a 2-D one, but to make the things a little challenging let's learn about 3-D image handling in NIFTI. As in the previous section, this will set you up and prepare for the image segmentation case study ahead.

You are going to use the BRATS 2020 dataset from the Perelman School of Medicine at `www.med.upenn.edu/cbica/brats2020/data.html`. The BRATS 2020 data contains NIFTI files in various modes (made by varying pulse sequences in the MRI machine), namely

- Native (T1)

- Post-contrast T1-weighted (T1CE)

- T2-weighted (T2)

- T2 Fluid Attenuated Inversion Recovery (T2-FLAIR)

If you are interested in understanding the differences between pulse sequences, you can visit `https://radiopaedia.org/articles/mri-pulse-sequences-1?lang=us` and learn more.

Since your data is going to be 3-D data, let's understand what exactly makes it 3-D. In the medical system, our body can be divided into three planes:

- Axial/traverse: Top to bottom

- Sagittal: Left to right of the body

- Coronal: Posterior to anterior (back to front)

This is what gives three dimensions to a MRI images. In the DICOM images above, the images were shot only in the coronal plane and hence you saw a 2-D image. To learn more on this topic, please refer to `https://teachmeanatomy.info/the-basics/anatomical-terminology/planes/`.

Although the MRI data is taken from different clinical protocols and multiple scanners, they are already preprocessed in three ways:

- **Coregistered with the same anatomical template**: Since we are capturing multiple modes of a MRI, if a patient moves (even slightly) between acquiring these images it can cause misalignment when all the sequences are combined together for the segmentation task and hence a process called as *registration* is done to avoid such errors. Since this has already been done for you, you don't need to worry about it. See Figure 8-13.

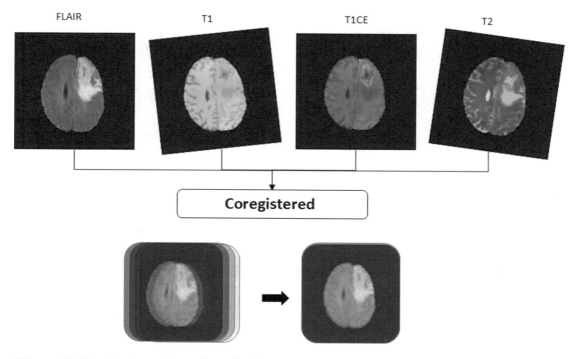

Figure 8-13. *Registration of medical images*

- **Interpolated with same resolution**: This just means that spatial information is uniform across the 3-D volume for all of the four sequences.

- **Skull-stripped**: In MRI images, it is a good practice to remove skull boundaries when solving tasks such as brain tumor segmentation for the simple reason that the skull boundary doesn't provide any information that helps solve the segmentation problem and hence we just strip it away. See Figure 8-14.

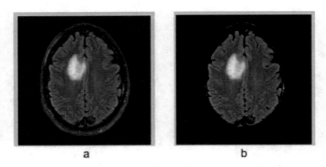

a   b

Figure 8-14. *Example of a skull-stripped image. (a) MRI image; (b) Skull-stripped MRI image. Source: "SVM-LWT Enabled Fuzzy Clustering-based Image Analysis for Brain Tumor Detection" by Arun et al in 2017*

Note   If tomorrow you start to use a different dataset, make sure you check for these three things for sure.

NIFTI Format

The NIFTI file format is not generated by scanners and hence the metadata information is not as rich compared to the DICOM file format, but it still has some metadata. Also, it represents the images series as a single file.

The coordinate system is a little different in the NIFTI files as compared to DICOM. It is good to know this difference because often you may want to keep files in the NIFTI format as the whole image series is present in a single file, unlike DICOM, so it easier to share and maintain. See Figure 8-15.

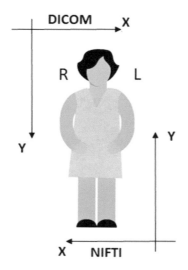

Figure 8-15. *Coordinate system in NIFTI images*

Finally, the units of measurement can be different in NIFTI and not fixed to mm like in DICOM. NIFTI stores the information on the unit of measurement separately (for example, pixel spacing info as you saw in DICOM).

Since NIFTI headers are not that elaborate compared to DICOM, in practice we rarely use NIFTI header info. Some of the important information to look out for is the following:

- Pixel spacing

- Dimensions for the three planes

- XYZ-T units

Introduction to MRI Image Processing

Let's quickly set up your input pipeline.

```
BASE_DIR = "./Data/3d_brain_tumor_segmentation/MICCAI_BraTS2020_TrainingData/"
label_paths = glob.glob(os.path.join(BASE_DIR,"**","*seg.nii"))
flair_paths = glob.glob(os.path.join(BASE_DIR,"**","*flair.nii"))
t1_paths = glob.glob(os.path.join(BASE_DIR,"**","*t1.nii"))
t1ce_paths = glob.glob(os.path.join(BASE_DIR,"**","*t1ce.nii"))
t2_paths = glob.glob(os.path.join(BASE_DIR,"**","*t2.nii"))

# Let's create a dictionary of dictionary to order the data
```

```
    full_data = {i:{'label':label,
        'flair':flair,
        't1':t1,
        't1ce':t1ce,
        't2':t2} for i, (label,flair,t1,t1ce,t2) \
 in enumerate(zip(label_paths,
                    flair_paths,
                    t1_paths,
                    t1ce_paths,
                    t2_paths))}
```

You already know that there are four different sequences and each of them can be viewed in three different ways across the axial, sagittal, and coronal planes.

```
    patient_id = 5
    k=1
    plt.figure(figsize=(20,20))
    for i,seq in enumerate(["flair","t1","t1ce","t2"]):
        img = io.imread(full_data[patient_id][seq], plugin='simpleitk')
        for j in range(3):
            if (j==0):
                plt.subplot(4,3,k)
                plt.imshow(img[100,:,:])
            # x-y plane
                plt.title("Axial/Traverse View")
                plt.ylabel(seq.upper())
                k=k+1
            elif (j==1):
                plt.subplot(4,3,k)
                plt.imshow(img[:,100,:])
                plt.title("Coronal View")
                k+=1
        else:
                plt.subplot(4,3,k)
                plt.imshow(img[:,:,100])
                plt.title("Sagittal View")
                k+=1
```

In Figure 8-16, you can clearly see how different modalities highlight different parts of the brain across different views and provide complementary information.

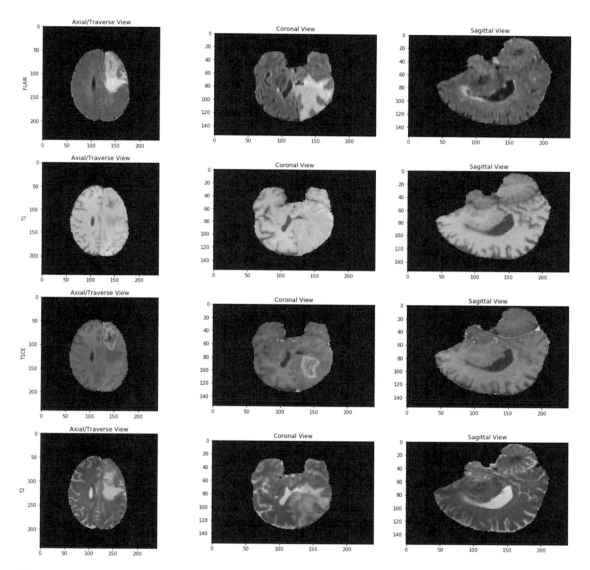

Figure 8-16. *Cross-ciew of MRI modes and views*

For the same patient, let's also have a look at the target label.

```
# For the same patient let's also have a look at the target label
    img = io.imread(full_data[patient_id]['label'], plugin='simpleitk')
    plt.figure(figsize = (20,20))
    k = 1
    for i in [50, 75,100, 125]:
        plt.subplot(1,4,k)
    plt.imshow(img[i,:,:])
        plt.title("Labels:- " + ", ".join([str(i) for i in
        np.unique(img[i,:,:])]))
        k+=1
```

As you can see in Figure 8-17, there are four different labels for the segmentation task. The tumor part is labeled with green, yellow, and blue (1, 2, and 4) while the background is labeled with purple (0)

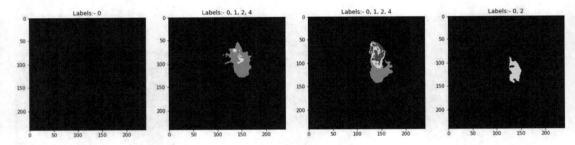

Figure 8-17. *Segmentation labels (in axial view)*

From the above plots in Figures 8-16 and 8-17, it is clear that

- Not all slices are important.

- Pixel intensities are not evenly distributed for different sequences.

- There is high imbalance in the pixel intensities of the segmentation labels (as most of the image has the purple color, followed by label 2, the yellow color).

Let's explore points 1 and 2 above and see what you get from these observations.

Non-Even Pixel Distribution

Let's quickly see how different sequences make pixel intensities vary. This will help you decide a normalization strategy for each of the sequences.

```python
import seaborn as sns
    sns.set_style('whitegrid')

    fig, axes = plt.subplots(nrows=4, ncols=4)
    fig.tight_layout(pad=1, w_pad=1, h_pad=0.5)
    fig.set_size_inches(20,20)
    k=1
    for patient_id in [5,10,20,50]:
        for i,seq in enumerate(["flair","t1","t1ce","t2"]):
            img = io.imread(full_data[patient_id][seq], plugin='simpleitk')
            if (i==0):
                plt.subplot(4,4,k)
                plt.hist(x= img.reshape(-1,1))
            plt.title(seq.upper())
                plt.ylabel("Patient "+str(patient_id))
                k=k+1
        else:
                plt.subplot(4,4,k)
                plt.hist(x= img.reshape(-1,1))
            plt.title(seq.upper())
                k+=1
```

You can clearly observe in Figure 8-18 that

- Most of the pixels have a 0 level of intensity and are right-skewed.

- For different sequences, different cutoffs can be observed for outlier treatment. For T1 and T1CE, it is around 500, while for FLAIR and T2, it varies from 300 t0 600.

- You must normalize this and deal with skewness.

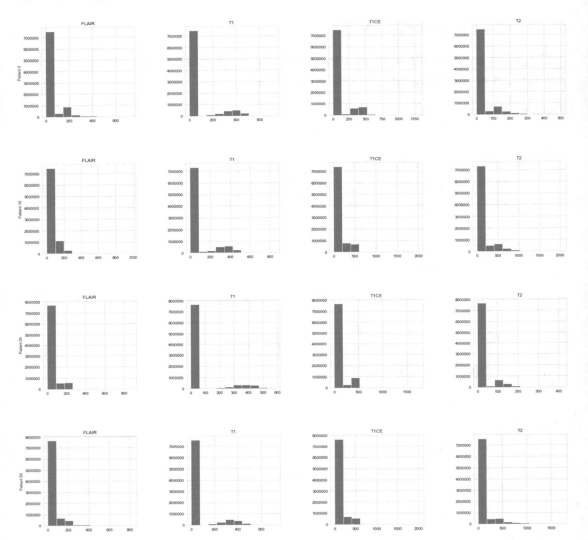

Figure 8-18. *Intensity variation across different MRI sequences across patients*

Correlation Test

To analyze whether you need to consider all of the slices or not, you can do a correlation test across the depth dimension. You will iterate across the depth of the image and calculate the correlation. To make your job easier, you will just convert this into a pandas dataframe and then calculate the correlation. The idea is that if the pixel intensities of adjacent or near adjacent slices don't vary, they will yield the correlation as NA because their covariance is 0.

Let's quickly plot some graphs to see which slices are not correlated.

```
    k = 1
from itertools import chain
    fig, axes = plt.subplots(nrows=1, ncols=4)
    fig.tight_layout(pad=0.5, w_pad=2, h_pad=0.5)
    fig.set_size_inches(13,5)
    for i,seq in enumerate(["flair","t1","t1ce","t2"]):
    _indices = []
        for patient_id in range(5,85,10):
            img = io.imread(full_data[patient_id][seq], plugin='simpleitk')
            depth_dimension = img.shape[0]
            _slice = np.array([list(img[i,:,:].reshape(-1,1)) for i in
            range(depth_dimension)])
            _slice = np.squeeze(_slice,axis = 2).T
        slice_df = pd.DataFrame(_slice)
        # correlation matrix
        _df = slice_df.corr()
        # indices or slice numbers whose correlation is nan
            _indices.append([y for x in np.argwhere(_df.isnull().all(axis=1).
            values) for y in x])
        plt.subplot(1,4,k)
    plt.hist(x= list(chain.from_iterable(_indices)))
    plt.title(seq.upper())
        k+=1
```

From Figure 8-19, you can clearly observe that

- Slice numbers from 0-5 and 140-154 in a general trend show no variation in intensities across all sequences and hence these slices can be ignored.

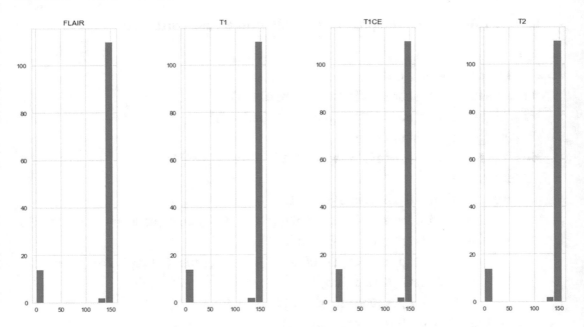

Figure 8-19. *Non-varying intensities across slices*

Cropping and Padding

There are other types of preprocessing that can be done, such as cropping the slices
to a lower dimension and then padding them to a standard one. This is usually done
to reduce the volume size. You will follow another method to reduce unnecessary
convolutions over the image volume. But you must be sure that after doing this there is
no misalignment, as illustrated in Figure 8-20.

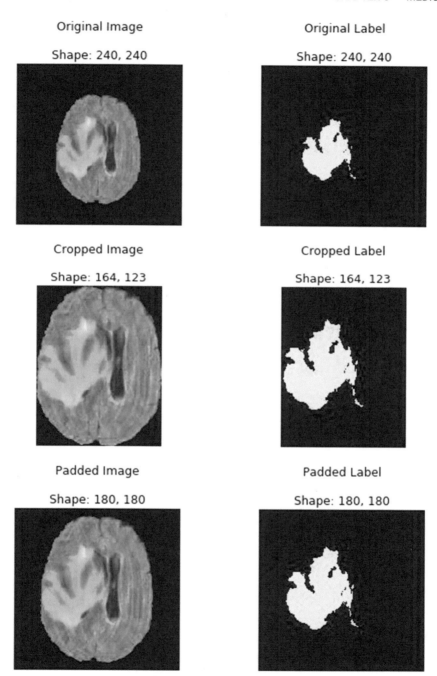

Figure 8-20. *Cropping the original image to reduce dimensions*

Although you can visibly see that the size has reduce without any loss of information, I think the most effective way is to handle it while creating a 3-D patch of the volume training data by setting thresholds on the patch volume, say at least 10% or 5% non-zero pixel intensity. More on this in later sections.

Image Classification on 2-D Images

The section called "Handling 2-D Images" covered in length many of the data attributes and what all you can do with them. Remember the discussion around pixel spacing and how you should resample your images to evenly distribute the spatial information? This preprocessing step helps you make processing using CNNs effectively such that kernels learn the same information from a unit of image. Kernels are filters (2-D matrices) that are used to extract features from images.

Image Preprocessing

Histogram Equalization

Sometimes due to poor contrast X-ray images need to be enhanced to highlight small textures and details. This is done basically to expand the range of values of pixels of the image. See Figure 8-21.

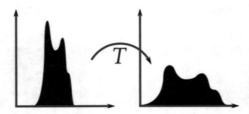

Figure 8-21. *Histogram equalization. Source: Wiki*

Now if your whole image is confined within a range of pixels, you can simply map the current pixel distribution to a wider and uniform distribution, but if there already exist regions of high and low intensity (a.k.a. larger range of pixel values) you must go local and apply something called *adaptive histogram equalization.*

Specifically you are going to use the CLAHE method. It can enhance the image local contrast and enhance the visibility of the edges and curves in each part of an image.

- **Contrast limiting**: If any of the histograms of the region are above the contrast limit, they are clipped.

- **Adaptive histogram equalization**: The image is divided into small blocks called tiles. These tiles are histogram equalized.

You will be using the OpenCv to histogram normalize your images. See the results in Figure 8-22.

```python
def histogram_equalization(img, clip_limit, grid_size):
    """

    Histogram Equalization
    """

    clahe = cv2.createCLAHE(clipLimit = clip_limit,
                            tileGridSize = grid_size)
    img_clahe = clahe.apply(img)

    return img_clahe
```

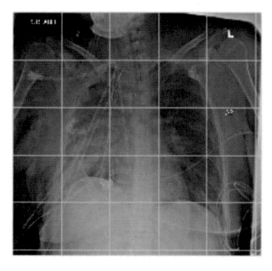

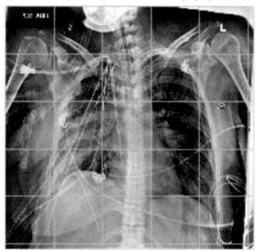

Figure 8-22. *Result of the histogram equalization*

Isotropic Equalization of Pixels

In order to ensure uniform pixel spacing, you must interpolate and resample your image.

```
def resample(img, x_pixel, y_pixel):
    new_size = [1, 1]

size = np.array([x_pixel, y_pixel])

img_shape = np.array(img.shape)

new_shape = img_shape * size
new_shape = np.round(new_shape)
resize_factor = new_shape / img_shape

resampled_img = scipy.ndimage.interpolation.zoom(img, resize_factor)

return resampled_img
```

Although your pixels are now properly spaced, this leads to a lower-shaped image, which means that different pixel spacing will lead to different image sizes, so now you must reshape them by cropping/padding/interpolation. I generally prefer interpolation to a fixed size because the difference between original and target shape isn't much. You will be using Opencv for the same.

Model Creation

Since you found some important information in the DICOM metadata, you will be creating a two-input, single-output neural network where one branch ingests a batch of 2-D images and another branch ingests scaled feature columns. See Figure 8-23.

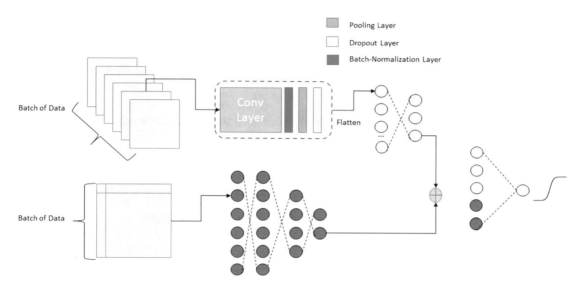

Figure 8-23. *Medical image classification model*

Some of you might not know the different layers and terms I am going to use next. I recommend going through this excellent guide shared by Dumoulin et al titled "A Guide to Convolution arithmetic for Deep Learning."

Let's start by importing the relevant libraries from the TensorFlow library.

```
from tensorflow.keras.models import Model, Sequential
from tensorflow.keras.layers import (
    Input,
    Conv2D,
    Dropout,
    MaxPooling2D,
    concatenate,
    BatchNormalization,
    Flatten,
    Dense
)
from tensorflow.keras.optimizers import Adam

METRICS = [
        tf.keras.metrics.AUC(name='auc'),
]
```

Next, you create a function that acts as the convolution block (shown by the dotted lines in Figure 8-23). You provide several controls to create this convolution block, namely

1) A convolution layer with any number of filters and a convolution of a specific `kernel_size`.

2) A `BatchNormalization` layer to normalize data in a batch such that covariate shifts between data are reduced.

3) `pooling` to reduce the feature space of an image by condensing information by using the maximum of pixel intensities in a kernel.

4) `dropout` to prevent overfitting by randomly dropping neurons while training.

```python
def convolution_block(input_layer, num_filters, kernel_size,
                      strides, padding = 'valid',
                      activation = 'selu',
                 batch_normalization = False,
                 pool_kernel = None, dropout_rate = None):

layer = Conv2D(num_filters, kernel_size, strides = strides,
               padding=padding, activation=activation)(input_layer)
if batch_normalization:
    layer = BatchNormalization()(layer)
if pool_kernel:
    layer = MaxPooling2D(pool_kernel)(layer)
if dropout_rate:
    layer = Dropout(dropout_rate)(layer)
return layer
```

Now you can build your main function that creates your intended network.

- Start by creating two input layers, which tells the model what size of input to expect.

- Then, depending on how many parameters you want to train, you can keep adding to the convolution block and choose the kernel and pooling accordingly. I generally prefer to start with large kernel size and no pooling. Then I introduce both in deeper layers.

```python
def build_model():
    input_img = Input(TARGET_SHAPE+(1,))
    input_feats = Input((6,))
    cb1 = convolution_block(input_img, num_filters = 128, kernel_size = 8,
                    strides = 1, padding = 'valid',
                batch_normalization = True,
                    activation = 'selu',
                pool_kernel = None, dropout_rate = None)
    cb2 = convolution_block(cb1, num_filters = 32, kernel_size = 8,
                    strides = 1, padding = 'valid',
                    activation = 'selu',
                    pool_kernel = 2, dropout_rate = None)
    cb3 = convolution_block(cb2, num_filters = 8, kernel_size = 8,
                    strides = 1, padding = 'valid',
                    activation = 'selu',
                    pool_kernel = 2, dropout_rate = 0.2)
    cb4 = convolution_block(cb3, num_filters = 4, kernel_size = 8,
                    strides = 1, padding = 'valid',
                    activation = 'selu',
                    pool_kernel = 2, dropout_rate = 0.2)

conv_flat = Flatten()(cb4)
    cl1 = Dense(128, activation='selu')(conv_flat)
    cl2 = Dense(64, activation='selu')(cl1)
    cl3 = Dense(32, activation='selu')(cl2)

# Feature block
    fl1 = Dense(4, activation='selu')(input_feats)

concat_layer = concatenate([cl3, fl1], axis = 1)

# prediction block
    pl1 = Dense(16, activation = 'selu')(concat_layer)
    pl2 = Dense(8, activation = 'selu')(pl1)
    output = Dense(1, activation = 'sigmoid')(pl2)

return Model([input_img, input_feats], output)
```

Preparing Input Data

Out-of-the-box generators in Keras don't support such multi-inputs so you must create your own custom generator.

You start with one-hot encoding the view position and the age bins, the two most important feature variables you found to be correlated with the target variable.

```
bin_labels = ['0_20', '20_40', '40_60', '60_80', '80_plus']
train_labels_w_md['age_bucketed'] = pd.cut(train_labels_w_md['age'].
astype(int),

                              bins = [0, 20, 40, 60, 80, max(train_
                              labels_w_md['age'].astype(int))],
                    labels = bin_labels)
```

View position is already a categorical variable and hence it can be directly one-hot encoded.

```
from sklearn.preprocessing import LabelBinarizer

age_binarizer = LabelBinarizer()
    age_binarizer.fit(train_labels_w_md['age_bucketed'])
    transformed_age = age_binarizer.transform(train_labels_w_md['age_bucketed'])
transformed_age_ohe = pd.DataFrame(transformed_age)
    transformed_age_ohe.columns = ["age_bin_trans_"+str(i) for i in
    range(len(age_binarizer.classes_))]

view_pos_binarizer = LabelBinarizer()
    view_pos_binarizer.fit(train_labels_w_md['view_pos'])
    transformed_view_pos = view_pos_binarizer.transform(train_labels_w_md[
    'view_pos'])
transformed_view_pos_ohe = pd.DataFrame(transformed_view_pos)
    transformed_view_pos_ohe.columns = ["view_pos_trans"]

    data = pd.concat([train_labels_w_md, transformed_age_ohe,
    transformed_view_pos_ohe], axis=1)
```

Next, you define a preprocessing function for your image array. Besides histogram equalization and isotropic equalization, you convert the images to a standard shape and also normalize pixel values by dividing each pixel by 255 (the maximum value of a pixel for your images).

You also add another dimension that acts as a channel. This is done to satisfy the Conv2D layer requirements.

```
def get_train_images(dicom_path, target_shape):
 img = pydicom.read_file(dicom_path)
    img_equalized = histogram_equalization(img.pixel_array, 4, (8,8))
    img_isotropic = resample(img.pixel_array, img.PixelSpacing[1],
    img.PixelSpacing[0])
 img_standardized = cv2.resize(img_isotropic, target_shape,
 interpolation = cv2.INTER_CUBIC)
 # Pixel Standardization
    img_standardized = np.array(img_standardized)/255
    res = np.expand_dims(img_standardized, axis = 2)
 return res
```

You create your training and validation sets.

```
from sklearn.model_selection import train_test_split
   train, val = train_test_split(data,test_size=0.25, random_state=42)

   TARGET_SHAPE = (224,224)
   BATCH_SIZE = 32
```

Finally, you create your generator, similar to the one you created in Chapter 4. You yield your multi-input to the network.

```
def get_data_generator(df, target_shape, shuffle = True, batch_size=32):
    """

    Generator function which yields the input data and output for
    different clusters
    """
 img, feat_set, y = [], [], []
 if shuffle:
        df = df.sample(frac=1).reset_index(drop=True)

 while True:
     for i,row in df.iterrows():
            feat_set.append(np.array(row[[x for x in df.columns if
            "_trans" in x]].tolist()))
```

```
            img.append(get_train_images(os.path.join(DATA_DIR,
            "Train",row['patientId'] + ".dcm"), TARGET_SHAPE))
            y.append(np.array([row['Target']]))

        if len(feat_set) >= batch_size:
            yield (np.array(img), np.array(feat_set)), y
            img, feat_set, y = [], [], []
```

Training

In training, you call the generator function separately for the training and validation sets. Please note that creating generators in such a fashion is not always recommended as the data pipeline is not optimized for things like prefetching and many of the data operations while creating batch data. You can avoid this if you have more compute and RAM to preprocess and store data in desired formats.

```
train_generator = get_data_generator(train, TARGET_SHAPE, True, BATCH_SIZE)
val_generator = get_data_generator(val, TARGET_SHAPE, True, BATCH_SIZE)

model = build_model()

    model.compile(optimizer= 'adam',
            loss = tf.keras.losses.BinaryCrossentropy(from_logits=True),
            metrics=METRICS)
```

As you can see in Figure 8-24, based on architecture, the number of training parameters is 526,217, which is nowhere close to what we expect from very large image models such as ImageNet. Hence, depending upon your compute resources, feel free to make a different architecture and experiment performance and convergence rate.

```
history = model.fit(train_generator,
                steps_per_epoch= len(train)//BATCH_SIZE,
                    epochs=10,
                validation_data=val_generator,
                validation_steps= len(val)//BATCH_SIZE)
```

```
concatenate (Concatenate)        (None, 36)          0          dense_2[0][0]
                                                                dense_3[0][0]
_____
dense_4 (Dense)                  (None, 16)          592        concatenate[0][0]
_____
dense_5 (Dense)                  (None, 8)           136        dense_4[0][0]
_____
dense_6 (Dense)                  (None, 1)           9          dense_5[0][0]
================================================================================
Total params: 526,473
Trainable params: 526,217
Non-trainable params: 256
```

Figure 8-24. *Model summary*

Image Segmentation for 3-D Images

I already discussed in depth various image analysis methodologies when I covered key challenges and key developments/solutions for each of these methodologies. In this section, you are going to focus on the image segmentation problem of a 3-D image.

Let's quickly recap key things about image segmentation:

- **What is it?** Image segmentation partitions a given image into various segments, also known as regions of interest, based on training data.

- **Key challenges for biomedical segmentation:**

  - Noise in a captured image can lead to non-uniform intensities.

  - The target organ or lesion may vary hugely in size and shape from patient to patient.

  - Class imbalance where the lesion/target organ occupies a very small area of the whole image can lead to ML models learning more about the background or local minima.

Image Preprocessing

Based on your analysis of the BRATS data in the section above and other general preprocessing recommended for MRI images, you will be doing the following preprocessing:

- Bias field correction

- Removing unwanted Slices

You will standardize your center pixel intensity and ignore empty volumes when creating patches for training.

Bias Field Correction

When capturing MRI images, a bias field can blur images by reducing high frequency content such as edges. It also affects the intensity of pixels such that the same tissue shows gray-level variation.

For the naked eye, the difference doesn't mean much, but for ML algorithms it can create a huge difference. Let's correct for this bias. You will be using the SimpleITK library for this, which provides N4 field correction. The N4 bias field correction algorithm is a popular method for correcting low frequency intensity non-uniformity present in MRI image data known as a bias or gain field. More details are at `https://simpleitk.readthedocs.io/en/master/link_N4BiasFieldCorrection_docs.html`

Since the edges/contours are affected by the bias field, you must use a thresholding algorithm to separate the background and foreground pixels. For this, you will use Otsu's Method. Note there are other automatic thresholding algorithms in the SimpleITK library such as Maximum Entropy, Triangle, etc. I urge you to try such different variations.

Otsu's Method is quite computationally extensive, so it can take a good amount of time to complete, so you will save the result of this bias correction in a separate folder.

```
NEW_BASE_DIR = os.path.join(os.path.split(BASE_DIR)[0],
                "PROCESSED_IMAGE")
```

You start by reading the image and then creating a mask using Otsu's method. This mask just contains 1 and 0 separating the foreground and background pixels. After this you field correct the input image using the threshold mask.

```
def correct_bias_field(input_path, output_path):
inputImage = sitk.ReadImage(input_path)
maskImage = sitk.OtsuThreshold( inputImage,
                        0, # Background Value
                        1, # Foreground Value
                        250 # Number of Histograms
                )
```

```
# Casting to allow real pixel value
inputImage = sitk.Cast( inputImage, sitk.sitkFloat32 )
corrector = sitk.N4BiasFieldCorrectionImageFilter()
output = corrector.Execute( inputImage, maskImage)
# Since our original image followed the 16-bit pixel format
outputCasted = sitk.Cast(output,sitk.sitkVectorUInt16)
sitk.WriteImage(outputCasted,output_path)
```

You call the above function for each patient and each image sequence and correspondingly save the results.

```
processed_full_data = {}
for patient_id,v in full_data.items():
    processed_full_data[patient_id] = {}
    for seq,input_path in v.items():
            print(f"Started Bias Correction for Patient {patient_id} and
            Sequence {seq.upper()}")
            folder_name = os.path.split(os.path.split(input_path)[0])[-1]
            file_name  = os.path.split(input_path)[-1]
        output_path = os.path.join(NEW_BASE_DIR,folder_name, file_name)

        # Automatically create the directory that doesn't exist
        if not os.path.exists(os.path.join(NEW_BASE_DIR,folder_name)):
            os.makedirs(os.path.join(NEW_BASE_DIR,folder_name))

        # Updating the new paths for 4 sequences
            if seq == "label":
            processed_full_data[patient_id].update({seq:input_path})
        else:
            processed_full_data[patient_id].update({seq:output_path})
            correct_bias_field(input_path, output_path)
    break
```

Removing Unwanted Slices

This is the last step of the preprocessing pipeline before creating the training data. Save the results in the HDF5 file format, which allows stitching individual data together in a single file.

You are going to save the final image file with all sequences stacked together to create a 4-D volume of size 4,135,240,240 and the label volume of size 135,240,240. You are going to use the h5py Python package to save the HDF5 files.

```python
import h5py
    NEW_BASE_DIR = os.path.join(os.path.split(BASE_DIR)[0],
                    "PROCESSED_IMAGE","SLICE_CORRECTED")

# Automatically create the directory that doesn't exist
if not os.path.exists(NEW_BASE_DIR):
    os.makedirs(NEW_BASE_DIR)
```

You run consecutive for loops to loop through the paths and save the h5py file in the new directory created above.

```python
for patient_id,v in processed_full_data.items():
    image_vol_w_seq = {}
    image_mask = []
    for seq,input_path in v.items():
        image_volume = io.imread(input_path, plugin='simpleitk')
        slices_to_keep = np.array([_slice for i,_slice in enumerate(
        image_volume) if i not in (list(range(5))+list(range(140,155)))])
        if seq == "label":
            # To enable one-hot encoding of these categories
            # we make a continous range of classes from 0 to 3
            slices_to_keep[slices_to_keep == 4] = 3
            image_mask = np.copy(slices_to_keep)
        else:
            image_vol_w_seq[seq] = slices_to_keep

    final_image = np.stack((image_vol_w_seq['flair'],
                    image_vol_w_seq['t1'],
                    image_vol_w_seq['t1ce'],
                    image_vol_w_seq['t2'])).astype('float')

    # Check individual size of mask and train images
    assert image_mask.shape == slices_to_keep.shape
        assert final_image.shape == (4, ) + slices_to_keep.shape
```

```
# Initialize the HDF5 File
    _path = os.path.join(NEW_BASE_DIR, f'{str(patient_id+1).zfill(3)}.h5')
    _hf = h5py.File(_path, 'w')

# Use create_dataset to give dataset name and provide numpy array
    _hf.create_dataset('X', data = final_image)
    _hf.create_dataset('Y', data = image_mask)

# Close to write to the disk
_hf.close()
```

Model Creation

The 3D U-Net architecture was inspired from the U-Net architecture which amassed huge popularity after being the SOTA for some time for medical image segmentation. The architecture was introduced by the University of Freiburg in collaboration with Google's Deepmind Team in the paper titled "3D U-Net: Learning Dense Volumetric Segmentation from Sparse Annotation." Figure 8-25 is an image from the same paper showcasing the U-Net architecture.

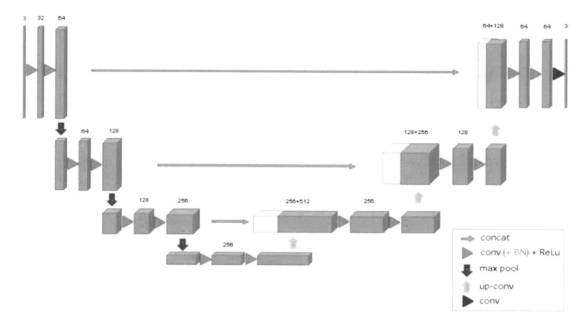

Figure 8-25. *The 3D U-Net architecture. The blue boxes represent feature maps. The number of channels is denoted above each feature map*

A U-Net architecture consists of a **contracting path (left side)** and an **expansive path (right side)**.

The contracting path follows the typical architecture of a convolutional network.

A convolution layer is followed by non-linear activation and a pooling operation to prevent overfitting. Sometimes BatchNormalization or its variants are added to make sure that covariate shifts in a batch of data don't abruptly affect the gradient learning process. Covariate shits are observed changes in data distribution across batches.

At each downsampling step, the feature channels are doubled whereas the expansive path consists of upsampling and concatenation followed by regular convolution operations. In this path you try to restore the condensed features by expanding the feature dimension. You upsample in a way that you meet the desired shape of the feature map from the contracting path denoted by green arrows in Figure 8-25.

The main win for U-Net is that while upsampling you also concatenate the feature maps from the encoder/contracting network.

Let's get coding. You start by importing the relevant layers required to create the model.

```python
from tensorflow.keras.models import Model
from tensorflow.keras.layers import (
    Input,
    Activation,
    Conv3D,
    Conv3DTranspose,
    MaxPooling3D,
    UpSampling3D,
    SpatialDropout3D,
    concatenate,
    BatchNormalization
)
from tensorflow.keras.optimizers import Adam
```

You create the convolution block, which basically creates both the contracting and expanding path. Just like in previous chapters you continue to use SELU as your go-to activation.

You are also going to use a batch normalization layer, which handles covariate shits across a batch of data. You can control the use of it by using a flag variable.

One thing to note is the use of `data_format = 'channels_first'`. This is done to tell the layers that the input image has channels as the first dimension. Don't be confused; your input image is actually a 5-D tensor.

```
5+D tensor with shape: batch_shape + (channels, conv_dim1, conv_dim2,
conv_dim3) if data_format='channels_first' or 5+D tensor with shape:
batch_shape + (conv_dim1, conv_dim2, conv_dim3, channels) if data_
format='channels_last'
```

```python
def convolution_block(input_layer, n_filters, batch_normalization=False,
                      kernel=(3, 3, 3), activation='selu',
                      padding='same', strides=(1, 1, 1)):
    """
    Creates Convolutional Block
    """
    layer = Conv3D(n_filters, kernel, activation = 'selu', data_format
    = 'channels_first', padding = padding, strides = strides)
    (input_layer)

    if batch_normalization:
            layer = BatchNormalization(axis=1)(layer)

    return layer
```

Sometimes to prevent overfitting you might want to add a dropout layer after max-pooling but for simplicity, let's not introduce it. For those who want, you can add `SpatialDropout3D` layer by passing the max-pooling output to the Dropout layer.

In a similar manner, for the expanding path you define an up-convolution operation. To get the image of the same size, there are various methods. In the function below, you can see two of them, which are deconvolution and upsampling.

- **Deconvolution**: Use filters, kernels, padding, and strides just as the convolution layers to get an image of desired size.

- **Upsampling**: Resizes images to the desired size by passing the pool size used to compress the image.

```python
def up_convolution(n_filters, pool_size, kernel_size = (2, 2, 2),
                   strides = (2, 2, 2),
                   deconvolution = False):
```

```
if deconvolution:
        return Conv3DTranspose(filters=n_filters, data_format =
        'channels_first',
                            kernel_size=kernel_size, strides=strides)
else:
        return UpSampling3D(size=pool_size,  data_format =
        'channels_first')
```

You create the architecture shown in Figure 8-25 and return the model for training.

```
def unet_model_3d(loss_function, input_shape=(4, 24, 160, 160),
                    pool_size = 2, n_labels = 3,
                    initial_learning_rate = 0.001,
                    deconvolution=False, depth = 4, n_base_filters = 32,
                    metrics=[],
                batch_normalization = True):

    """
    U-Net 3D Model
    """

# Input Layer for the Image patch
inputs = Input(input_shape)
current_layer = inputs
levels = list()

# add levels with max pooling
for layer_depth in range(depth):
    layer1 = convolution_block(input_layer = current_layer,
                                    n_filters = \
                                n_base_filters * (2 ** layer_depth),
                                        batch_normalization = \
                            batch_normalization)
    layer2 = convolution_block(input_layer=layer1,
                                    n_filters = \
                                n_base_filters * (2 ** layer_depth)* 2,
                                        batch_normalization = \
                            batch_normalization)

    # Do Max-Pooling until reaching the bridge
```

```python
        if layer_depth < depth - 1:
            current_layer = MaxPooling3D(pool_size = pool_size,  data_
            format = 'channels_first')(layer2)
        levels.append([layer1, layer2, current_layer])
    else:
        current_layer = layer2
        levels.append([layer1, layer2])

# add levels with up-convolution or up-sampling
    for layer_depth in range(depth - 2, -1, -1):
    up_convolution_layer = up_convolution(pool_size = pool_size,
                                    deconvolution = deconvolution,
                                    n_filters = \
current_layer.shape[1])(current_layer)

    # Concatenate Higher and Lower Dimensions
        concat = concatenate([up_convolution_layer, levels[layer_depth]
        [1]], axis=1)

    current_layer = convolution_block(
            n_filters = levels[layer_depth][1].shape[1],
        input_layer = concat, batch_normalization = batch_normalization)

    current_layer = convolution_block(
            n_filters=levels[layer_depth][1].shape[1],
        input_layer=current_layer,
        batch_normalization=batch_normalization)

    final_convolution = Conv3D(n_labels, (1, 1, 1),
                            data_format = 'channels_first',
                        activation = 'sigmoid')(current_layer)

model = Model(inputs = inputs, outputs = final_convolution)

if not isinstance(metrics, list): metrics = [metrics]

model.compile(optimizer=Adam(lr = initial_learning_rate),
            loss = loss_function,
            metrics=metrics)
return model
```

Preparing Input Data

To prepare input data, you need to understand how segmentation ideally works given the model explained above.

Ideally, you would like the whole volume of information, be it channels/seq, the depth dimension, etc., to be used for creating training labels, but as you can see from the file size of one HDF5 file, the image size will be huge when uncompressed. Besides, this would lead to larger kernel size when convolving and hence many more parameters to learn.

So you are left with either of these two approaches:

1) Train the segmentation model by inputting each slice from the stacked image at a time and the corresponding slice from the label image, just like you would do a 2-D convolution, but then you are knowingly letting go of spatial information present along the depth dimension, which can play a pivotal role in determining the type of tumor. Some tumors might look small in the axial view but might be very visible in the sagittal view and hence this technique doesn't provide good results.

2) You can also create small patches of 3-D volume from your volume cube and capture the spatial information across all dimensions. Now this isn't a perfect technique since you might miss out on some colocation information, but it allows you to capture much more information at a time and hence it is preferred.

As shown in Figure 8-26, you will create your training data. You repeat this process for n number of tries depending upon how many maximum patches you want per image volume.

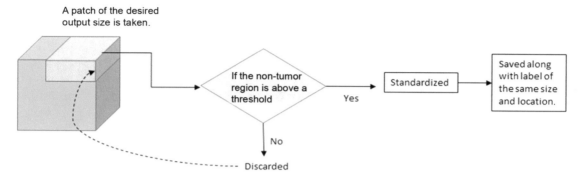

Figure 8-26. *Detail flow to create the training data patches*

You start by first creating the standardize function, which centers your pixel intensity to a mean of 0 and a standard deviation of 1. For each sequence you loop across the depth and on the $(240,240)$ image you center-scale it and then stack them back at the same place.

```
import tensorflow as tf

    def standardize(image):
        """

        Centers the image with mean of zero and sd = 1
        """

    # initialize to array of zeros, with same shape as the image
    standardized_image = np.zeros(image.shape)

    # iterate over sequences
        for c in range(image.shape[0]):
        # iterate over the depth dimension
            for z in range(image.shape[1]):
            image_slice = image[c,z,:,:]

            # subtract the mean from image_slice
            centered = image_slice - np.mean(image_slice)

            # divide by the standard deviation (only if it is different
            from zero)
            if np.std(centered):
                centered_scaled = centered / np.std(centered)
                standardized_image[c, z, :, :] = centered_scaled
```

```
        else:
            standardized_image[c, z, :, :] = image_slice

    return standardized_image
```

Next, you create the patches you want for the training data. For this you create a new folder for the new images.

```
NEW_BASE_DIR = os.path.join(os.path.split(BASE_DIR)[0],
            "FINAL_TRAIN_IMAGE")

# Automatically create the directory that doesn't exist
if not os.path.exists(NEW_BASE_DIR):
    os.makedirs(NEW_BASE_DIR)
```

There are a lot of things happening in the function, but these are the broad steps that are happening.

1) You start by taking your desired patch size, number of classes in the label image, and how many tries you want for getting a desired number of patches from a patient image. You need to try multiple times because you want the threshold to have at least 4% tumor region.

2) You select a random patch by selecting a random start point for all the axes: x, y, and z.

   a) Since you are selecting multiple patches, it can happen that a patch's starting point can be the same. For this you can maintain a separate list for already-selected starting points to avoid any overlap.

   b) You can either compare an axis tuple or individual axis points. I chose the former one but you can try either one.

3) On the label image you introduce a new dimension that one-hot encoded the tumor labels. As you can see in the code example below, a new dimension is introduced.

You are going to use `tf.keras.utils.to_categorical` to do this.

Converts a class vector (integers) to binary class matrix.
Read more at https://www.tensorflow.org/api_docs/python/tf/keras/utils/to_categorical

```
tf.keras.utils.to_categorical([0,1,2,3], num_classes=4)
```

Output:-

```
array([[1., 0., 0., 0.],
       [0., 1., 0., 0.],
       [0., 0., 1., 0.],
       [0., 0., 0., 1.]], dtype=float32)
```

```
tf.keras.utils.to_categorical([[0,1,0,3],[0,0,2,3]], num_classes=4)
```

Output:

```
array([[[1., 0., 0., 0.],
        [0., 1., 0., 0.],
        [1., 0., 0., 0.],
        [0., 0., 0., 1.]],

       [[1., 0., 0., 0.],
        [1., 0., 0., 0.],
        [0., 0., 1., 0.],
        [0., 0., 0., 1.]]], dtype=float32)
```

4) You remove the background class because you are not interested in predicting it. But keep in mind that this still doesn't change the sparsity you will have due to imbalance.

5) If the background ratio is passed, you standardize the input image and save it along with the label.

Note   For those of you thinking how to decide the output dimension, revisit the cropping image exercise. You can see that after cropping for the skull you are left with a dimension of 164,123 and hence you can take a desired dimension of (180, 160).

```python
def get_multiple_patchs(image, label, patient_id,
                    save_dir,
                        out_dim = (180,160,24),
                        num_classes = 4,
                        max_tries = 1000,
                        num_patches = 5,
                        background_threshold=0.96):
    """
    Extract random sub-volume from original images.
    """

    num_channels, orig_z, orig_x, orig_y =  image.shape
    out_x, out_y, out_z = out_dim

    all_patches = []
    tries = 0

    # try until you fail :P
    prev_start = []
    while (tries < max_tries) and (len(all_patches) < num_patches):

        # Start from the corner randomly sample a voxel (volume box)
        start_x = np.random.randint(0, orig_x - out_x + 1)

        start_y = np.random.randint(0, orig_y - out_y + 1)

        start_z = np.random.randint(0, orig_z - out_z + 1)

        # Make sure you are choosing a unique starting point each time
        while (start_x,start_y,start_z) in prev_start:
            start_x = np.random.randint(0, orig_x - out_x + 1)
            start_y = np.random.randint(0, orig_y - out_y + 1)
            start_z = np.random.randint(0, orig_z - out_z + 1)

        # extract relevant area of label
        y = label[start_z: start_z + out_z,
                start_x: start_x + out_x,
                start_y: start_y + out_y]

        # One-hot encode the tumor categories to add a 4-th dimension
```

```
y = tf.keras.utils.to_categorical(y,num_classes)

# compute the background ratio
    bgrd_ratio = np.sum(y[:,:,:,0])/(out_x*out_y*out_z)

# increment tries counter
    tries += 1

# check if background ratio is less than the maximum background
# threshold
if bgrd_ratio < background_threshold:

    # make copy of the sub-volume and take all the channels/seq
    X = np.copy(image[:,
                    start_z: start_z + out_z,
                    start_x: start_x + out_x,
                    start_y: start_y + out_y])

    X_std = standardize(X)

    # we will also make sure that we bring the num class dimension
    # as the first axis
        y = np.moveaxis(y, 3, 0)

    # Exclude the background class as we don't want to predict it
        y = y[1:, :, :, :]

    all_patches.append([X_std, y])

    # Initialize the HDF5 File
        _path = os.path.join(save_dir, f'{str(patient_id).zfill(3)
        + "_" + str(len(all_patches))}.h5')
        _hf = h5py.File(_path, 'w')

    # Use create_dataset to give dataset name and provide numpy array
        _hf.create_dataset('X', data = X_std)
        _hf.create_dataset('Y', data = y)

    # Close to write to the disk
    _hf.close()

return all_patches
```

Finally, you save all the patches to the training directory.

```
processed_path =
glob.glob(os.path.join(os.path.join(os.path.split(BASE_DIR)[0],
            "PROCESSED_IMAGE","SLICE_CORRECTED"),"*.h5"))

for _path in processed_path:
    with h5py.File(_path, 'r') as f:
        _image = f.get("X")
        _label = f.get("Y")
        _patient_id = int(os.path.split(_path)[-1].replace(".h5",""))
    x = get_multiple_patchs(_image, _label, _patient_id, NEW_BASE_DIR,
                            out_dim = (180, 160,24),
                            num_classes = 4,
                            max_tries = 1000,
                            num_patches = 5,
                            background_threshold=0.96)
```

You are now all set to train your model.

Training

Since you are dealing with a lot of images of significant sizes, it is generally not recommended to load all of your images at once. You will load them using a generator.

Not all of the out-of-the-box generators in TensorFlow-Keras expect an image file. There are some remarkable generators but sadly they won't work for HDF5 data and hence you would have to write one on your own.

Note   For those interested, check flow_from_* functions at this repo:
https://keras.io/api/preprocessing/image/.

I am leveraging code from this excellent tutorial. Follow it to broaden your understanding: https://stanford.edu/~shervine/blog/keras-how-to-generate-data-on-the-fly. The code for the generator is shared in the GitHub repo of the book. Do check it out.

In order to train your model, the last piece is to decide on a loss function. Most likely, when dealing with multiple classes you would be inclined to choose cross-entropy loss but cross-entropy loss doesn't work that well with highly imbalanced dataset.

Let's understand it. Figure 8-27 shows an image patch with foreground pixels represented by 1 and background pixels represented by 0.

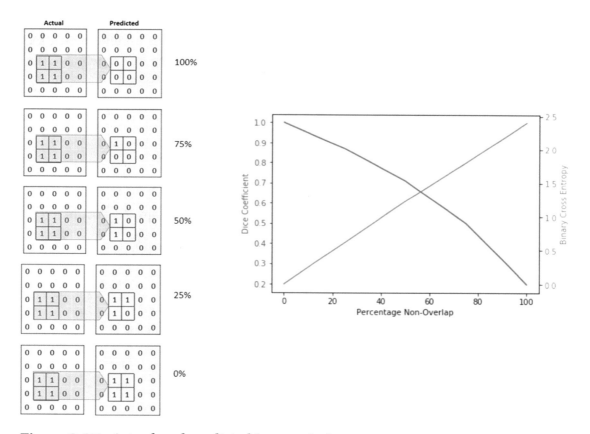

Figure 8-27. *Actual and predicted image pixels*

You can see how binary cross entropy almost linearly increases as the non-overlapping region increases whereas the dice coefficient doesn't touch 0 even with no overlap and there is no linear decrease, hence it handles imbalance better.

The paper titled "Statistical Validation of Image Segmentation Quality Based on a Spatial Overlap Index" by Zou et al discusses dice coefficient in detail with statistical validation. I strongly recommend you have a look at it.

You can further tune the loss function to your use case. Since your DL model actually outputs and not just probabilities, you can modify the actual Dice function to work on probabilities and not the actual binary values.

The code for the Soft Dice function is shared in the GitHub repo of the book, so check it out. Also, please note that while reading some papers you will not find any mention of epsilon, but in implementation you will. Don't be scared; it's a common practice to use laplace smoothing to avoid division errors in real-world implementations.

Having finally decided on the loss function, you now need a performance metric for evaluating the trained model. For this you will be using the dice coefficient, which is the standard metric for evaluating the performance of segmentation models.

```python
from tensorflow.keras import backend as K
K.set_image_data_format("channels_first")

    def dice_coefficient(y_true, y_pred, axis=(1, 2, 3),
                          laplace_smoothing_factor=0.00001):

        dice_numerator =2 *K.sum(y_pred*y_true,axis) + laplace_smoothing_
            factor
    dice_denominator = K.sum(y_pred,axis) + K.sum(y_true,axis) + laplace_
    smoothing_factor

    # For multiple classes take the mean across each axis
    dice_coefficient = K.mean(dice_numerator/dice_denominator)

    return dice_coefficient

    def soft_dice_loss(y_true, y_pred, axis=(1, 2, 3),
                        laplace_smoothing_factor=0.00001):
        """
        Compute mean soft dice loss over all Multiple classes.
        """
        dice_numerator =2 *K.sum(y_pred*y_true,axis) + laplace_smoothing_
            factor
        dice_denominator = K.sum(y_pred**2,axis) + K.sum(y_true**2,axis) +
        laplace_smoothing_factor
        dice_loss = 1 - K.mean(dice_numerator / dice_denominator)

    return dice_loss
```

For details, refer to `https://en.wikipedia.org/wiki/` `S%C3%B8rensen%E2%80%93Dice_coefficient`.

```
    model = unet_model_3d(depth = 3,
                          pool_size= 2,
                          input_shape=(4,180, 160,24),
                          n_base_filters = 32,
                 loss_function=soft_dice_loss, metrics=[dice_coefficient])
```

```
import h5py
    NEW_BASE_DIR = os.path.join(os.path.split(BASE_DIR)[0],
                "FINAL_TRAIN_IMAGE")

    all_patches = glob.glob(os.path.join(NEW_BASE_DIR,"*.h5"))
```

```
from sklearn.model_selection import train_test_split
    train_data, val_data = train_test_split(all_patches, test_size=0.33,
    random_state=42)
```

```
    BATCH_SIZE = 5
# Get generators for training and validation sets
    train_generator = BatchDataGenerator(train_data, batch_size =
    BATCH_SIZE, dim = (180, 160, 24))
    valid_generator = BatchDataGenerator(val_data, batch_size = BATCH_SIZE,
    dim = (180, 160, 24))
```

For training a generator, you pass something called `steps per epoch`. This number of steps is the number of samples to train in a batch. If there are 100 train samples and you want 5 batches, then `steps per epoch = ceil(num_samples/batch_size)`.

```
steps_per_epoch = len(train_data)//BATCH_SIZE
    n_epochs=10
validation_steps = len(val_data)//BATCH_SIZE
```

```
history = model.fit(train_generator,
        steps_per_epoch=steps_per_epoch,
        epochs=n_epochs,
        use_multiprocessing=False,
        validation_data=valid_generator,
        validation_steps=validation_steps)
```

```
Epoch 1/10
120/120 [==============================] - 860s 7s/step - loss: 0.3559 -
dice_coefficient: 0.4725 - val_loss: 0.4446 - val_dice_coefficient: 0.4008
Epoch 2/10
120/120 [==============================] - 802s 7s/step - loss: 0.3350 -
dice_coefficient: 0.5026 - val_loss: 0.3232 - val_dice_coefficient: 0.5164
Epoch 3/10
120/120 [==============================] - 4914s 41s/step - loss: 0.3214 -
dice_coefficient: 0.5237 - val_loss: 0.5040 - val_dice_coefficient: 0.3589
Epoch 4/10
120/120 [==============================] - 505s 4s/step - loss: 0.3194 -
dice_coefficient: 0.5305 - val_loss: 0.3561 - val_dice_coefficient: 0.4605
Epoch 5/10
120/120 [==============================] - 517s 4s/step - loss: 0.3023 -
dice_coefficient: 0.5525 - val_loss: 0.4168 - val_dice_coefficient: 0.4328
Epoch 6/10
120/120 [==============================] - 518s 4s/step - loss: 0.3066 -
dice_coefficient: 0.5552 - val_loss: 0.3478 - val_dice_coefficient: 0.5206
Epoch 7/10
120/120 [==============================] - 521s 4s/step - loss: 0.3054 -
dice_coefficient: 0.5596 - val_loss: 0.3900 - val_dice_coefficient: 0.4615
Epoch 8/10
120/120 [==============================] - 238s 2s/step - loss: 0.2914 -
dice_coefficient: 0.5746 - val_loss: 0.3515 - val_dice_coefficient: 0.5378
Epoch 9/10
120/120 [==============================] - 294s 2s/step - loss: 0.3022 -
dice_coefficient: 0.5697 - val_loss: 0.3471 - val_dice_coefficient: 0.5286
Epoch 10/10
120/120 [==============================] - 374s 3s/step - loss: 0.2864 -
dice_coefficient: 0.5864 - val_loss: 0.3279 - val_dice_coefficient: 0.5300
```

Performance Evaluation

See Figure 8-28 to get the Performance and Loss graphs for your model. Note that the model performs decently with the dice coefficient improving with each epoch. There are multiple ways to improve the model further by using a higher filter size and dropouts to prevent overfitting and more depth.

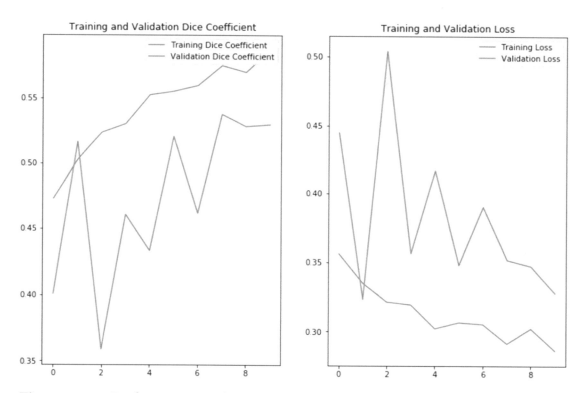

Figure 8-28. *Performance and Loss graphs for the 3-D U-Net Model*

Transfer Learning for Medical Images

Transfer learning is a way to unlock knowledge from a large pretrained network trained on huge annotated datasets to solve tasks outside the domain or the purpose it was trained for. Almost all computer vision problems now use transfer learning and achieve SOTA.

But unlike natural images, which consistently consist of three channels and less variation between different sets, medical images can be fundamentally different.

They can not only have varying channel length but also the pixel intensity of these images is decided based on the medical device and physics it applies.

Therefore, let's develop an understanding about whether transfer learning is applicable for medical images and, if not, what can we do to make it happen.

This section mainly picks up ideas from Google Brain and Cornell University's paper published in NIPS 2019 titled "Transfusion: Understanding Transfer Learning for Medical Imaging."

The authors tried to understand it by doing the following:

- **Performance evaluation**: Compare models trained from random initialization and applied directly on tasks to those pretrained on ImageNet for the same task.

- **Representation analysis**: Compare and contrast hidden representation from different models using the canonical correlation analysis.

- **Effects on convergence**: Time taken for the model to converge is significantly reduced as features are reused.

On the basis of these three experiments, this is what the authors concluded:

1) Transfer learning does not significantly affect performance on medical imaging tasks. It means pretrained models are over-parameterized.

   a) For context, ImageNet has 1000 classes whereas medical images have much smaller prediction vectors.

   b) The sizes of the input images are very different. While the natural images that are part of ImageNet have a size of 224 X 224, medical images can have much larger sizes, like 512 X 512, 1024 X 1024, etc. Such images are too large to be directly fed to a neural network.

2) Using pretrained weights from the last two layers of the network is found to have the biggest effect on convergence.

I think that transfer learning for medical images is not as effective as it is for natural images. For medical images, we should still stick to the approach of training our own network based on the modality of the image and task at hand.

Conclusion

Congratulations on making through such a long chapter. This chapter covered a wide spectrum of information related to medical images and the application of AI. You explored the different modalities used to capture medical images and how some modalities can be useful for certain anatomy. We then discussed two different formats, DICOM and NIFTI, which store these images, and how to leverage metadata associated with the images to broaden your understanding of the images you receive. Often, this is neglected by the more fascinating deep-learning applications but metadata contains a lot of insights. Lastly, you looked at 2-D and 3-D images and different architectures that can be used to solve classification and segmentation problems.

There is a huge real-world value in what you learned in this chapter. Classification and localization can be used for screening of diseases and also in emergent diagnosis and incidental findings. Very recently, with the onslaught of COVID cases leading to an unforeseen shortage of medical staff, techniques like segmentation were used to diagnose patients for critical conditions and thus they were given care first. Segmentation also helps identify tumor contours and sensitive areas for radiation therapy in oncology.

Lastly, the field of deep learning and medical AI isn't limited to just classification or segmentation. There are various other areas where there is huge potential to apply advanced AI techniques, such as registration of images captured from different sequences, reconstruction of images from the device to what is available to physician, and also image retrieval with clinical context that can help physicians track what's been done in the past for a case.

References

1. B. H. Menze, A. Jakab, S. Bauer, J. Kalpathy-Cramer, K. Farahani, J. Kirby, et al, "The Multimodal Brain Tumor Image Segmentation Benchmark (BRATS)," IEEE Transactions on Medical Imaging 34(10), 1993-2024 (2015) DOI: 10.1109/TMI.2014.2377694.

2. S. Bakas, H. Akbari, A. Sotiras, M. Bilello, M. Rozycki, J.S. Kirby, et al, "Advancing the Cancer Genome Atlas Glioma MRI Collections with Expert Segmentation Labels and Radiomic Features," Nature Scientific Data, 4:170117 (2017) DOI: 10.1038/sdata.2017.117.

3. S. Bakas, M. Reyes, A. Jakab, S. Bauer, M. Rempfler, A. Crimi, et al, "Identifying the Best Machine Learning Algorithms for Brain Tumor Segmentation, Progression Assessment, and Overall Survival Prediction in the BRATS Challenge," arXiv preprint arXiv:1811.02629 (2018).

4. S. Bakas, H. Akbari, A. Sotiras, M. Bilello, M. Rozycki, J. Kirby, et al, "Segmentation Labels and Radiomic Features for the Pre-operative Scans of the TCGA-GBM collection," The Cancer Imaging Archive, 2017. DOI: 10.7937/K9/TCIA.2017.KLXWJJ1Q.

5. S. Bakas, H. Akbari, A. Sotiras, M. Bilello, M. Rozycki, J. Kirby, et al, "Segmentation Labels and Radiomic Features for the Pre-operative Scans of the TCGA-LGG collection," The Cancer Imaging Archive, 2017. DOI: 10.7937/K9/TCIA.2017.GJQ7R0EF.

6. www.frontiersin.org/articles/10.3389/fnins.2019.00810/full

CHAPTER 9

Machines Have All the Answers, Except What's the Purpose of Life

We have covered so much thus far. Kudos to us. In all of the past cases, you knew what you were looking for and what the outcome would be, whether it was the readmission rate of at-risk patients, ICD-9 code prediction, or tumor identification. But sometimes all we have are questions and we don't know the possible answers. Be it healthcare or any other industry, there is so much knowledge embedded into research, company documents, or any public information, and sometimes we are not aware as it becomes a little overwhelming to go over such an extensive set of information. So, let's put the machine to work.

In this chapter, I will briefly review how Q&A systems are built and then you will build one for yourself using the COVID-19 dataset. With the pandemic situation we all have faced, we know so little about the side effects of present medication and how comorbidities can affect treatment. Also, understanding information about the SARS family of viruses, which was embedded into millions of documents in such a short time, wouldn't be possible without technologies like Q&A. So let's get right into it.

Introduction

People working in the healthcare profession as well as the general public need fast and effective access to biomedical information via a system that understands complex biomedical concepts and can find the best document to support a particular response.

The research in Q&A and particularly biomedical Q&A has been fueled by various competitions and conference tracks such as **TREC [Text REtrieval Conference (TREC)]**

© Anshik 2021
Anshik, *AI for Healthcare with Keras and Tensorflow 2.0*, https://doi.org/10.1007/978-1-4842-7086-8_9

and **BioASQ.** BioASQ organizes challenges on biomedical semantic indexing and question answering (QA). The challenges include tasks relevant to hierarchical text classification, machine learning, information retrieval, QA from texts and structured data, multi-document summarization, and many other areas.

There are various datasets released through independent research and competitions in various areas of healthcare such as scientific (CORD-19), clinical (emrQA) or consumer health (MediQA, LiveQA-Med).

Despite an active interest, there are still many challenges:

- **Small and non-complex datasets**: Most of the datasets available are small in size in comparison to SQUAD v1 and v2 datasets (general domain) and generally do not require complex reasoning.

- **Ontologies and KB are not utilized**: NCBI and BioPortal host a bunch of Ontologies and Knowledge Graphs pertaining to the medical domain but often a standalone deep-learning-based solution fails to utilize them. Certain recent papers are coming up that are enriching either the embeddings while training or reranking retrieved documents using existing KBs.

- **Lack of explainability**: Due to the nature of the healthcare domain, sometimes an explanation of a specific answer can help the user understand the reasoning better and accordingly instill confidence.

As a general overview, there are roughly four major types of Q&A systems:

- Open/closed domain: In retriever (information retrieval) and reader/generator (machine comprehension) frameworks, a large number of passages from the knowledge source are encoded and stored in memory. A retrieval model is able to query the memory to identify the top relevant passages, which have the maximum inner product with the question embedding.

- Knowledge base: Converts queries to RDF triplets and answers questions based on KGs or ontologies such as DbPedia or Semantic Map.

- Question entailment: Reuses answers from similar questions in the training database to formulate responses.

- Visual Q&A: Answers questions from images.

You are going to work on an IR-based QA system. These systems find and extract a text segment from a large collection of documents and are the closest implementation of a real world QA as you are first deciding which documents to find an answer from and then finding the answer.

Unless you live under a rock, you have used Google. Let's search for a question on Google, which very "simply" is an IR system with recently integrated QA capabilities. See Figure 9-1.

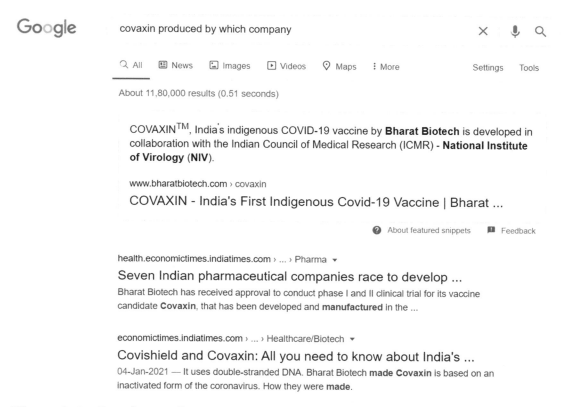

Figure 9-1. *Google search*

As you can see, the query produced

- A list of links with relevant paragraphs from each of the links highlighting certain keywords

- A snippet box giving the actual answer

Google at the back end uses multiple technologies to

- Retrieve documents

- Highlight important keywords/paragraphs in those documents

- Give a final answer

- Reformulate multiple queries from the given query

- Search history

But for us mere mortals, we can understand this IR-QA to work simply as shown in Figure 9-2.

- The retriever serves as a search engine, ranking and retrieving relevant documents.

- Comprehension is generally a seq-seq model that tries to probabilistically identify which phrase from the context is highly likely to be seen given the question and, yes, you guessed right: this generally done using question answering datasets.

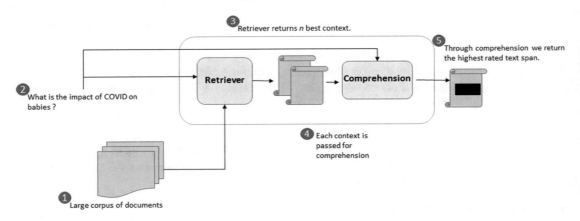

Figure 9-2. *Flow diagram for IR-QA system*

Getting Data

You are going to use CORD-19 dataset to build your Q&A model. It consists of over 400,000 scholarly articles about COVID-19, SARS-CoV-2, and related coronaviruses. You can obtain this dataset from Kaggle by signing up for the CORD-19 research challenge competition at www.kaggle.com/allen-institute-for-ai/CORD-19-research-challenge.

The CORD-19 dataset comes with `metadata.csv`, a single file that records basic information on all papers available in the CORD-19 dataset. This is a good place to start exploring!

Along with metadata, there are full text articles taken from PubmedCentral and PDFs (Research journals - Microsoft) in the `document_parses` folder on Kaggle. These are JSON files containing information about the full text article/PDF such as SHA-ID, list of authors, list of paragraphs in the abstract, full text, bibliography, etc.

For this case study, you will only be working with the `metadata.csv`, which contains an article's title and abstract information. You can easily expand upon the principles you learn here to include paragraphs from full text as well. This is something you should experiment with.

So for now, download the `metadata.csv` from Kaggle and put it in the `./Data` folder of your working directory.

Note   Note the presence of `metadata.readme`. This keeps track of the changes the data went through. This data is maintained by Allen AI along with other collaborators.

Load the metadata and see what's present:

```python
import os
import pandas as pd
    data_dir = "./Data/"
    metadata_path = os.path.join(data_dir,"metadata.csv")
    metadata_df = pd.read_csv(metadata_path, dtype={'Microsoft Academic
    Paper ID': str, 'pubmed_id': str})
    metadata_df = metadata_df.dropna(subset=['abstract', 'title']).reset_
    index(drop=True)
    metadata_df = metadata_df.drop_duplicates(['abstract', 'title']).reset_
    index(drop = True)
```

Here you load the metadata, ensuring that full-text IDs are stored as strings. You remove rows that are missing the abstract and title or are duplicated at the abstract and title level. This can happen because the main document can have multiple sources of information or reference multiple documents (full text). But you can ignore these nitty-gritties and move forward with the analysis.

Keep the columns that we are concerned with for this case study.

```
#Subsetting Columns
    final_metadata = metadata_df[['abstract', 'title']]
    final_metadata["id"] = [str(i) for i in range(final_metadata.shape[0])]
```

For those who plan to integrate full text as well as the abstract and title, please visit `https://github.com/allenai/cord19#metadatacsv-overview` to get a good idea about what the different columns mean.

Since you are dealing with transformer-based language models, you know that they only capture a limited amount of context, which is fixed to a maximum length of 512 tokens. This means that if the abstract is greater than 512 tokens, it will not be used entirely and the remaining tokens will be missed. Moreover, these 512 tokens are not something you get from whitespace splitting but the transformer's own internal tokenization mechanism (wordpiece for BERT architectures) and the vocabulary it is using.

To handle this, you will run a window of a fixed length and stride and split the abstract into several smaller chunks to capture context as decided by the window length. Figure 9-3 shows how to create your data for retrieval and comprehension.

Since you are going to use Covid-BERT fine-tuned for MedNLI, you will load it to decide upon tokenization length (discussed in the "Retrieval Mechanics" section). For now, you can imagine it to be like a BERT model used for encoding information from text.

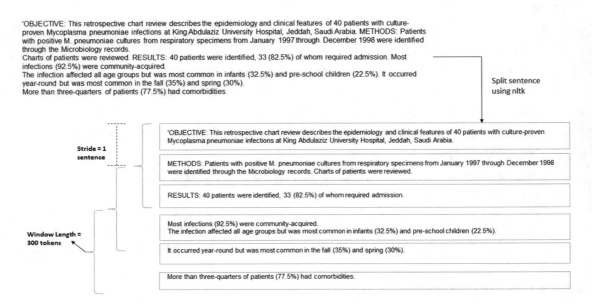

Figure 9-3. *Running a window over an abstract to prevent abrupt loss of context*

You can download a pretrained model from https://huggingface.co/Darkrider/ covidbert_mednli and create a folder named pretrained_model in your working directory and save it there, or you can directly pass the string /Darkrider/covidbert_ mednli to AutoTokenizer.from_pretrained().

Then you can load the model using Hugging Face's transformers package.

```
from nltk.tokenize import sent_tokenize
import numpy as np
from transformers import AutoTokenizer
    TOKENIZER = AutoTokenizer.from_pretrained('./pre_trained_model/
    training_nli_covidbert-mednli/0_Transformer')
    MAX_LEN = 300
    STRIDE = 1
```

Next, write a function that splits the abstract into different paragraphs.

```
    def get_para_segments(text, stride, max_len, id_, title, tokenizer):
        """
        Get Running length window of certain length with a particular stride
        """
#       tokenizer = AutoTokenizer.from_pretrained('./pre_trained_model/
training_nli_covidbert-mednli/0_Transformer')
    text_map = {i:sent for i, sent in enumerate(sent_tokenize(text))}
    text_lenmap = {i:len(input_id) for i,input_id in
    enumerate(tokenizer(list(text_map.values()))['input_ids'])}

    para = []
        i = 0
        if len(text_map) > 1:
        while i < len(text_map):
            for j in text_map.keys():
                if j > i:
                    new_para_sub_len = np.sum(list(text_lenmap.values())[i:j])
                        if j == (len(text_map) -1):
                            para.append("".join(list(text_map.values())
                            [i:(j+1)]))
                            i = 999999 # some big value
                    if new_para_sub_len <= max_len:
                        continue
```

```
                    else:
                        para.append( "".join(list(text_map.values())
                        [i:j]))
                    i = i+stride
        else:
            para.append(text_map[0])
        # at least 5 words should be there in the paragraph
        para = [paragraph for paragraph in para if len(paragraph.split()) > 5]
        return [[id_, str(id_) + "_" + str(i), title, paragraph] for
i,paragraph in enumerate(para)]
```

There are three main things happening in the code above:

1) You provide an ID to each sentence of the abstract. These
   sentences are obtained from nltk's sentence tokenization.

2) You also create a mapping using the same ID and get the length
   post tokenization from the BERT model.

3) You keep on iterating on each sentence until you hit the maximum
   length or it is the end of possible sentences.

Finally, you call the function over chunks of your metadata dataframe. But before
you do this, please make sure you create a folder named passage inside the Data folder.

Pickle is used to serialize Python objects into byte streams (1s and 0s). This makes
loading data into your work environment easy.

```
from tqdm import tqdm
import pickle

    for i,df in enumerate(np.array_split(final_metadata, 10)):
    print(i)
        passage_list = [get_para_segments(row["abstract"],STRIDE,
        MAX_LEN,row["id"], row["title"], TOKENIZER) for i,row in tqdm
        (df.iterrows())]
        with open('./Data/passage/passage_'+str(i)+'.pkl', 'wb') as f:
        pickle.dump(passage_list, f)
        del passage_list
```

Designing Your Q&A

As shown in Figure 9-2, there are multiple components in a Q&A system. Mainly the functionalities are divided between the Retriever and Reading/Comprehension modules. Each module further contains multiple parts which can be removed or added depending on the complexity of the use case and expected performance. Let's deep dive into each of them and see what all makes up a Retriever module and a Reading module.

Retriever Module

A retriever module is made up of three main parts:

- Query paraphrasing

- Retrieval mechanics (core)

- Reranking

Query Paraphrasing

Query paraphrasing is the process of asking semantically the same query but changing it linguistically. For example, **"What are the benefits of taking covaxin?"** can be paraphrased to **"What are the advantages of using covaxin?"**

There can be multiple ways in which queries can be paraphrased. This is captured extremely well by a NeurIPS 2016 paper titled "Paraphrase Generation with Latent Bag of Words" by Fu et al. They propose that lexical substitutions from WordNet like ontologies and seq2seq models (generative models) do not fully capture all linguistic aspect of the sentence. These linguistic aspects can be

1) **Morphology**: Study of words and parts of words such as root words, prefixes, suffixes, etc. (e.g. speak-speaking-spoken)

2) **Synonym**: Words similar to other words (e.g. big-large, airplane-jet)

3) **Entailment**: If sentence A entails sentence B then sentence A can't be true without B being true as well (e.g. sky-airplane, court-racket)

4) **Metonymy**: Search engines like Google, Quora, etc.

The authors use the words from the source sentence to predict their neighbors and use the words in the target sentence as the target BOW. See Figure 9-4.

Quora

Input	why do	people	ask	questions on	quora	instead of	googling it
Neighbor			post	quora	quora		google
			answer	questions	questions		search
BOW sample	ask, quora, people, questions, google, googling, easily, googled, search, answer						
Output	why do people ask questions on quora that can be easily found on a google search ?						
Input	how do	i	talk	english fluently ?			
Neighbor			speak	english fluently			
			better	improve confidence			
BOW sample	english, speak, improve, fluently, talk, spoken, better, best, confidence						
Output	how can i improve my english speaking ?						

MSCOCO

Input	A	tennis player	is	walking while	holding	his	racket
Neighbor		court holding		walks	carrying		court
		racket man		across	holds		racquet
BOW sample	holding, man, tennis, walking, racket, court, player, racquet, male, woman, walks						
Output	A man holding a tennis racquet on a tennis court						
Input	A	big	airplane flying	in	the	blue	sky
Neighbor		large	airplane sky			blue	clear
		large	jet	airplane		clear	flying
BOW sample	blue, airplane, flying, large, plane, sky, clear, air, flies, jet						
Output	A large jetliner flying through a blue sky						

word morphology	synonym	entailment	metonymy

Figure 9-4. *Example from the deep generative BOW model*

The datasets used in the paper can't be used in specialized domains like biomedical. There are datasets like MedSTS that give a pair of similar biomedical sentences, which can be used to try the ideas from the paper.

Another paper titled "BERT-QE: Contextualized Query Expansion for Document Re-ranking" by Zheng et al focuses on not actually creating new queries but trying to find contextual evidence from within the paragraphs that are to be retrieved. This reduces the false positives due to spurious query generation that can happen due to use of ontologies (which doesn't address polysemy and/or semantics of the usage) or other methods based on syntactic correctness.

It does so in three phases:

- **Phase 1**: Take the top n documents from BM25 (term-based matching, discussed in the next section) and find the relevance score using a fine-tuned BERT model trained on the MSMARCO and ROBUST04 datasets. This selects the relevant document given the query.

- **Phase 2**: For each of these documents you now select chunks, which are subphrases taken from the docs with a sliding window of size m such that two neighboring chunks are overlapped by up to m/2 words. This selects the relevant chunks given the query. See Figure 9-5.

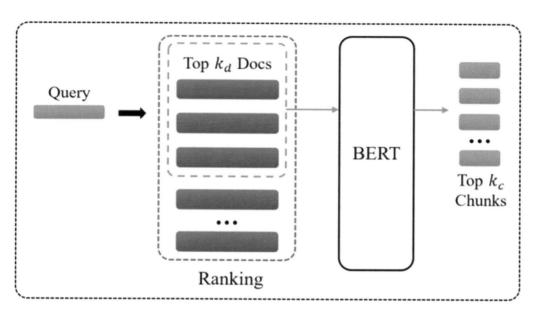

Figure 9-5. *Phase 1 and 2 of the BERT-QE model*

- **Phase 3**: The chunks selected from phase two are used in combination with the original query to compute a final reranking. You start by evaluating the relevance of a document using the selected feedback chunks and the query relevance score as weights to chunk and document relevance.

$$rel(C,d) = \sum_{c_i \in C} \text{softmax}_{c_i \in C} \left(rel(q,c_i) \right) \cdot rel(c_i,d)$$

With α as the hyperparameter, you weigh the importance of relevancy score of (query, document) and (chunk, document).

$$rel(q,C,d) = (1-\alpha) \cdot rel(q,d) + \alpha \cdot rel(C,d)$$

You will use the second approach because it is domain agnostic and you can capture semantics by using a COVID-specific corpus. You will be using deepset's Covid fine-tuned model from `https://huggingface.co/deepset/covid_bert_base`.

Retrieval Mechanics

A retriever generates a set of candidate passages. Since the number of documents can be very large, especially for open-domain question answering systems, it is very important to have an efficient retrieval mechanism. It can be either term-based **or** semantic-based.

Term/Phrase-Based

Both the query text and the context text are represented by a vector where each dimension represents a word in the vocabulary. Now, since each context only contains a subset of possible terms, their term vectors are often sparse.

The similarity between two texts, for instance a document and a query, can be computed by a dot product between these vectors while also accounting for term importance using techniques like TF-IDF or BM25.

BM25 helps saturate term frequency and takes into account the document length by penalizing larger docs containing no relevant term for the query. If you're interested in knowing more, go to `www.kmwllc.com/index.php/2020/03/20/understanding-tf-idf-and-bm25/`.

To efficiently do term-based matching at scale, you need to create an inverted index of the content. An inverted index is a type of hashmap that maps words to the documents they are found in. All major search engines like Elasticsearch, Solr, and Anserini use inverted indexing to fetch documents given a set of words.

There are three main steps to create an inverted index:

1) Load the document.

2) Analyze it.

    - Remove stop words like "I", "the", "we", "is", "an," etc.

    - Stem the root word to normalize the words.

3)   Make an inverted index.

   – In a general search, you find a document and then the word in it, but with
     an inverted search, you directly query over terms and then find the docu-
     ment IDs pertaining to them.

For more information on how inverted indexes work, refer to
`www.elastic.co/guide/en/elasticsearch/guide/current/inverted-index.html`.

Semantic-Based

Almost all search engines provide the ability to pass synonyms for the indexed words but
the potential terms in the vocabulary can be really large. Here comes our old good friend
embeddings, which basically tries to quantify the proportion of your text to different
semantic categories.

There are various ways to train these embeddings for semantic retrieval. Let's
discuss some of them. Before you dive deeper, you need to understand that any kind of
embeddings can be used here but you want embeddings that are trained on "similarity"
tasks such as end-to-end Q&A, sentence similarity, natural language inference (NLI), etc.

- **Dense passage retrieval**: Two independent BERT networks are used
  to encode passages and queries to take into account their different
  nature such as length, style, and syntax to optimize the dot product of
  the two encodings to perform better on ranking query-passage pairs.

- **NLI-based**: Natural language inference is the task of determining
  whether a "hypothesis" is true (entailment), false (contradiction), or
  undetermined (neutral) given a "premise."

- **Sentence similarity**: Given a pair of sentences and flag 1/0, which
  shows whether the sentence is similar or not, model weights are fine-
  tuned to reduce binary cross-entropy loss between the target and
  predicted labels.

Since you are mostly concerned with optimizing on the similarity task, which in
turns means you need to adopt a method closest to understanding the natural language,
I'll only discuss NLI-based methods in detail.

Given a pair of texts, you predict the similarity by predicting for three classes:
entailment (meaning similar), contradiction (meaning not similar at all), and neutral

(meaning the premise and hypothesis are completely independent). With the addition of a third state, the model is better able to understand sentences. See Figure 9-6.

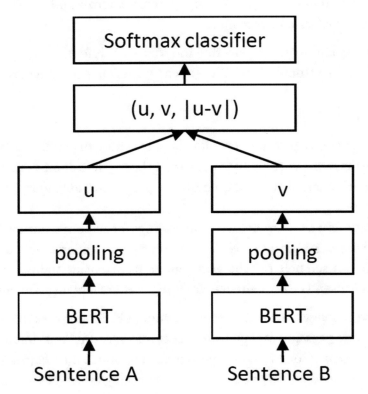

Figure 9-6. *Using NLI to create sentence representation*

The idea to use NLI for sentence representation was presented in the paper titled "Supervised Learning of Universal Sentence Representations from Natural Language Inference Data" by Conneau et al.

You will be using a pretrained model that uses different NLI datasets, particularly related to the biomedical domain. These MedNLI datasets are obtained from PhysioNet, the same website from which you accessed to MIMIC 3 dataset for your first case. The good news is you don't have to go through any training to access to this new dataset. See Figure 9-7.

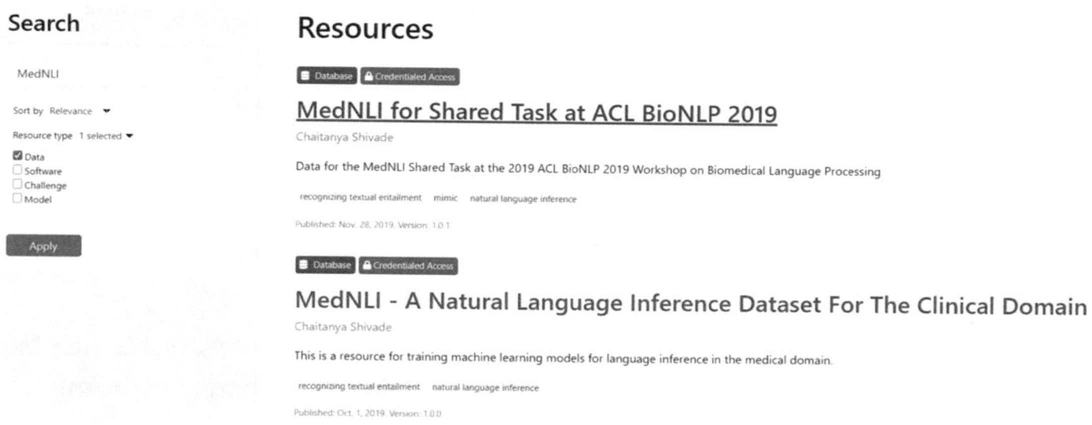

Figure 9-7. *PhysioNet MedNLI data*

Since you are going to use large dimensional embeddings on your list of paragraphs, it is recommended to index them for fast retrieval. You are particularly going to use FAISS for this.

FAISS is a C++ library with Python bindings that is used to do vector similarity matching over millions or billions of vectors. More details can be found at `https://engineering.fb.com/2017/03/29/data-infrastructure/faiss-a-library-for-efficient-similarity-search/`.

Reranking

Reranking is the final nail in the coffin for getting the best ranked passages on which your Q&A model can run.

MS-MARCO is the most widely used dataset when it comes to passage reranking. For reranking, you need a query against a set of positive and negative passages. You are free to choose any ratio of positive to negative passage for a query. This ratio also determines the size of your training data. You can read more about it at `https://github.com/microsoft/MSMARCO-Passage-Ranking#ranking-task`.

You can't directly use the MS-MARCO dataset for your domain as most of the questions in the dataset are not medically related, causing a domain mismatch between the training and evaluation data.

To overcome this challenge, MacAvaney et al in their paper titled "SLEDGE-Z: A Zero-Shot Baseline for COVID-19 Literature Search" used MedSyn, a lexicon of layperson and expert terminology for various medical conditions, to filter for medical questions.

Yes, you are right to think here that you can also replace it with the UMLs ontologies that we discussed previously, but the beauty of this ontology is that the terms are more general human conversation lingo and not terms based on scientific literature.

Hence you will be using a CovidBert transformer fine-tuned for the ranking task for reranking of your results.

Comprehension

There are various machine comprehension/question answering models/techniques that leverage state-of-the-art deep-learning methodologies, such as the neural variational inference model (VS-NET), RNNs with self-matching attention, and even convolutional networks. But for this case study, you will be leveraging the transformer architecture via BERT models to learn what machine comprehension is and how BERT does it.

You learned a lot about the BERT architecture in Chapter 4. If you haven't read that chapter, go through the section "Understanding How Language Modeling works" to understand more about it.

In a question-answering task, you are given a question along with a paragraph containing an answer to the question. The goal is to extract the answer from the paragraph for the given question.

BERT for Q&A

To prepare the input for training a Q&A model on BERT, there are five major steps. You won't be coding each step because they are handled by the use of external libraries.

1) When using BERT for the question answering task, you represent the input question and passage as a single packed sequence.

2) The [CLS] token is added to the beginning of the question. It plays no role in picking up the answer but condenses the question's context.

3) The [SEP] token is added at the end of the question as well as the passage.

4) BERT also uses segment embeddings to differentiate between the question and the passage that contains an answer. BERT creates two segment embeddings, one for the question and other for the passage, to differentiate between the question and passage. Then these embeddings are added to a one-hot representation of tokens (BERT tokenization using token embedding) to segregate between the question and passage.

5) A positional embedding is also added to each token to indicate its position in the sequence. See Figure 9-8.

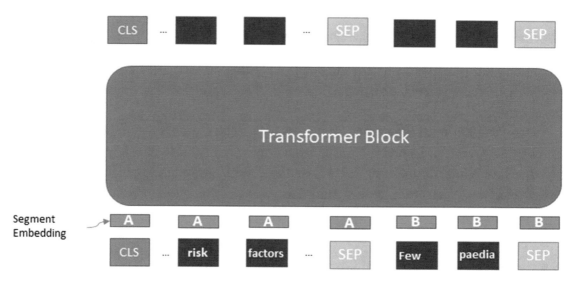

Figure 9-8. *Input of the BERT for QnA*

When I say that the model must extract an answer from the paragraph, it essentially has to return the text span containing the answer. This is done by finding the start and end index of the text span.

You only introduce a start vector S and an end vector E during fine-tuning. The probability of word i being the start of the answer span is computed as a dot product between T_i and S, followed by a Softmax over all of the words in the paragraph. Similarly, an E vector is present to calculate the end index.

One thing to note here is that both S and E are 768-dimension vectors, which is equal to the dimension of the token's embedding. For one iteration the same weights are applied to each token embedding. See Figure 9-9.

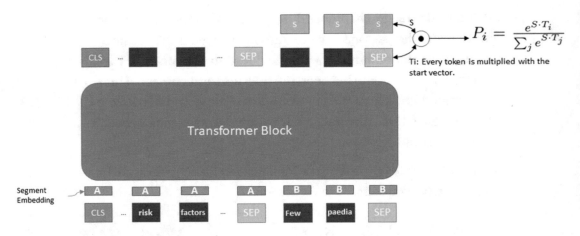

$$P_i = \frac{e^{S \cdot T_i}}{\sum_j e^{S \cdot T_j}}$$

Ti: Every token is multiplied with the start vector.

Figure 9-9. *Calculating the start index for the answer span*

I hope this provides a very succinct review of how you set up BERT for Q&A training. In this case study, you will be using a fine-tuned BERT model and will not be training from scratch.

If you want to learn how BERT does its magic on Q&A, read the paper titled "How Does BERT Answer Questions? A Layer-Wise Analysis of Transformer Representations" by Aken and Winter. It does this analysis on three main parameters, which are interpretability, transferability, and modularity.

Fine-Tuning a Q&A Dataset

More often you will not be training a transformer model from scratch for just the question/answering task. You will mostly be fine-tuning it for various tasks. It works just like the transfer learning examples you saw in the past chapters.

Question answering comes in many forms. In this case study, you are going to do extractive QA that involves answering a question using a passage as the context for comprehension and then highlighting the segment of the passage that answers the question. This involves fine-tuning a model that predicts a start position and an end position in the passage.

One popular dataset for such a task is the SQUAD dataset. It consists of 100k+ questions on a set of Wikipedia articles, where the answer to each question is a text snippet from corresponding passages. SQUAD 2.0 takes it a step further by combining the 100k questions with 50k+ unanswerable questions that look similar to the answerable ones.

There's a fine-tuned BERT model on the SQUAD dataset available at `https://huggingface.co/graviraja/covidbert_squad`. You will use this model for your comprehension task.

If you want to learn how to fine-tune a pretrained model from scratch, Hugging Face provides a very good tutorial on how to do so at `https://huggingface.co/transformers/custom_datasets.html#question-answering-with-squad-2-0`.

Recently COVID-QA (`https://github.com/deepset-ai/COVID-QA`), which is a question answering dataset consisting of 2,019 question/answer pairs annotated, was released. It can be used to further fine-tune your comprehension model. I leave this as a task for you to try.

Final Design and Code

Based on your understanding of the different components of QnA, let's quickly lay out the steps needed to design it. See Figure 9-10.

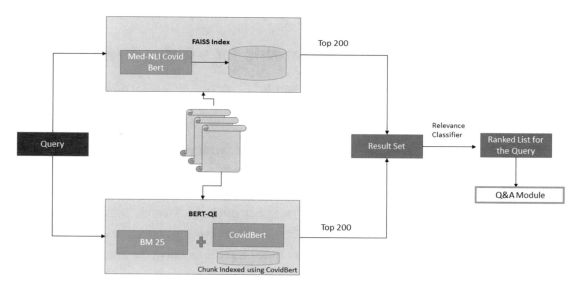

Figure 9-10. *Q&A system design*

Step 0: Preparing the Document Data

You start by loading the pickle file that you saved after converting the abstracts to passages.

```python
import glob
import pickle
import pandas as pd
all_metadata = []
    for i,files in enumerate(glob.glob("./Data/passage/passage_*.pkl")):
        with open(files, 'rb') as f:
            data_list = pickle.load(f)
            all_metadata.extend([data_pair for data in data_list \
                            for data_pair in data])

    all_metadata_df = pd.DataFrame(all_metadata, columns = ["id","passage_
    id","title","passage"])
```

Step 1: BERT-QE Expansion

Step 1.1: Extract the Top k Documents for a Query Using BM-25

Since there are a lot of documents, I will be randomly sampling 50,000 passages from the all_metadata_df to carry out relevancy tasks. If you have a very large amount of RAM, you can try with the full or partial data.

Since BM-25 works on terms, you need to tokenize your passages to these terms to create an inverted index and then retrieve them using BM-25. For this exercise, you are going to use the rank-bm25 package.

For tokenizers, you are going to use a base spacy package. Please note that spacy has released v3.0, which extensively uses transformers for accuracy but is not efficient for our purpose, which is tokenization. Previous spacy pipelines are quite accurate, so you will use the en_core_web_sm spacy package for this purpose.

```python
from spacy.tokenizer import Tokenizer
from spacy.lang.en import English
nlp = English()
# Create a blank Tokenizer with just the English vocab
tokenizer = Tokenizer(nlp.vocab)
```

You are going to create a class called BM25RankedResults which basically **indexes your data** and **allows you to query and return** the top 200 documents.

```python
from rank_bm25 import BM25Okapi
import numpy as np

    class BM25RankedResults:
        """
        BM25 Results from the abstract.

        Usage:

        bm25 = BM25RankedResults(metadata_df) # metadata_df is a pandas
        dataframe with 'title' and 'abstract' columns
        topbm25 = bm25.search("What is coronavirus", num=10) # Return `num`
        top-results
        """

        def __init__(self, corpus: pd.DataFrame):
        self.corpus = corpus
        self.columns = corpus.columns
        token_list = pd.Series([[str(token) for token in doc if str(token)] \
            for doc in tokenizer.pipe(corpus.passage,
                                      batch_size=5000)])
        self.index = token_list.to_frame()
            self.index.columns = ['terms']
        self.index.index = self.corpus.index
        self.bm25 = BM25Okapi(self.index.terms.tolist())

        self.bm25 = BM25Okapi(token_list)

        def search(self, query, num = 200):
            """
            Return top `num` results that better match the query
            """
        search_terms = query.split()
        doc_scores = self.bm25.get_scores(search_terms) # get scores

            ind = np.argsort(doc_scores)[::-1][:num] # sort results
```

```
    results = self.corpus.iloc[ind][self.columns] # Initialize results_df
        results['score'] = doc_scores[ind] # Insert 'score' column
        results = results[results.score > 0]
    return results.passage_id.tolist()

  passage_data = all_metadata_df.sample(50000)
bm25 = BM25RankedResults(passage_data) # Covid Search Engine
```

If you want to work with full data and have a decent amount of RAM, you can also load a prebuilt Lucene index and use Pyserini (v 9.3.1) to query using BM-25. It is faster and very scalable.

I already have the index built for the configuration I used to create the passage, which is stride of 1 and maximum length of 300 tokens for the passage. You can get those files from https://drive.google.com/file/d/1A824rH3iNg8tRjCYsH2aD50YQMNR6FVI/view.

Now load the prebuilt binary and call the SimpleSearcher class.

```
from pyserini.search import SimpleSearcher
    bm25 = SimpleSearcher('./Data/indexes')

# Example
search_hits = bm25.search('what is coronavirus', k= 200)
    bm25_passage = [hit.docid for hit in search_hits]
```

I am going to use the pyserini method for the rest of the code because it is super-fast, but the BM25RankedResults class offers more flexibility in terms of handling text (cleaning, lemmatization, etc.) and can be used as well.

Step 1.2: Relevance Score on the Top 200 Documents

To calculate the relevance score, there are three phases, as discussed in the section above. Although the authors have experimented with different transformer models in different phases, for your use case you will use the covidBert model from deepset available at https://huggingface.co/deepset/covid_bert_base.

To load this model, you will use the sentence-transformer library. It is an excellent library that quickly helps to compute dense vector representations for sentences and paragraphs. It supports various transformer networks like BERT, RoBERTa, XLM-RoBERTa, etc.

If you have cuda set up on your laptop, you can also pass the device for the model to perform operations on. For NVIDIA-GPU cards you can pass device = 'cuda'.

```python
from sentence_transformers import SentenceTransformer,util
    covid_bert = SentenceTransformer("deepset/covid_bert_base",
    device = 'cuda')
```

Since BERT-QE is based on finding the top n passages/chunks, let's write a single wrapper function to get the top k values based on cosine similarity between two vectors.

You start by encoding all the of text present in the list using the covidBert model.

Then you use a built-in function from the sentence-transformer utility file to compute cosine scores and then return the top k matches based on cosine similarity.

There is a flag variable that you can use if you want to directly work with the cosine score metric.

```python
def get_top_k_vals(list1, list2, k = 100, model = covid_bert, return_
cosine_mat = False):
# Compute embedding for both lists
embeddings1 = model.encode(list1, convert_to_tensor = True)
embeddings2 = model.encode(list2, convert_to_tensor = True)

# Compute cosine-similarity
cosine_scores = util.pytorch_cos_sim(embeddings1, embeddings2)

if return_cosine_mat:
    return cosine_scores.numpy()

# Select top kd documents/passage
    _topkd = np.argsort(cosine_scores.numpy()[0])[::-1][:k]

    return _topkd, cosine_scores.numpy()[0][_topkd]
```

You also need to calculate the Softmax of the query with top chunks, so let's define a Softmax function that can work with a NumPy array.

```python
def softmax(x):
    """Compute softmax values for each sets of scores in x."""
e_x = np.exp(x - np.max(x))
    return e_x / e_x.sum(axis=0)
```

You are now ready to write the main function. The steps are as laid out in the original paper. I have commented the code into separate phases for better understanding.

```python
from collections import OrderedDict
    def bert_qe(query, bm25_model, passage_id_map, bert_model = covid_bert,
                alpha = 0.4, document_size = 500, chunk_size = 8):
        """
        Re-ranks BM-25 document based on relevancy of query to chunks of a
        passage.
        """

        print("\tPhase 1")
    # Phase 1
    topbm25 = bm25_model.search(query, document_size)

    #doc index to passage map
    passage_index_map = OrderedDict({idx:passage_id_map[passages] if
    isinstance(passages,str) \
                            else passage_id_map[passages.docid] for
                            idx,passages in enumerate(topbm25)})
    passageid_index_map = OrderedDict({idx:passages if
    isinstance(passages,str) \
                            else passages.docid for idx,passages in
                            enumerate(topbm25)})

    _topdocidx, _topdocscores = get_top_k_vals([query],
                                    list(passage_index_map.values()),
                                    k = document_size, model = bert_model)
    # Store Top Contextually matching docs
    passage_scores = {idx:score for idx,score in zip(_topdocidx,
    _topdocscores)}

        print("\tPhase 2")
    # Phase 2
    # Create chunks of length "n" and stride them with a length of "n/2"
        _chunks = [[" ".join(phrase) for i, phrase in enumerate(nltk.
        ngrams(passage_index_map[idx].split(),
        chunk_size)) if i%(chunk_size/2)==0] for idx in _topdocidx]
```

```python
# Flatten the list
all_chunks = list(chain.from_iterable(_chunks))

# Get top chunks based on relevancy score with the query
_topchunkidx, _topchunkscores = get_top_k_vals([query],
                                    all_chunks,
                                        k = int(len(all_chunks)/2),
                                        model = bert_model)

top_chunks = np.array(all_chunks)[_topchunkidx]

# Apply softmax over query and chunk relevancy score,
# This acts as weights to chunk and document relevancy
_topchunksoftmax = softmax(_topchunkscores)

# Phase 3
    print("\tPhase 3")
scores = get_top_k_vals(list(passage_index_map.values()),
                        list(top_chunks),
                        k = len(top_chunks),
                        model = bert_model,
                        return_cosine_mat = True)

# Multiply the weights of chunk with query to relevancy of chunk with
the document
# and sum over all the top chunks (kc in the paper)
    docchunk_score = np.sum(np.multiply(_topchunksoftmax,
    np.array(scores)), axis = 1)

# weighing importance of query relevance and query chunk-doc relevance

    final_score = alpha*_topdocscores + (1-alpha)*docchunk_score

passage_score = dict(zip([passageid_index_map[idx] for idx in
_topdocidx],final_score))

return passage_score
```

Step 2: Semantic Passage Retrieval

To achieve semantic retrieval at a considerable pace, you will leverage Faiss. Faiss is a library for efficient similarity searching and clustering of dense vectors. It contains algorithms that search in sets of vectors of any size, even ones that do not fit in RAM.

Faiss uses only 32-bit floating point matrices. This means that you must change the data type of the input before building the index.

Here, you will use the IndexFlatIP index. It's a simple index that performs a maximum inner product search.

For a whole list of the index, you can visit
`https://github.com/facebookresearch/faiss/wiki/Faiss-indexes`.

You start by loading the covidbert-nli model to get the encoding of all the passages you have. This is the same model that you used for tokenization to create running length passages from your abstract.

```
# Instantiate the sentence-level covid-BERT NLI model
    from sentence_transformers import SentenceTransformer,util
    covid_nli = SentenceTransformer('./pre_trained_model/training_nli_
    covidbert-mednli', device = 'cuda')
```

```
# Convert abstracts to vectors
embeddings = covid_nli.encode(passage_data.passage.to_list(), show_
progress_bar=True)
```

You can now write the code for Faiss indexing. Please note that Faiss doesn't support string IDs and hence an external map needs to be created for the `passage_ids` that are mapped to an integer value.

Also, to create an index with the passage vectors, you will

- Change the data type of the passage vectors to float32.

- Build an index and pass it the dimension of the vectors it will operate on.

- Pass the index to `IndexIDMap`, an object that enables you to provide a custom list of IDs for the indexed vectors.

- Add the passage vectors and their ID mapping to the index.

```
import faiss

# Building FAISS Index
    embeddings = np.array([embedding for embedding in embeddings]).
    astype("float32")

# Instantiate the index
    embedding_index = faiss.IndexFlatIP(embeddings.shape[1])

# Pass the passage index to IndexIDMap
embedding_index = faiss.IndexIDMap(embedding_index)

# Numerical map
passage_num_map = {int(i):x for i,x in enumerate(all_metadata_df.passage_
id.values)}

# Add vectors and their IDs
embedding_index.add_with_ids(embeddings, np.array(list(passage_num_map.
keys()), np.int64))
```

You can now save this index using the Faiss library. You can use this index later to deploy your Q&A model in the next chapter.

```
faiss.write_index(index, "./Data/faiss_cord-19-passage.index")
```

You can load a Faiss index by using the read_index command.

```
embedding_index = faiss.read_index("./Data/faiss_cord-19-passage.index")
```

Step 3: Passage Reranking Using a Fine-Tuned Covid BERT Model on the Med-Marco Dataset

You are at the final step of your retriever steps where you use the passages from both BERT-QE and semantic retrieval to rerank using the BERT model trained on the reranking tasks on the Med-Marco dataset.

You can download the pretrained model from https://huggingface.co/ Darkrider/covidbert_medmarco and create a folder named pretrained_model in your working directory and save it there. Or you can directly pass the string /Darkrider/ covidbert_medmarco to CrossEncoder().

Once you download it, you can place it in your `pre_trained_model` folder.

```
from sentence_transformers.cross_encoder import CrossEncoder
    covid_marco = CrossEncoder("./pre_trained_model/training_medmarco_
    covidbert")
```

Sentence transformers provide two wrapper functions to compare a pair of sentences. The first is a bi-encoder and the second is a cross-encoder.

Bi-encoders produce for a given sentence a sentence embedding. You pass the sentences A and B to a BERT independently, which results in the sentence embeddings u and v. These sentence embedding can then be compared using cosine similarity. In contrast, for a cross-encoder, you pass both sentences simultaneously to the transformer network. It produces an output value between 0 and 1, indicating the similarity of the input sentence pair.

Since for your passage ranking task you are not concerned about individual embeddings but how similar two sentences are, you will use cross-encoders. See Figure 9-11.

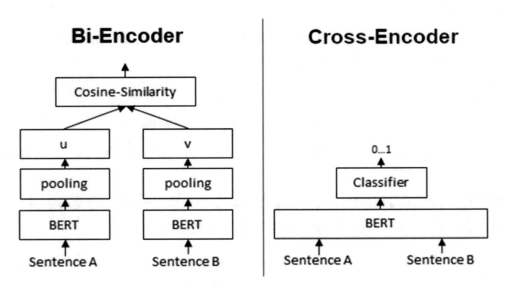

Figure 9-11. *Bi-encoder vs. cross-encoder for a sentence pair*

As per Figure 9-10, you now have important passages from the BERT query expansion technique and the semantic vector matching. You are ready to rerank them using a fine-tuned BERT model on the Med-Marco dataset explained in the "Retriever" section.

For this you first write a wrapper function that collates the results from step 1 and 2. This function basically takes the passage IDs from Step 1 and 2 and passes them to the Marco-trained model (Step 3).

```
def get_ranked_passages(query, bm25_model, bert_model, passage_id_map,
faiss_index, bert_qe_alpha = 0.4):

    print("Step 1 : BERT-QE Expansion")
#BERT-QE
bertqe_dict = bert_qe(query, bm25_model = bm25_model, passage_id_map =
passage_id_map,
        bert_model = bert_model, alpha = 0.4, document_size = 500,
        chunk_size = 8)

    print("Step 2 : Semantic Passage Retrieval")
# Semantic Search
    _,indices = faiss_index.search(np.expand_dims(covid_nli.
    encode(query), axis = 0), k=500)
    semantic_passage_ids = [passage_num_map[idx] for idx in indices[0]]

# passages to be re-ranked
total_passage_ids = list(bertqe_dict.keys())+ semantic_passage_ids

    return list(set(total_passage_ids))
```

Finally, based on the query, you retrieve the final ranked documents.

```
# Some queries we want to search for in the document
    queries = ["What is Coronavirus"]

# Map of Passage id to Passage Text
passage_id_map = pd.Series(all_metadata_df.passage.values,index=all_
metadata_df.passage_id).to_dict()

#Search in a loop for the individual queries
for i,query in enumerate(queries):
        print(f"Ranking Passages for {i+1} of {len(queries)} query/queries")
    passage_ids = get_ranked_passages(query, bm25_model = bm25, passage_id_
    map = passage_id_map,
                                bert_model = covid_bert,
```

```
                                 faiss_index = embedding_index,
                                    bert_qe_alpha = 0.4)
```

#Concatenate the query and all passages and predict the scores for the pairs [query, passage]
```
model_inputs = [[query, passage_id_map[passage_id]] for passage_id in passage_ids]

    print("Step 3 : Passage Re-ranking using Fine-Tuned Covid BERT ")
scores = covid_marco.predict(model_inputs)
```

#Sort the scores in decreasing order
```
    results = [{'input': inp, 'score': score} for inp, score in
    zip(passage_ids, scores)]
    results = sorted(results, key=lambda x: x['score'], reverse=True)
```

Output

```
Ranking Passages for 1 of 1 query/queries
Step 1 : BERT-QE Expansion
          Phase 1
          Phase 2
          Phase 3
Step 2 : Semantic Passage Retrieval
Step 3 : Passage Re-ranking using Fine-Tuned Covid BERT
```

Note that result is a dictionary containing the passage_id and the ranked score. You are now finally ready to do comprehension. You can also subset the results based on the score. Let's keep a cutoff of 0.3

```
    final_results = {res_dict['input']:res_dict['score'] for res_dict in
    results if res_dict['score'] > 0.3}

len(final_results)
```

Output

107

You see how by using intelligent retrieval techniques you are able to reduce your document search space from 0.6 million to just ~100 odd documents/passages.

Step 4: Comprehension

Hugging Face provides a simple interface for model inference using pipelines. These are objects that abstract out most of the complex code for model inference. They cover many tasks, such as

- `ConversationalPipeline`

- `FeatureExtractionPipeline`

- `FillMaskPipeline`

- `QuestionAnsweringPipeline`

- `SummarizationPipeline`

- `TextClassificationPipeline`

- `TextGenerationPipeline`

- `TokenClassificationPipeline`

- `TranslationPipeline`

- `ZeroShotClassificationPipeline`

- `Text2TextGenerationPipeline`

- `TableQuestionAnsweringPipeline`

Well, each of these tasks deserves a chapter in of its own, but for this case study you are concerned with just the `QuestionAnsweringPipeline`.

```
from transformers import pipeline
comprehension_model = pipeline("question-answering", model='graviraja/
covidbert_squad',tokenizer='graviraja/covidbert_squad', device=-1)
```

The parameters are

- `task(str)`: The task defining which pipeline will be returned. "question-answering" returns a `QuestionAnsweringPipeline`.

- `model(str or PreTrainedModel(pytorch) or TFPreTrained Model(Tensorflow))`: The model that will be used by the pipeline to make predictions. This can be a model identifier (string) or an actual instance of a pretrained model inheriting from `PreTrainedModel` (for PyTorch) or `TFPreTrainedModel` (for TensorFlow).

- `tokenizer (str or PreTrainedTokenizer)`: The tokenizer that will be used by the pipeline to encode data for the model. This can be a model identifier or an actual pretrained tokenizer inheriting from `PreTrainedTokenizer`. If not provided, the default tokenizer for the given model will be loaded (if it is a string).

- `use_fast (bool)`: Whether or not to use a fast tokenizer if possible. Fast tokenizers are implemented using Rust.

- `device` is a kwarg parameter. You use "-1" to enable GPU use.

To use this, you need to pass the question and the context.

```
# sample example
comprehension_model(question="What is coronavirus", context=all_
metadata_df.passage.tolist()[0])
```

Output

```
{'score': 0.02539900690317154,
 'start': 529,
 'end': 547,
 'answer': 'community-acquired'}
```

Now on Kaggle's CORD-19 task, there are sets of questions that are divided across nine tasks:

1. What is known about transmission, incubation, and environmental stability?

2. What do we know about COVID-19 risk factors?

3. What do we know about virus genetics, origin, and evolution?

4. What do we know about vaccines and therapeutics?

5. What do we know about non-pharmaceutical interventions?

6. What has been published about medical care?

7. What do we know about diagnostics and surveillance?

8. What has been published about information sharing and inter-sectoral collaboration?

9. What has been published about ethical and social science considerations?

Each of these tasks has a set of questions that are often asked in a COVID-Literature search, so you will include them as well. Thanks to @kaggle/dirktheeng for compiling these questions.

Here is a small snippet of these questions:

```
covid_kaggle_questions = [
    {
        "task": "What is known about transmission, incubation,
        and environmental stability?",
        "questions": [
            "Is the virus transmitted by aerosol, droplets, food,
            close contact, fecal matter, or water?",
            "How long is the incubation period for the virus?",
            •••
        ]
    },
    {
        "task": "What do we know about COVID-19 risk factors?",
        "questions": [
            "What risk factors contribute to the severity of
            2019-nCoV?",
            "How does hypertension affect patients?",
            "How does heart disease affect patients?",
            •••
        ]
    }
]
```

Let's go back and modify the question for loop that ranks the passages for comprehension and create a dataframe for each task's question.

Using the Q&A pipeline from Hugging Face, you basically get a dictionary of the form.

```
{'score': 0.622232091629833, 'start': 34, 'end': 96, 'answer':
'COVID-19 happens in respiratory tract'}
```

Since you pass a list of passage_ids (a.k.a. context), you get a list of this dictionary. When creating the comprehension output (comp_output variable) make sure to pass the passage_id and the passage_rank score. You are storing this information to use it later in deployment (Chapter 10).

Finally, you store all of the answers for each question from all of the tasks in a dataframe named all_comprehension_df.

```
# Map of Passage id to Passage Text
passage_id_map = pd.Series(all_metadata_df.passage.values,index=all_
metadata_df.passage_id).to_dict()

# Numerical map for semantic passage retrieval
passage_num_map = pd.Series(all_metadata_df.passage_id.values,index=pd.
Series(range(len(all_metadata_df)))).to_dict()

# Map of Passage id to Paper Title
passage_id_title_map = pd.Series(all_metadata_df.title.values,index=all_
metadata_df.passage_id).to_dict()

all_comprehension_df_list = []
#Search in a loop for the individual queries
for task_query_dict in covid_kaggle_questions:
        for i,query in enumerate(task_query_dict["questions"]):
            print(f"Ranking Passages for {i+1} of {len(task_query_
            dict['questions'])} query/queries")
            passage_ids = get_ranked_passages(query, bm25_model = bm25,
            passage_id_map = passage_id_map,bert_model = covid_bert, faiss_
            index = embedding_index, bert_qe_alpha = 0.4)

        #Concatenate the query and all passages and predict the scores for
        the pairs [query, passage]
        model_inputs = [[query, passage_id_map[passage_id]] for passage_id
        in passage_ids]
```

```python
    print("Step 3 : Passage Re-ranking using Fine-Tuned Covid BERT ")
scores = covid_marco.predict(model_inputs)

#Sort the scores in decreasing order
    results = [{'input': inp, 'score': score} for inp, score in
    zip(passage_ids, scores)]
    results = sorted(results, key=lambda x: x['score'], reverse=True)

# Filtering passages above a certain threshold
    final_results = {res_dict['input']:res_dict['score'] for res_
    dict in results if res_dict['score'] > 0.3}

    print("Step 4 : Comprehension ")
# Comprehension
    comp_output = [[comprehension_model(question="What is coronavirus",
                            context = passage_id_map[pass_id]),
                        pass_id, pass_score] \
            for pass_id, pass_score in final_results.items() if
            len(passage_id_map[pass_id].split()) > 5]

# Adding pass id and score to the comprehension
    [comp_output[i][0].update({'pass_id': comp_output[i][1],
                        'pass_rank_score': comp_output[i][2]}) for
                    i in range(len(comp_output))]

# Converting list of dictionaries of ranked results to dataframe.
    comprehension_df = pd.DataFrame([comp_[0] for comp_ in comp_output])

# adding query and the task
    comprehension_df["query"] = query
    comprehension_df["task"] = task_query_dict["task"]

# Finally, using passage_id to replace with actual Paper Title and
Context
    comprehension_df["title"] = [passage_id_title_map[pass_id] for
    pass_id in comprehension_df.pass_id]

all_comprehension_df_list.append(comprehension_df)

all_comprehension_df = pd.concat(all_comprehension_df_list, axis = 0)
```

Now you save the pandas dataframe.

```
all_comprehension_df.to_csv("all_question_comprehension.csv",
index = None)
```

Conclusion

You learned a lot in this chapter. You started with the different types of Q&A systems and then you built a system design for a closed-domain Q&A system involving multiple ways of ranking the right document before comprehension can be applied. You also learned new technologies such as FAISS for inner product search. This has applications beyond Q&A and can be used in any large-scale production environment.

Feel free to play around with different questions. Although you are using the questions of the CORD-19 task for the next chapter, you can still pass in your own queries and understand COVID better.

CHAPTER 10

You Need an Audience Now

A very large percentage of ML research and modeling today is left to gather dust in Jupyter notebooks or multiple Python scripts. It takes a great amount of understanding of other IT systems and enterprise architecture for a data scientist to take things to production and go live on a real system. Trends have changed in the industry from just a "data scientist" to a "full-stack data scientist."

All of our modern ML application code is nothing but libraries with a complicated setup process with data munging. In this chapter, you will learn how to take models to production with the help of Docker, which can reproduce the environment you used to develop your ML code, which then leads to reproducible outputs and hence provides portability. You will also deploy your app with a live URL using Heroku.

Demystifying the Web

Most enterprise applications today are web applications. Gone are the days of downloading an .exe file to run the latest software. Most software today runs in the cloud. This has led to a change in the scale, experience, and cost for both companies and consumers. We are putting larger computing powers into smaller devices and are living in an "always connected" world via the Internet. With changing times, a change in technology is warranted.

Modern software systems follow a CI/CD approach (continuous integration and continuous deployment). Continuous integration aims at integrating the source code with proper testing, and deployment takes that code and packages it for deployment. For AI to be successful, it needs to be a part of this system.

© Anshik 2021
Anshik, *AI for Healthcare with Keras and Tensorflow 2.0*, https://doi.org/10.1007/978-1-4842-7086-8_10

A data scientist, when given a problem, will start with a Jupyter notebook/Python script and create a model that solves the problem. Once the model achieves the required accuracy, it will be stored in file formats such as `.h5`, `.pkl`, or `.onnx` so that it can be loaded and used by another data scientist or end user. To integrate it into modern applications, which are traditionally written in JS/C#/Java or C++, we have to write a wrapper that can call such a model inside its environment, as most of the data pipelines are written in such languages. This isn't just a problem of integration but also of storing and making available the compute resources to run such a model, as most likely the model will require a GPU. Hence we can't just keep exchanging files. We need to manage the model lifecycle just like software development.

How Does an Application Communicate?

A web application connects to a web server, which is nothing but a remote computer unit (like a CPU). Figure 10-1 explains how the web technology evolved from just static HTML to advance applications such as Gmail, Facebook, etc. One important thing that gets missed in discussion is the evolution of database technologies. Although traditional applications were built on a SQL DB, now more advanced DB technologies are available such as MongoDB, Cassandra, Neo4J, etc.

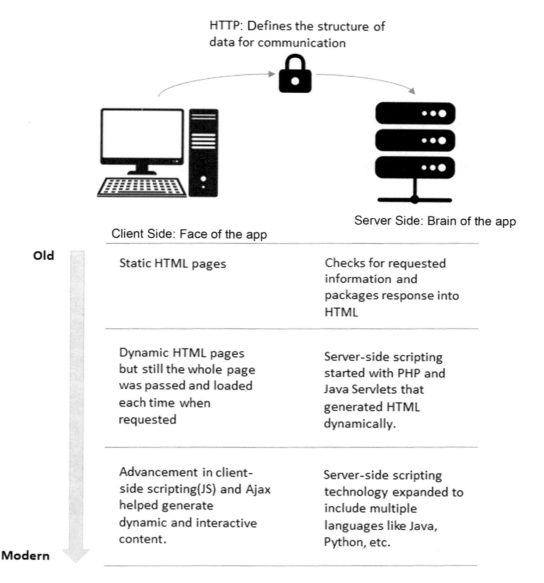

HTTP: Defines the structure of
data for communication

Client Side: Face of the app

Server Side: Brain of the app

Old

Static HTML pages	Checks for requested information and packages response into HTML
Dynamic HTML pages but still the whole page was passed and loaded each time when requested	Server-side scripting started with PHP and Java Servlets that generated HTML dynamically.
Advancement in client-side scripting(JS) and Ajax helped generate dynamic and interactive content.	Server-side scripting technology expanded to include multiple languages like Java, Python, etc.

Modern

Figure 10-1. *Evolution of web technologies*

Generally these websites were supported by local servers maintained by a company's IT but as the applications became complex and extremely connected (with data, people, and other applications), it was difficult to scale the servers proportionately. It didn't make business sense and the resources weren't available to maintain such a highly performant system.

Cloud Technology

And then came cloud technology. For the uninitiated, the cloud is an on-demand computer system available to many users over the Internet. This on-demand system helps us get desired storage and processing power through virtualization (i.e. dividing (through resource-locking via software) servers into smaller virtual machines).

With the cloud making enterprise-scale technology available at a really low cost, many services started to pop up. A view of such technologies is shown in Figure 10-2.

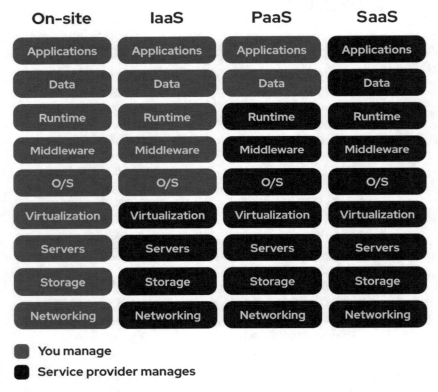

Figure 10-2. *Various cloud-based services. Source:* `redhat.com`

On-site is very rare these days. It might be used for some internal software/websites that can only be accessed via a company's intranet.

In IaaS, only the infrastructure is rented (i.e. a machine with certain storage, RAM, and compute resources is commissioned to you). Imagine buying a CPU. Now you can do anything: install software, make applications, or even start a website. Yes, you can host a website with your computer but can you guarantee uptime and speed?

While using PaaS you are only concerned with developing your code and data scripts. You are not concerned with how many VMs you need to run your code efficiently and also provision the OS, library versions, and so on for each VM separately.

SaaS are generally web-based tools like Google Colab, Facebook, LinkedIn, etc. They are so called because you don't need to set up anything in order to use them. All you need is an Internet connection that communicates to the cloud.

Docker and Kubernetes

Why Docker?

Modern web apps contain a lot of dependencies. Some of them are OS dependent. Some of them are dependent on versions of different libraries that are used. This situation is only expected to grow as more and more libraries are developed independently. You could be using one library from one developer and another one from another, and thus is the case in ML.

This can be very troublesome if you have to integrate code tested on multiple machines (in development) and then integrate it finally to a staging server. To manage issues like this, a new development paradigm is emerging called *containerized applications*. It basically keeps the code, libraries used to run it, and OS-level information as a separate, isolated unit. This isolated unit can be run on another machine as is without worrying about configuring the machine for the application code to run. Docker is the most widely used container technology today and is very popular in the ML community.

OS Virtualization

Docker containers run on top of a host operating system and provide a standardized environment for code running within the container. Docker is suitable when the development environment's operating system and testing operating system are the same. These containerized units basically solve the DevOps issue in ML because you now, along with code, get all of the dependent libraries with the right version and even the OS (i.e. an exact replica of the developer's environment).

This OS virtualization using Docker allows you to achieve efficient use of resources as compared to hardware virtualization done using VM creation with applications such as Hypervisor because you can now dynamically allocate resources between Docker containers, although they all use the same server compared to VMs, which block resources to their respective unit.

Kubernetes

Now, imagine a full-fledged app like Amazon that uses multiple such images of a container. One is allowing search results to come up, one is recommending new items, and one is capturing user behavior and interaction touchpoints with the web app. Can we scale all of them dependent on their usage? Yes. For orchestrating independent Docker containers, we use Kubernetes.

Covering Kubernetes or Docker in more detail than I have is out of the scope for the book but there are some excellent resources online such as articles on `https://mlinproduction.com/`.

Deploying the QnA System

I have covered the basics. You are ready to now deploy your Q&A setup and create a web app.

First, you need a framework to handle your deployment and integration needs such as front-end and backend communication, client- and server-side scaling, etc. You will use Flask for this purpose. Let's dive into it.

Building a Flask Structure

Flask is a microservices web-based framework that allows you to expose any business logic/functions via an API. Although I am not going to cover a lot of Flask, for those of you using Flask for the first time, here are some basics.

Start by creating a folder named `covidquest`. You will use this as the folder for your application.

Install Flask so you can download the latest Flask via a pip channel.

After setting it up, let's create the Flask app.

There are two essential things that are required to make your Flask app, one that handles the client side (front end) and another that handles the server side (back end).

The web application setup contains two files. Hence you will create these two files as follows:

- **app.py**: A Python script to handle client communication and generate responses.

- **index.html**: Your GUI interface. It allows users to submit inputs (a.k.a. requests) for computation and renders the returned result, exactly like you studied in the section "How Does an Application Communicate?"

You can clone the app files from `https://github.com/NeverInAsh/covidquest`. This will serve as your starting point, but let's quickly see the basics of what's in each of your files.

Deep Dive into app.py

```python
from flask import Flask, render_template, request
import pandas as pd
import numpy as np
import sys

    app = Flask(__name__, template_folder='./templates/')

@app.before_first_request
    def at_startup():
    global answer_df, question_map, top_k_map

        answer_df = pd.read_csv("./all_question_comprehension.csv", index_col=None)
        question_map = {'1': 'Is the virus transmitted by aerosol,
        droplets,  food, close contact, fecal matter, or water?',
    ... skipped lines
                        '30': 'Can 2019-nCoV infect patients a second time?'}

        top_k_map = {'0': 5, '1': 10, '2': 20, '3': 30, '4': 50}

@app.route('/')
    def home():
        return render_template("index.html")
```

```
def create_answer(text, start, end):
    output = [text[0:start],
             text[start:end],
             text[end:len(text)]]
    return output

@app.route('/top_k_results', methods=['GET', 'POST'])
    def top_k_results():
        question_select = "0"
        weight = "0.2"
        top_k = "0"
        if request.method == "POST":
            question_select = request.form.get('question_select', '')
            weight = request.form.get('weight', '')
            top_k = request.form.get('top_k', '')

    query = question_map[question_select]
    # Filtering answer dataframe for the query
        _df = answer_df[answer_df['query'].isin([query])]
        _df = _df.drop_duplicates(subset=['passage_id']).reset_index(drop=True)

        _df["final_score"] = np.float(
            weight)*_df["score"] + (1-np.float(weight))*_df["pass_rank_score"]

    _df = _df.sort_values(
            'final_score', ascending=False).reset_index(drop=True)

    # results-dictionary
        results = [{'passage': create_answer(row['passage'], row['start'],
        row['end']),
                    'title':row['title'],
                    'task':row['task']} for i, row in _df.head(top_k_map[
                    top_k]).iterrows()]

        return render_template("index.html", question_select=question_
        select,
                        weight=weight, top_k=top_k, results=results)
```

```
if __name__ == '__main__':
    port = int(os.environ.get("PORT", 5000))
    app.run('0.0.0.0', port)
```

Your app.py is organized in the following way:

1) You start by importing all the relevant libraries used to write your backend logic.

2) You then create an app object, which is an instance of the Flask object. Using it, you can configure your entire application. For example, you make sure that Flask knows which web page to render by explicitly giving the link to the templates folder. The templates folder is used to store all of the HTML files of the app, whereas all of the CSS and .js files (other technologies used for front-end/client side) are stored in static folders.

3) The app object also helps set up routes for the endpoints/functions, which in turn invoke a URL. (A URL is the addresses of an endpoint.) This is done using the decorator @app.route(<url>, methods), which is an HTTP method for communication.

4) The most common data communication/transfer methods are GET and POST. Whereas GET sends unencrypted information to the server, POST masks this information and passes the data in the request's body.

5) You use the home endpoint as the landing page for your website. It simply renders the index file.

6) You also use decorators like @app.before_first_request, which makes sure that all of the required files/variables needed to generate a response to a request are loaded before the server is ready for communication.

7) **app.route()** is used to map the specific URL with the function. For example, you are mapping the landing page/home page of the website with the URL "/". Similarly, you're mapping "/top_k_results" with the function **top_k_results.**

8) **render_tempalte()** is used to render HTML that is the skeleton of the UI for the client to interact with. Flask uses the Jinja template library to render templates. Read more about it at `https://jinja.palletsprojects.com/en/2.11.x/`.

9) The main code logic is stored in the `top_k_results()` endpoint, which collects data from the website form (Figure 10-3). This data is

   a) Query

   b) Weight of comprehension score in the final score, which is a linearly weighted sum of the comprehension score and the med-marco rank score

   c) Top k results to show for the question asked

10) The above data is returned via the POST method in the request body and is all string, so you convert it into the write datatype and also get an actual value and not an HTML element's value.

11) You return with a `render_template()` function to render the HTML or URL associated with the endpoint. Note that you pass a number of variables along with `render_template()`. This helps you embed logic into the markup using backend data. This is done using a Jinja template (discussed more below).

12) Finally, you run the Flask app by calling it with the address and the port number for the server to listen to for the requests.

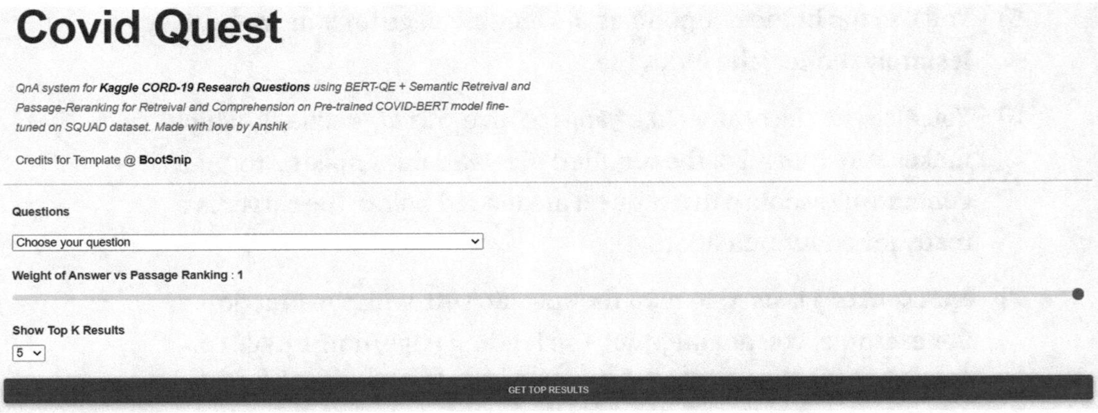

Figure 10-3. *Form for getting user input*

Understanding index.html

Your index file looks something like

```
<form action="{{url_for('top_k_results',_anchor='resultsView')}}"
method="post">
        <div class="container my-4">
          <p class="font-weight-bold">Questions</p>
          <select class="mdb-select md-form" id="question-select"
          name="question_select">
            <option value="" disabled selected>Choose your question
            </option>
            <option value='1' {% if question_select=='1' %} selected {
            % endif %}>Is the virus transmitted by aerosol,
              droplets, food, close contact, fecal matter, or water?
              </option>
            <option value='2' {% if question_select=='2' %} selected
            {% endif %}>How long is the incubation period for
              the virus?</option>
....
  <button type="submit" class="btn btn-primary btn-block btn-large">
  Get Top Results</button>
      </form>
    </div>
```

You use a form to get post requests from the front end. The weird template {{}} you see is called a Jinja template. It helps create HTML, XML, and other markup formats, which are returned to the user via an HTTP response.

You can use any variable passed as a response from the endpoint you interacted with. It is very helpful. In your use case, you don't have any pre-hand knowledge of how many responses a user would like to see for the question asked, so this is something that can't be static.

See how easy it is easy to replicate a template for the number of results you want?

```
<ul class="timeline">
        {% for result in results %}
        <li class="timeline-item bg-white rounded ml-3 p-4 shadow">
          <div class="timeline-arrow"></div>
```

```
            <h2 class="h5 mb-0">{{result.title}}</h2><span class=
            "small text-gray"><i class="fa fa-clock-o mr-1"></i>
            {{result.task}}</span>
            <p class="text-small mt-2 font-weight-light">{{result.
            passage[0]}}<strong><span

                style="color:orange">{{result.passage[1]}}</span>
                </strong>{{result.passage[2]}}</p>
        </li>
        {% endfor %}
      </ul>
```

By now you should have a good idea of your Flask app and how it is structured. Before I close this section, I would like you to see the directory tree of your Flask app.

```
|    all_question_comprehension.csv
|    app.py
|
+---static
|    |    favicon-32x32.png
|    |
|    +---css
|    |         bootstrap.min.css
|    |         choices.min.css
|    |         font-awesome.min.css
|    |         index.css
|    |         jquery.mCustomScrollbar.min.css
|    |
|    \---js
|              bootstrap.bundle.min.js
|              choices.min.js
|              index.js
|              jquery-3.3.1.slim.min.js
|              jquery.mCustomScrollbar.concat.min.js
|
+---templates
|         index.html
|
```

To run the Flask app, go to the project folder directory using the command line tool of your OS and type flask run, as shown in Figure 10-4.

```
(tfdeploy) C:\Users\bansa\Desktop\Book\Chapter 10\covidquest>flask run
 * Environment: production
   WARNING: This is a development server. Do not use it in a production deployment.
   Use a production WSGI server instead.
 * Debug mode: off
 * Running on http://127.0.0.1:5000/ (Press CTRL+C to quit)
```

Figure 10-4. *Windows command of flask run to launch the app on a local host*

Dockerizing Your Application

So far, you have built your application. Now it can be deployed on the server. Although for your use case it is not absolutely necessary to dockerize your application because you're not using very many libraries and packages, this is something that can change with time and hence can cut short the lifetime for your application.

Also, you are coding on Windows but most deployment servers are Unix-based kernels. It is very likely that when you make this app live, there will be package issues and also hardware resource usage issues if the code leverages a GPU.

So to create an isolated and portable machine that can stay true to your present configuration, you will need Docker to sail smoothly through the journey of taking your app from your laptop to the production environment.

> **Note**   To install Docker on your system, please refer to the very simple guide at `https://docs.docker.com/desktop/`.

Creating a Docker Image

In order to create a Docker image, which is a single file containing all the config and dependency information required to run the app, you must create a Dockerfile. It contains all the startup commands that are executed once the container is spun off. Containers are running instances of an image. For example, a house's blueprint is the image and the actual house is the container. In the same way that you can use a blueprint to create many houses, a Docker image can be used to create many instances that are run in separate containers.

The following commands are used to create a Dockerfile:

- FROM

- COPY

- WORKDIR

- EXPOSE

- RUN

- CMD or ENTRYPOINT

Base Image and FROM Command

Every Docker container is an image with a read/write layer on top of a bunch of read-only layers. What this means is you start with an OS distribution, say Linux Ubuntu, which is your read-only layer, and then keep on adding different layers like Anaconda to set up your Python environment and libraries like Flask, pandas, and NumPy to run your application. See Figure 10-5.

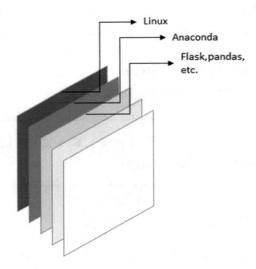

Figure 10-5. *Docker containers are stacked images*

You use the FROM command to get the base image. This is a necessary command to build a Dockerfile. For your application, you are going to use the continuum Anaconda distribution. This image can be found on the Docker hub, which is a collection of container applications: https://hub.docker.com/r/continuumio/anaconda3.

COPY and EXPOSE

Using COPY command you essentially pass your files and folders to the Docker image. This, in your case, is the `covidquest` folder that contains your Flask app. Once copied, you will be able to fire the app from inside the Docker image.

The EXPOSE command tells the Docker OS's network to open some ports for the server to listen for requests.

WORKDIR, RUN, and CMD

WORKDIR helps you set up the work directory, which in your case is where the `app.py` file resides. This is typically the directory you copied your files into using the COPY command.

The RUN command helps you to install a set of dependencies and libraries to run the app inside the container. Instead of installing each dependency separately, you make use of a `requirement.txt` file that contains all of the required files with particular versions.

This can also be used to run not just library installations but any other command line command. Obviously, it varies with the base image you choose.

The last command in the Dockerfile is CMD, which is the startup command for the container. It's just like when you ran `flask run` on your local.

Dockerfile

Now that you are armed with this knowledge, you can finally use these commands to build your Docker image.

You start by copying your `covidquest` folder and renaming it to `covidquest_docker`. Inside this folder you create your Dockerfile. It will be an extension-less file. Your directory will now look something like this:

```
|   Dockerfile
|
\---covidquest
    |   all_question_comprehension.csv
    |   app.py
    |   requirements.txt
    |
```

```
+---static
|   |     favicon-32x32.png
|   |
|   +---css
|   |         bootstrap.min.css
|   |         choices.min.css
|   |         font-awesome.min.css
|   |         index.css
|   |         jquery.mCustomScrollbar.min.css
|   |
|   \---js
|             bootstrap.bundle.min.js
|             choices.min.js
|             index.js
|             jquery-3.3.1.slim.min.js
|             jquery.mCustomScrollbar.concat.min.js
|
\---templates
            index.html
```

Add the following commands to your Dockerfile. You can use any text editor, but make sure that there is no extension to the Dockerfile.

```
FROM continuumio/anaconda3
    MAINTAINER Anshik, https://www.linkedin.com/in/anshik-8b159173/
RUN mkdir /app
COPY ./covidquest /app
WORKDIR /app
EXPOSE 5000
RUN pip install -r requirements.txt
CMD flask run --host 0.0.0.0
```

One more thing to note is that requirements.txt is kept inside the app folder because multiple containers that are spun off using this image will know exactly what libraries are used to build this app logic.

Building Docker Image

Finally, you use the following command to build your Docker image (see Figure 10-6):

```
docker build -t <docker_image_name> .
```

Note   The -t flag is used to give a name to the newly created image.

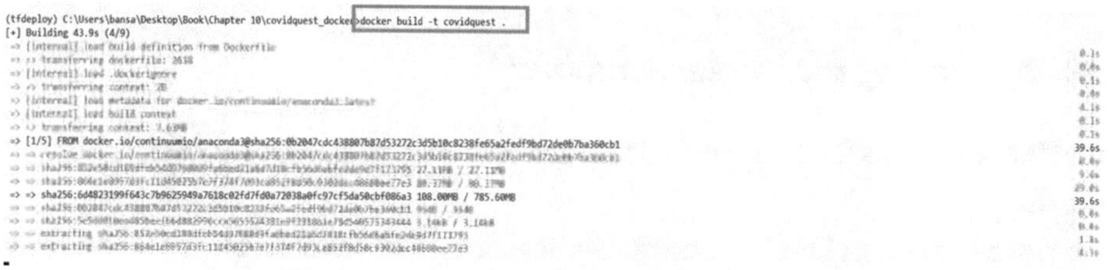

Figure 10-6. *Building the Docker image*

The process can take some time depending upon your network speed. Figure 10-7 shows whether the image has been created.

```
(tfdeploy) C:\Users\bansa\Desktop\Book\Chapter 10\covidquest_docker>docker images
REPOSITORY    TAG        IMAGE ID        CREATED           SIZE
<none>        <none>     077c3f468991    13 minutes ago    2.72GB
covidquest    latest     9f40f4671834    19 minutes ago    2.72GB
<none>        <none>     b478568374fc    19 minutes ago    2.72GB
<none>        <none>     cad0767f8fc1    About an hour ago 2.72GB
```

Figure 10-7. *Docker image list*

After the image gets created, you can run the container using the following command. The command below the -p flag is used to publish a container's port to the host. Here, you're mapping port 5000 inside your Docker container to port 5000 on your host machine so that you can access the app at localhost:5000. See Figure 10-8.

```
(tfdeploy) C:\Users\bansa\Desktop\Book\Chapter 10\covidquest_docker>docker container run -p 5000:5000 covidquest
 * Environment: production
   WARNING: This is a development server. Do not use it in a production deployment.
   Use a production WSGI server instead.
 * Debug mode: off
 * Running on http://0.0.0.0:5000/ (Press CTRL+C to quit)
172.17.0.1 - - [08/Mar/2021 21:38:52] "GET / HTTP/1.1" 200 -
172.17.0.1 - - [08/Mar/2021 21:38:52] "GET /static/favicon-32x32.png HTTP/1.1" 200 -
172.17.0.1 - - [08/Mar/2021 21:39:02] "POST /top_k_results HTTP/1.1" 200 -
172.17.0.1 - - [08/Mar/2021 21:39:02] "GET /static/fonts/fontawesome-webfont.woff2?v=4.7.0 HTTP/1.1" 404 -
172.17.0.1 - - [08/Mar/2021 21:39:02] "GET /static/fonts/fontawesome-webfont.woff?v=4.7.0 HTTP/1.1" 404 -
172.17.0.1 - - [08/Mar/2021 21:39:02] "GET /static/fonts/fontawesome-webfont.ttf?v=4.7.0 HTTP/1.1" 404 -
172.17.0.1 - - [08/Mar/2021 21:39:09] "POST /top_k_results HTTP/1.1" 200 -
172.17.0.1 - - [08/Mar/2021 21:39:09] "GET /static/fonts/fontawesome-webfont.woff2?v=4.7.0 HTTP/1.1" 404 -
172.17.0.1 - - [08/Mar/2021 21:39:09] "GET /static/fonts/fontawesome-webfont.woff?v=4.7.0 HTTP/1.1" 404 -
172.17.0.1 - - [08/Mar/2021 21:39:09] "GET /static/fonts/fontawesome-webfont.ttf?v=4.7.0 HTTP/1.1" 404 -
```

Figure 10-8. *Running the Docker container*

Even after you press Ctrl + C or CMD + C, the container will still run in the background.

Please note that each Docker container is associated with an ID. You can find out how many containers are running by using the command docker container ls, as shown in Figure 10-9.

```
(tfdeploy) C:\Users\bansa\Desktop\Book\Chapter 10\covidquest_docker>docker container ls
CONTAINER ID   IMAGE       COMMAND             CREATED        STATUS        PORTS                    NAMES
1c0757cc2cf4   covidquest  "/bin/sh -c 'flask r…"  4 minutes ago  Up 4 minutes  0.0.0.0:5000->5000/tcp  epic_germain
```

Figure 10-9. *Listing the Docker containers*

Make sure to kill the container after use (Figure 10-10). If you don't, it can throw an error like this:

```
(tfdeploy) C:\Users\bansa\Desktop\Book\Chapter 10\covidquest_
docker>docker run -p 5000:5000 -d covidquest
4778247c6c95a5a5093edd1279b03a1e41e243afb6ab84788752c9629fbaf69b
docker: Error response from daemon: driver failed
programming external connectivity on endpoint funny_jemison
(dc7d4acc7671b41c701558a8c4200406ec9f0474e360e8aea38b075cc1c2d5d0): Bind
for 0.0.0.0:5000 failed: port is already allocated.
```

```
(tfdeploy) C:\Users\bansa\Desktop\Book\Chapter 10\covidquest_docker>docker stop 1c0757cc2cf4
1c0757cc2cf4
```

Figure 10-10. *Kill the container*

When building Docker image `covidquest` and running the Docker container, you generate a lot of garbage, such as

- Stopped containers

- Networks not used by at least one container

- Images (see Figure 10-7)

- Build cache

You can delete all of these unwanted files and reclaim space by running the command

```
docker system prune
```

Making It Live Using Heroku

Now that you have dockerized your application, you can take it anywhere you want and deploy it to an actual address. But before you do that, let's understand a bit about development servers.

What you have been using until now was Flask's very own development server. This server is very limited in a sense that it can't handle multiple users or multiple requests well.

When running a web app in production, you want it to be able to handle multiple users and many requests such that there are no noticeable amounts of time for the pages and static files to load.

To make the server more "production-ready," you can use Gunicorn. Gunicorn is a pure-Python HTTP server for WSGI (Web Service Gateway Interface) applications. It allows you to run any Python application concurrently by running multiple Python processes over the machine commissioned by Heroku (also called dynos).

For your application to run in a production environment, you need to make certain changes. You need to change the Docker file:

```
FROM continuumio/anaconda3
    MAINTAINER Anshik, https://www.linkedin.com/in/anshik-8b159173/
## make a local directory
RUN mkdir /app
COPY ./covidquest /app
# Not required by Heroku
```

```
# EXPOSE 5000
WORKDIR /app
RUN pip install -r requirements.txt
# CMD flask run --host 0.0.0.0
    CMD gunicorn app:app --bind 0.0.0.0:$PORT --reload
```

You also add a Procfile. Procfile is a format for declaring the process types that describe how your app will run. A process type declares its name and a command-line command. This is a prototype that can be instantiated into one or more running processes such as your Docker container.

It is an extensionless file that contains the following process, which is basically a gunicorn process telling the app.py file it has to run since it contains the function/endpoint that processes the request:

```
web: gunicorn app:app --log-file=-
```

Your covidquest_docker directory now looks like this:

```
|   Dockerfile
|
\---covidquest
    |   all_question_comprehension.csv
    |   app.py
    |   Procfile
    |   requirements.txt
    |
    +---static
    |   |   favicon-32x32.png
    |   |
    |   +---css
    |   |       bootstrap.min.css
    |   |       choices.min.css
    |   |       font-awesome.min.css
    |   |       index.css
    |   |       jquery.mCustomScrollbar.min.css
    |   |
    |   \---js
```

```
|               bootstrap.bundle.min.js
|               choices.min.js
|               index.js
|               jquery-3.3.1.slim.min.js
|               jquery.mCustomScrollbar.concat.min.js
|
\---templates
        index.html
```

You are finally ready to deep-dive into Heroku. Heroku is a PaaS system that helps build data-driven apps with fully managed data services. To learn more about Heroku, see the video "Heroku Explained: Icebergs, Lumberjacks, and Condos."

You will do so by using the Heroku CLI. The Heroku command line interface (CLI) makes it easy to create and manage your Heroku apps directly from the terminal. It's an essential part of using Heroku. You can follow the CLI installation from `https://devcenter.heroku.com/articles/heroku-cli`.

To check whether you have successfully set up Heroku or not, run the command shown in Figure 10-11.

```
(base) C:\WINDOWS\system32>heroku --version
heroku/7.50.0 win32-x64 node-v12.16.2
```

Figure 10-11. *Checking the Heroku version*

Next, you must log in to Heroku. You can do it from the command line by typing the command `heroku login`, which redirects you to the browser for login. After successfully logging in (Figure 10-12), close the tab and return to the CLI.

```
C:\WINDOWS\system32>heroku login
heroku: Press any key to open up the browser to login or q to exit:
Opening browser to https://cli-auth.heroku.com/auth/cli/browser/672a2352-7baf-4e51-96b5-0abd51a9a162?requestor=SFMyNTY.g
2gDbQAAAA4xODMuODMuMjExLjE4Nm4GAGex4BN4AWIAAVGA.i_eFq67BT_yiChhCREnpyMqkV17rSzkF4jdoRNwT3cI
Logging in... done
Logged in as bansal.anshik@gmail.com
```

Figure 10-12. *Heroku login*

You can now create your Heroku app by using the command `heroku create <app-name>`. This prepares Heroku to receive your source code. Heroku doesn't allow you to take names that are already taken. But before that, make sure you move to the app directory (Figure 10-13).

```
C:\Users\bansa\Desktop\Book\Chapter 10\covidquest_docker>heroku create covidquest
Creating ▢ covidquest... done
https://covidquest.herokuapp.com/ | https://git.heroku.com/covidquest.git
```

Figure 10-13. *Creating a Heroku app*

Heroku runs a container registry on `registry.heroku.com`. With the CLI, you can log in with the command

`heroku container:login`

or via the Docker CLI

```
docker login --username=<email-id> --password=$(heroku auth:token)
registry.heroku.com
```

But before you push the app to the Heroku container registry, you need to tell the Heroku CLI which app you want to run this command for. For this, you convert your folder to a Git repository using `git init`. If it is already a Git repo, then you don't need to worry.

After this, you add the app name for the repo and create a git remote. Git remotes are versions of your repository that live on other servers. You deploy your app by pushing its code to a special Heroku-hosted remote that's associated with your app.

`heroku git:remote -a <your_app_name>`

To build an image and push it to container registry, make sure that your directory contains a Dockerfile and run the command `heroku container:push web`. See Figure 10-14.

```
C:\Users\bansa\Desktop\Book\Chapter 10\covidquest_docker>heroku container:push web
=== Building web (C:\Users\bansa\Desktop\Book\Chapter 10\covidquest_docker\Dockerfile)
[+] Building 2.9s (9/9) FINISHED
 => [internal] load build definition from Dockerfile                                          0.0s
 => => transferring dockerfile: 288B                                                          0.0s
 => [internal] load .dockerignore                                                             0.0s
 => => transferring context: 2B                                                               0.0s
 => [internal] load metadata for docker.io/continuumio/anaconda3:latest                       2.7s
 => [internal] load build context                                                             0.1s
 => => transferring context: 7.63MB                                                           0.1s
 => [1/4] FROM docker.io/continuumio/anaconda3@sha256:0b2047cdc438807b87d53272c3d5b10c8238fe65a2fedf9bd72de0b7ba3  0.0s
 => CACHED [2/4] COPY ./covidquest /usr/local/python/                                         0.0s
 => CACHED [3/4] WORKDIR /usr/local/python/                                                   0.0s
 => CACHED [4/4] RUN pip install -r requirements.txt                                          0.0s
 => exporting to image                                                                        0.0s
 => => exporting layers                                                                       0.0s
 => => writing image sha256:9f40f4671834b47731ea6e7c349126a9f68164fa5d36af7b6e4c8c6d6a479526  0.0s
 => => naming to registry.heroku.com/covidquest/web                                           0.0s
=== Pushing web (C:\Users\bansa\Desktop\Book\Chapter 10\covidquest_docker\Dockerfile)
Using default tag: latest
The push refers to repository [registry.heroku.com/covidquest/web]
a140e2263a46: Pushed
5f70bf18a086: Pushed
917469180d46: Pushed
5f19d44a0a55: Pushing [>                    ]  14.09MB/2.427GB
2dc54177d545: Pushing [==>                  ]  12.61MB/210.7MB
f5600c6330da: Pushing [=======>             ]  9.777MB/69.24MB
```

Figure 10-14. Build and push a Docker image with Heroku

After you've successfully pushed an image to the container registry, you can create a new release. Whenever you deploy code, change a config var, or modify your app's add-on resources, Heroku creates a new release and restarts your app. You can do so by using

```
heroku container:release web
```

Finally, you can open your app using the following command. This will open the app in the browser (Figure 10-15).

```
heroku open
```

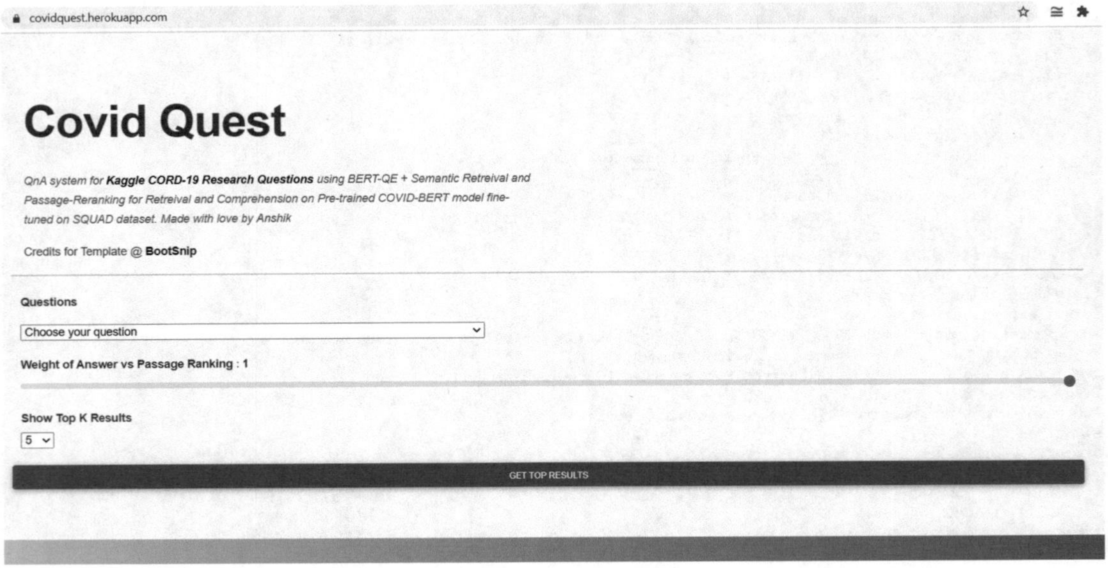

Figure 10-15. *Deployed app with a URL*

Since you are using the free tier, the app will go down after 30 mins of idle time. To keep your app up forever, you can explore paid apps.

Conclusion

It has been a long journey. If you made it to this chapter, you are a rock star. I hope in this journey of over seven case studies you felt curious and are excited about the kind of opportunity the current healthcare system offers and why you need to apply advanced AI and ML skills to take healthcare to scale.

You learned how different ethnic groups can have different adoption rates (Chapter 3) and how to extract ICD-9 codes from EHR text to help the insurance system that deals with billions of dollars using the latest flag-bearer of language understanding models, transformers. Then you explored advanced models like GCNs that leverage not just entity information but the linkages between them to learn better from the available data.

In Chapter 6, you explored the biggest pain point for any industry, especially healthcare, given the amount of expertise required to get any training data for the models. You learned about Snorkel, an upcoming power-packed package that makes semi-supervised learning tenable.

Chapter 7 introduced you to another way of looking at training ML models using federated learning. Healthcare has the right balance of consumers (patients), creators (pharma companies), and distributors (physicians and government organizations). Since there are so many stakeholders involved with inequitable power and resources, it begs the question of how we can protect the rights of an individual's privacy and yet advance science. You learned how this can be done using privacy-preserving mechanisms.

Chapter 8 discussed in length various types of medical image data and their various formats. You also looked at handling two different and highly prevalent image structures, 2-D and 3-D, and solved some of the most important tasks of detection and segmentation, respectively, on these images. You also learned how to optimize your data pipelines using iterators.

Chapter 9 took you to the future of how we will be interacting with computer systems. In the previous decade, the number of clicks to do a task (like buying clothes) has reduced considerably. With advances in UI and financial technologies, we are heading towards a time when we will just be chatting with machines, and QnA is the first step towards it.

Finally, you deployed what you built because if the world can't see it, it won't benefit anyone.

I hope you carry forward the learnings from this book and that this knowledge has sparked the flame in you to embrace, develop, and deploy the next great ML app idea you have in your mind.

Index

A

Accountable care organizations (ACOs), 7
Adaptive histogram equalization, 280
Adjacency matrices, 158
Anaconda Windows installation, 31
Autoencoders, 70, 71
AutoGraph, 26
AWS Public Dataset program, 43

B

BERT architecture, 318
BERT-QE model, 323
Bidirectional Encoder Representations
    from Transformers (BERT)
    ImageNet movement, 114
    input
        representation, 115
        segment embeddings, 116
        token embeddings, 115, 116
    training
        masked language
          mModeling, 117, 118
        next-sentence prediction, 118
Bi-encoders, 340
Bi-encoder *vs.* cross-encoder, 340
Biomedical images, 245, 247

C

Center for Medicare and Medicaid
    Innovation (CMMI), 3
Center for Medicare and Medicaid
    Services (CMS), 3
CLAHE method, 280
Clinically integrated
    networks (CINs), 7
Clinical modifications (CM), 100
Clinical notes
    attention, 106
    data
        DIAGNOSES_ICD, 105
        NOTEEVENTS, 101–105
    EHR data, 100
    encoder-decoder
        architecture, 106
    HHS, 100
    ICD codes, 99, 100
    modeling
        BERT deep-dive, 119–123
    paying attention
        classes, 109
        decoder and encoder states, 108
        feed-forward layer, 107
        fixed-length representation, 106
        information theory, 107

E

F

G

Printed in the United States
by Baker & Taylor Publisher Services